Dear Mr Snippet

ROSEANNA ROLPH

CRANTHORPE
— MILLNER —
PUBLISHERS

First published by Cranthorpe Millner Publishers (2025)

ISBN 978-1-80378-275-1 (Paperback)

www.cranthorpemillner.com

Cranthorpe Millner Publishers

Printed and bound by CPI Group (UK) Ltd
Croydon, CR0 4YY

MIX
Paper | Supporting
responsible forestry
FSC® C013604

In memoriam

E.J.R. & R.I.V.R.

O, do not pray for easy lives. Pray to be stronger men! Do not pray for tasks equal to your powers. Pray for powers equal to your tasks! Then the doing of your work shall be no miracle. But you shall be a miracle. Every day you shall wonder at yourself, at the richness of life which has come to you by the grace of God.

Phillips Brooks, 1835-1893

Written in Rita's handwriting at the back of John's 1944 diary.

For family:
past, present and future.

Prologue

Surrey
England
Spring 2024

Dear Reader,

It was during one of her last days that my mother, Rosemary, placed a rather ordinary looking cardboard box into my hands, a look of great expectation on her face, telling me that there was something very special about its contents. Looking inside revealed bundles of letters, tied with ribbon and written in emerald-green ink. These were my grandmother Rita's letters, written to my grandfather during World War II.

This was the moment their custody was handed to the next generation.

When clearing my mother's study, I found Rita's treasure chest; an old, battered hat box, displaying the faded remains of rose-pink stripes and summer blooms, promised to me a few years before. In amongst leatherbound diaries and black and white photographs sat a stack of letters in my grandfather's handwriting, the dates revealing that they were written during the Second World War years.

I wondered: could these letters speak to one another? Would they reveal a conversation over those years? What stories might they tell and what snippets of Rita and John's daily lives could be revealed? Gradually, I began to piece their story together, starting with the letters and then linking in John's military and personal diaries, blended into day-to-day accounts, and some of Rita's personal diary entries. Both being keen photographers, it has been magical linking their dated photographs to the letters of the time.

I discovered that, during this time, the postal system could be extremely efficient, with some letters sent within London arriving on the same day, whilst others were delayed for weeks. As such, there may be occasions when some of the diary entries detail events before the letter's arrival, and as you read you may, at times, know information before a replying letter. There are also periods of time where there are no letters. This was due to either the letters being lost, left behind or never delivered; illness or injury; or Rita being housed somewhere near to where John was training, enabling them to see each other regularly and, therefore, removing the need to write. During these years Rita stayed in over fifty different places to snatch as much time with John as she possibly could.

I have tried to keep to the original letters and diaries as much as possible, including spellings, word abbreviations and underlining of words, including Rita's creative and alternative use of punctuation (?!), used to relay her mischievous sense of humour. I hope you enjoy these snippets of their story and, like me, discover something new about the idiosyncrasies of living through World War II.

With best wishes,
Roseanna

Introduction

Although Rita had been reluctant to attend the New Year's Eve party in 1932 it had turned out to be rather an eventful evening. As part of a matchmaking game to partner guests for dinner, she had been paired with John Reed as Darby and Joan – a devoted and loyal folk tale couple who lived happily together into very old age. Having discovered Rita's fondness for cherries, John had shown great dedication in picking as many as he could out of the fruit trifle for her, and the time spent together wasn't marred by the fact he had two left feet and consistently crushed her toes during the dancing!

In conversation they had discovered that they were both nineteen and born two months apart. John, an only child, lived in Acton with his 'people', and Rita in Barnes, with Mummie, Sarah-Jane (who had cared for both her and her mother as children and a cherished member of the family), and their dog, Chicot. Rita was completing secretarial training ready to work for the International Tooth Company, and John was finishing a student placement on the production lines at the Ford Motor Company. He shared his love of rowing for Thames Rowing Club and said he could regularly be found on the river close to where she lived and where Rita was to be found the very next day, hiding behind a hedge, straining to catch a glimpse of John rowing past, whilst not wanting to appear too keen.

Their deep friendship and love for one another grew over the following years and one day, whilst driving through the South Downs John announced to Rita that he thought it might be very nice if they lived in the Downs, and asking her if she would like that? She took this as the one and only marriage proposal she might receive from him and quickly replied "Yes, I s'pose – yes I would like to live in the Downs very much".

Their engagement followed in the September of 1938.

John enlisted with the Honourable Artillery Company and began officer commission training in November 1938. While wedding plans were made with uncertainty for the summer of 1940, it progressively became apparent that Britain would go to war with Germany. At the end of August 1939 John was called up to the Territorial Army, his first orders to take part in the reinforcement of security at Armoury House, London; sandbagging the front of the building, digging trenches in the Artillery Ground, and then in error, the 1st XI cricket pitch, and sleeping in the Long Room.

On Friday 1st September, as Hitler invaded Poland, a sense of panic quickly pervaded civilian life, followed two days later with the

Prime Minister Neville Chamberlain's statement, broadcast from 10. Downing Street, stating that Britain was now at war with Germany. As John watched capture balloons rise into the London sky, Rita became inspired by her astrological diary which advised 'not to let over-much taking-of-thought turn her aside from action'.

Having agreed that they should get married if war broke out, and uncertain of their future, all in a hurry a dress, a wedding band engraved with 'Forever' and a cake were found. On Wednesday 6th September, whilst an air-raid warning threatened to hold proceedings up, John changed into his blues and motored his parents over to the church. Rita arrived only a few minutes later.

It was a beautiful September day, and although the ceremony was very different from what had been previously planned, they often said that whilst it was quick and very quiet, they wouldn't have changed it for any other kind that it was possible to have. It had felt as if it was just the two of them, pledging to each other, and for them that was the best kind of wedding you could have.

They honeymooned in the South Downs and every day the weather was perfect. Walking and driving through the lanes, sea- and sun-bathing, and enjoying a last-minute reprieve of an extension of leave of two days which Rita celebrated by dancing on the bed. They returned to London and John left immediately to join the Officer

Cadet Training Unit at Waterloo Barracks, alongside his friend George.

1939

Barnes
SW13
17-9-39

My belovedest husband, John,

This is just a tweeny note to tell you that I can't stop thinking of you, and I love you all of the time. I do hope you've had a good journey tonight, and that by now you're in bed (as I am), and sound asleep. You did look so tired tonight, darling, and the more I think about you, the more I want to put you into bed (with your wife, of course) and stroke your head till you go to sleep. I think I shall have to take a room one weekend, so that we can spend the whole time doing exactly what we want to (which will be, for me, loving you to suffocation!)

I went to Hammersmith after supper and found it terribly trying driving in the dark. Our lamps aren't dimmed, so I couldn't have any on at all.

I came to bed, but had to write to you, as I can't go to sleep for thinking of this time last night. I feel as lonely as our poor little Lonesome Lane and <u>do</u> miss you!

Goodnight and God bless you, my love. I love you and love you.

Your very lovesick wife,

Rita

Mrs John Reed

Waterloo Barracks
Aldershot
20-9-39

My darling wife,

It's a dreadful business having to be away so much, but today is Wednesday and tomorrow I put in for my weekend leave which is a

7

good spot in the week. We are working very hard and have no time to ourselves at all. We have to copy out and swot up on our notes every evening.

It will be great when Saturday arrives again. This war business certainly makes us appreciate our time to the full.

I must now get on with my notes. Do hope everything is going well for you at the office and at home.

I am always thinking of you. Heaps and heaps of love, darling.

Ever your loving husband,

John

Barnes

SW13

21-9-39

My darlingest one,

I can imagine how very busy you must be, but hope you enjoyed your 'evening off'. I haven't had one yet, so am looking forward to Saturday for mine! Tho' I shall probably have to use that evening for washing my hair, as there isn't another.

We are so frantically busy at the office now that we scarcely know what we're doing, and I seem to have a perpetual headache due to overtiredness and darkened windows. It's most depressing to work in all day. Added to this, travelling is getting worse, and I have to get up earlier, and arrive home later. Mrs John Reed is finding life very real and earnest lately!

I think the war seems to be a little better from our point of view, don't you?

All my love, my darling husband,

Your Rita

Dearest-husband-that-ever-there-was,

I had quite a good run home tonight and arrived at about 7 o'clock. No, darling, as promised, I didn't exceed 40 MPH, even tho' sorely tempted at times!

I hope, my love, that you've managed to get an early night, that you'll sleep well, and wake up without a sign of a sore throat. If only I could do the same again for you that we did last night, how perfectly happy I'd be! I'm feeling terribly 'wifely' again tonight (if you know what I mean!). It's awful not to have you. Never mind, my dearest, just imagine how wonderful it'll be later on! We'll more than make up for this, won't we?

The weather seems to be lovely still, tho' it's turning very cold. I do hope you're warm enough, especially in bed; your wife isn't, and misses her dear hot water bottle every night. How she will last out another 11 nights, I don't know!

Goodnight and God bless you, my sweet, precious better half. Every bit of my love,

Your wife

Waterloo Barracks
Aldershot
26-9-39

My dearest wife,

I am glad to say my throat has made a very good recovery thanks to your wonderful attention. The cold also has nearly gone so you see, you are very good for me, and if only you could be here with me now, I am sure I should never be ill at all.

I got to bed pretty early on Sunday, but the others came in rather pickled, and so kept us awake with much laughter.

All my love, precious.
Ever your loving,
John

Barnes
SW13
28-9-39

My dearest husband,

I'm very glad you're feeling much better. Yes, of course, I'd never let you be ill if I were with you now! So, you can look forward to an <u>extremely</u> healthy life when the war's over!

I've been wondering, my Mr Snippet, whether you'd like me to get you any underwear? It's all going up in price very considerably when existing stocks are cleared, and I think it would be wiser to buy now.

Well, darling, I must go to bed now. I'm sure I shan't sleep at all on Saturday night. I think of you such a lot and want you so.

Good night and God bless you. All my love, my precious,

Your 'Cabbage'

8-10-39

My most precious husband (world copyright reserved),

It was a lovely surprise this weekend, my love, and I think we took full advantage of it, don't you?! I can do with quite a few more surprises of that kind! I hope you caught your train and had a good journey.

I did so love this weekend, darling. Wasn't it marvellous being Lord and Lady Reed? Altho', of course, that wasn't anything like the best part! We can always manage that wherever we are, can't we?! A single room is enough!

I think of you these mornings too. It's getting quite wintry. I still queue up for the bus every day for 15-30 minutes and have been fighting to overcome a cold which now seems to be trying to overcome me!

I love you all the world, and it (the world) gets bigger every minute.

Your own, Rita

Waterloo Barracks
Aldershot
15-10-39

My dearest darling wife,

I have had a very miserable morning because when I got back from gun drill, I discovered that I had not got my wedding ring. When I saw your letter, I was very relieved because I thought you had found it. However, all is well. I went round to the Victoria at the first opportunity, and they had it. So, l left a tip for the honest finder and now feel quite happy again.

We obtained permission to go into Aldershot if we left someone in charge, so we have had a good Sunday lunch and feel much better for it. George sends his love and wishes you to know that he is keeping me in order. It is really the other way of course.

Heaps of love, darling. You are very dear to me.
Your John

Barnes
SW13
16-10-39

My dearly loved lord and master!

I was delighted to have your very dear letter waiting for me when

I got home tonight – it's better than the best cocktail going as a pick-me-up! I was sorry you'd had a shock about your ring, I know what a horrid feeling it is. I wonder where you'd left it, darling I had a good look round our room before I departed, and found the sweets you'd left, but didn't see the ring. Anyway, as long as you have it now, that's all that matters! It's my guardian angel for you, my love, so you mustn't lose it. It's <u>very</u> lucky, I'm sure!

I think the general situation is getting better for us. Hitler seems to be getting rebuffs on all sides, and if it goes on, I really can't see how he can last for long like this. If <u>only</u> something would 'happen' to him, and I could have you back with me all the time.

Please give my love to the boys again. Tell George I much appreciate the idea of keeping you in order, but 1) don't think it's needed, and 2) if it is, think it ought to be done by a fit and proper person!

I'll write again later on, my love. Do wish I could kiss you goodnight!

Your loving and obedient(?) spouse,

Rita

P.S. Darling, I left the letter open last night to see if I had any 'news' for you this morning. I can now inform you that we've done the trick again, and up to date there will be no little Reeds.

I love you!

Waterloo Barracks
Aldershot
18-10-39

Darling wife,
You must think I am very ungrateful but really when I am with you, I seem to forget everything else. I am jolly glad I got the ring back.

Just got your letter. Well done. Nice work. You have done very well so far.

All my best love to you, darling.
Ever yours,
John

Barnes
SW13
19-10-39

My darlingest one,

Thank you so much for your letter. I didn't expect one so soon – it was a lovely surprise! I'm glad you received my last one with the 'news' in it; I knew you'd be relieved!

I gave in my notice today. Mr Beaumont was rather cut up and wants me to leave it until the day before you finish your training, and then go back while I'm with you if it's within possible distance. Still, I shall definitely leave, as its very tiring, and also, it's not very pleasant for me there since I've been married. I think there's a certain amount of jealousy, and I shall be very glad to leave.

Well, my darling, only one whole day and two nights now! Whoopee!!

I love you,
Your Rita

23-10-39

My dearest darling,

I hope you managed to get a seat on the train last night and weren't <u>too</u> tired when you arrived. I do so hate seeing you go from all the warmth and comfort into that drab, cold place, darling. Anyway, we'll more than make up for it later on, and I'll love you and stroke your head until you don't want any more of it, even if it means investing in an arm-lifting machine!

I missed you dreadfully last night. I hugged Belinda, George (my hot water bottle), and in the end my pillow as well, but it didn't do any good. I loved Saturday night, didn't you? – and, of course, the whole weekend – and am longing for the next.

Am going to rush to catch the post now. I'll write again soon. Wish I could be with you!

I love you more than ever before (s'truth!)

Rita

26-10-39

My best beloved,

I went along to the Paradise Club. It is a queer place! Ever so dark and hidden away, and it took quite a time to find it. The girl informed me that we couldn't be sent invitations without being members, so I thought the only thing to do was to become one! I brought the application form home and filled it in for myself and posted it off. They will now send me an invitation, and I can take as many guests as I like 'on my own responsibility'. Your wife, Mr Reed, is now a member of a nightclub! At least, she will be, when we've paid 7/6d! We pay at the door; I hope it's not 7/6d each!

I'm just off to bed, my precious. Soon I'll be going with you. Whoopee!

All my love,

Your very own wife

Ps There's a wonderful model of the Maginot Line in Hamley's, which I thought you'd probably like to see.

My dearest Mr Snippet,

I'm glad you were firm at the Victoria. Let's hope it results in a double bed for the weekend! I'll do my best to catch the same train as last time, but the queuing up in Regent Street to get down the tube subway is getting worse every night. Did you notice the stations, darling?

Isn't it dreadfully dark at night now? I went to the dressmaker last night, and nearly got lost! I hear today that we are to be issued with ration books, and that bacon and butter are to be controlled. Thank goodness sugar isn't on the list!

I'm just longing for Friday, my love, and can hardly wait! I want to see you and hug you and love you and love you and love you!

Not much longer now, darling!

Your Rita

6-11-39

My dearest darling,

I do hope you didn't have to wait about for your train last night, and when it went you were sitting down in it! I did so hate seeing you off on such a horrible night; it's bad enough anyhow, but when the weather's so awful it's ten times worse. I had to wait ages for a bus at Hammersmith.

What terrific storms today! Poor old Chicot has been 'ick through it, and Mummie has seen to him, and that's made her bad now!

The girl who left the office to get married came in today and brought us each a small piece of wedding cake, which tonight I shall put under my pillow in the hope that I shall have sweet dreams of my lover. (Mind you turn up!) She made me very envious with her ravings of how marvellous it is to be just the two of you together in your very own little home. She assures me that 'nothing comes up to that'. Wouldn't it be wonderful if we had an attic between us?

I must stop now, my precious, as I want to catch the post. I love you all the world and would give anything to have you right now. I do want you so!

Your Rita

Waterloo Barracks
Aldershot
7-10-39

Dearest angel,

Yes, I got the train very well and had a seat in the restaurant car with another fellow I know. When we got to Aldershot it was absolutely pouring and rain soaked through my kit bag.

We have just finished our exam. Everybody thinks they have done badly. I know mine is a pretty good miss so now we await the results.

We were going out on night occupations tonight, but I don't imagine we shall, owing to inclement weather (that is an army term for rain). Instead, we shall probably go to the Hippodrome to drown our sorrows.

Heaps and heaps of love, darling.

Your loving husband,

John

Barnes
SW13
7-11-39

My darling Bless-it,

How have you got on today? I've been thinking of you. What a rotten day! I expect that by now you're enjoying yourself with the boys. I hope so!

I've just heard of the Belgian and Dutch peace conference offer on the news. I don't quite see how it can work, do you?

Today I've given my final 'notice' at the office, so they've jolly well had to accept it. Mr Beaumont was very nice, as usual, and I feel really sorry at leaving him, tho' I want to get away from some people there as soon as possible!

I've been wondering whether *Shipyard Sally* would be on at Ealing this week – it's on at most places. I don't think you'd appreciate *Goodbye, Mr Chips* very much! There are some deaths in it to <u>my</u> knowledge, and I thought you'd prefer, if possible, something cheerful darling?!

Hurry up, Saturday. I do want to see you.

I love you and love you,

Your Rita

Waterloo Barracks
Aldershot
9-11-39

My darling wife,

We have had a terrific rainstorm, and I am making full use of my second pair of trousers, but it is getting very difficult drying clothes. We have not yet had the results of our exam but are going over to the Larkhill ranges to watch a shoot.

I am glad to hear that you are definitely giving up at the office this week. You will then be a lady of leisure and be able take on more wifely duties.

Only two more nights and I shall be able to love and love you again.

All my love, darling,

Your John

My best in all the world,

I arrived home just now feeling quite sad and sorry for myself, to find your darling letter waiting for me. I have just left the office, and it's been quite heart-rendering saying goodbye to everyone (except the pigs, of course!) I was nearly on the point of collapsing into tears at the finish – they were all so sweet – and now, without you too, I feel so terribly lonely. I know just to see you will change all that, and I'm saying all the time inside, *Please God, let tomorrow come quicker than it ever has before.* I shall want you to love me more than ever this weekend! I know you won't mind!?

I'm so sorry, darling, about all this wet weather for you, and do hope that you won't catch cold through it.

I love you better than ever,

Your Rita

15-11-39

My dear Mr Snippet,

I'm glad I shall be free to come down to you for the weekends you are on duty, darling. It would be a crime if we couldn't have our Saturday night together! You tell the major that your wife wants you more than the army ever possibly could.

Well, my love, you'll be glad to hear that we've been clever again, and the curse finally arrived punctually, yesterday evening. I think it's wonderful the way it helps us out by arriving in the week, so that we don't have our weekends messed up, don't you? I was awake most of the night, of course, and shall be glad when today is over, but it might have been worse.

Unfortunately, Monday night was a catastrophe! I went to bed feeling extremely bilious, and during the night, in which I had no sleep at all, I succeeded in getting rid of my dinner and everything I had inside me, on four separate occasions! I feel as if I've been thoroughly spring cleaned! Mummie heard me, and came running out, assuring me that I must have 'fallen', so I was pleased to be able to inform her last night that I hadn't.

Yes, I am enjoying my 'life of freedom' very much. The only grudge I have is that I haven't my darlingest with me.

Three more days and nights to go, and then heaven again!

All my love,

Your Rita

Waterloo Barracks
Aldershot
16-11-39

My poor little angel,

I was so sorry to hear you had such a rotten gastric attack. I do hope you feel better now. Anyway, you have managed to get over both or rather two rotten things. There have been several fellows here feeling pretty dickie this week. It must be a kind of epidemic.

We have been filling up a form giving particulars of our training etc. and now know that we shall get a week's leave here from Dec 23rd.

Heaps of love darling and get quite well again.

Your loving,

John

My darling Bless-it,

Yes, thank you, I'm quite well again now, but can always do with being made even better by my husband!

I'm glad it's all right for this weekend and am longing to see you tomorrow. I feel all excited tingly inside when I think of it, and what a lovely time we'll have over Christmas now that we're sure of being together. They've only to post you somewhere where I can come and be with you all the time afterwards, and I shall really consider giving Mr Hore Belisha a bouquet, or at any rate a buttonhole.

Yesterday Mummie and I went to see *Wuthering Heights* at the Gaumont. A very good film, but rather heavy emotional stuff in it – true to Brontë type. It was a very tragic story, and your wife wept buckets!

Today I've been up to the West End to do some shopping. On the strength of the Xmas news, and the fact that I had a girl to serve me, I invested in two more boxes at 2/6d each, at Boots. The girl looked at me most speculatively!

I love you and love you and <u>will</u> love you tomorrow.

Your most loving wife,

Rita

20-11-39

My dearest Mr Snippet,

It was such a wonderful day that this morning I walked over the common to Sheen and back. Office life certainly makes you appreciate nature, doesn't it? (I don't mean nature in the raw – I can always appreciate that!)

I got the petrol station coupons and have noted that for the month of January there are only 2 units allowed, instead of 3, as now. However, they can always double the quantity of 1 unit, can't they?

I see that the 'nasties' have got a bit nearer London today. I'm sure they turned back because they saw Mrs John Reed out without her gasmask.

Well, my darlingest, it seems too wonderful to be true that the day after tomorrow I shall be with you again; shan't believe it until you've demonstrated that it's really you!

I love you and love you (still more than ever),

Your Rita

23-11-39

My dearest love,

I've just arrived home. It seemed such a dreadfully long way, leaving you behind me. I did so love seeing you, but I always miss you more than ever after it. Thank you again for last night, I did so enjoy it.

I enquired about a room for Saturday night, and the girl said that they were all booked with the exception of one very noisy one. I asked to see it, and it does look right over the street. She said that the troops would be marching past at about 4ish in the morning, and she was afraid that it would wake us. However, I'll tell you what I've done: I've booked it provisionally as I've realised that it will be Sunday morning, and I don't know whether there would be troop movements then?

Well, my precious, au revoir for a wee while. I <u>do</u> love you, darling, and am just longing for the time when we shall be together for always.

Your very loving little wife,

Rita

P.S. I will write to you from Eastbourne.

Sandhurst Hotel
Eastbourne
28-11-39

My dearest darling,

I had to write to <u>you</u> first of all, with my new pen. What do you think of the 'Quink'? I bought it in green to match my engagement ring; it's a special Parker product.

This morning the sun came streaming into my room, so I got up and went for a walk along the promenade, without my hat or coat; pretty good for November, wasn't it? We walked nearly all the morning and listened to the band, which plays here still. This afternoon we drove to Birling Gap, and went for another long walk, after which exercise I've worn a huge potato in my stocking heel!

Darling, I'm missing you more and more every hour. Everywhere we go, you and I were there together last time on our honeymoon, so you're really with me every second, tho' I'd give anything to have you in something more concrete!

I love you and love you, and <u>do</u> want you, my precious,

Your loving Rita

Barnes
SW13
7-12-39

My darling Mr Snippet,

I do hope you're feeling a little better this morning and have had a good night's rest. I rang up your father when I got in last night and he said he thought that it wasn't measles or anything like that the matter with you, but a chill caused through leaving off your thick khaki and going into a thin suit. It's quite possible that he's right; perhaps you'll be able to rake up something warmer next time.

I'm sorry, I forgot to thank you for the very nice dinner last night, and please thank George for taking care of you. You'll be glad to know that I now realise that you're not all mine. Perhaps it'll help us in our troubles! Tho' most annoyingly I find I still want to be all yours!

I love you all the world,
Your Rita

Waterloo Barracks
Aldershot
7-12-39

My darlingest wife,

I am feeling much better today. The feverishness has gone, and I have just the tail end of a cold left.

It was awfully nice seeing you yesterday and I am perfectly confident in our happiness within our two selves. We must take the greatest care to keep that absolutely sacred, for ever, wherever we may be, and I shall always do everything possible to give you every happiness.

I have just arrived in barracks, and to my great consternation I find I am without my whole bunch of keys now. There seems to be some evil influence over me with regard to keys. I think I must have had them when I left home, as you remember I let myself in twice before getting on my way. If you find them, will you bring them up to town with you please, darling?

    Heaps of love, my darling,
    Your loving John

15-12-39

My dearest darling,

    I have just got your letter. I shall be looking forward to seeing the fur coat, but I shall be looking forward still more to seeing <u>you,</u> which may damp my enthusiasm for the coat.

    We are all having to get polished up for the troop supper tonight. The Colonel and the Major and several officers will be there. George is to propose the health of the guests, but the poor fellow is still suffering from the ulcer on his tongue.

    My best of love darling
    From your John

Barnes
SW13
19-12-39

My dearest Mr Snippet,

    I'm so longing for Thursday that I don't know how I shall last out. There are also so many things to be done that I don't know what to do first. Yesterday I had quite a successful Christmas shopping day in town, and now I only have to get a few odds and ends. This morning, I did up all the presents, and this evening I shall get the cards ready, so that all and everything (including me) is waiting for you.

This morning I did the keep-fit exercises to the radio, at 7:30. It was <u>not</u> terribly successful, as a first go! Sarah-Jane thought it was most amusing, and kept on rushing in to watch me, and going off cackling loudly; Chicot came in and wiggle-waggled all round me whilst I was 'leg swinging', and got hit alternately on his chest and rear, after which he retired in disgust; Mummie kept on yelling out about the noise from the wireless and, to cap it all, I was just at the most crucial exercise of lying on my back with my legs over my head when I heard a slithering noise, and saw a small grey mouse body making for me at express rate! <u>That</u>, I regret to say, completely rounded off proceedings whilst I nearly brought the house down. Better luck on Thursday, I hope.

My love to the boys (you know the order, don't you?) and all my proper love to my belovedest,

From your Rita

1940

Subject: Postings - Officers No. 121/2/39

2/Lieut. A. J. Reed,
5, Montague Gardens,
Acton, W.3.

You have been posted to

63rd Med. Regiment, R.A. Melksham, Wilts.

and should join forthwith.

Authority - War Office Urgent Postal Telegram 112/Arty/8429.(A.G.6.(P) dated 11th January, 1940.

Railway Warrant is enclosed.

Aldershot.
12.1.1940.

B. Wilson
Lieutenant, R.H.A.
Adjutant, 121st Officer Cadet Training Unit, R.A. (HAC)

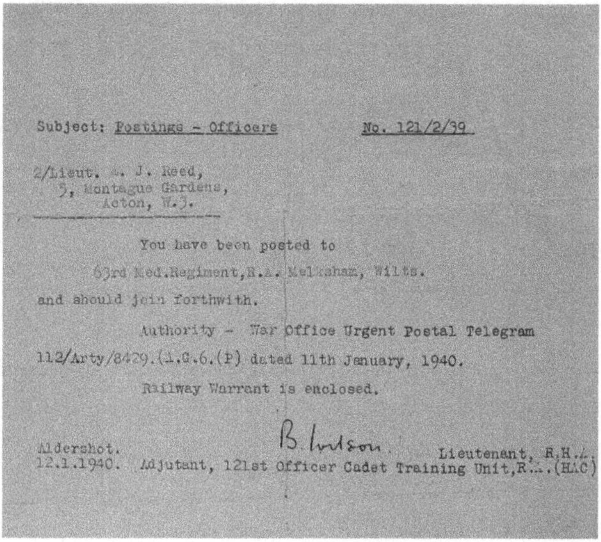

John's diary

Sunday 14th January 1940

Rita and I drive down to Melksham and arrive in what appears to be a rather wild and bewildered part of Wiltshire. We seem to be a whole lot of chaps, no guns or anything.

Sunday 21st January 1940

Medium guns have finally arrived. Old WW1 60- pounders, all on huge iron shod wheels; 1914 war stuff out of a museum. They are very, very heavy, and as solid as hell.

Rita's diary

Saturday 27th January 1940

Super party in the officers' mess tonight. John and I had a battle with soda water syphons, he on one side of the sofa and me on the other.

 *John's diary*

Wednesday 13th March 1940

Sent on army scheme to RAF Odiham – marvellous boys – mixing in with them and having a wonderful time. Working with an air observation post pilot of a Westland Lysander as a Forward Observation Officer, learning about artillery spotting and how to direct gunfire onto a target using views from the aircraft.

Thursday 14th March 1940

Final assessment for Army Air Observation Post scheme today. Went up in the Lysander and, having done my bit of spotting, was informed by the pilot that we'd do a bit of avoiding action! Played silly buggers doing looping the loop and twirls all over the place. When I deplaned I absolutely flaked out, my legs folding and buckling underneath me.

Rita's diary

Thursday 28th March 1940

The last few months we have been living in a very heightened state, on the edge of a volcano, with all our emotions very highly tuned. We're living in a way as we've never lived and feeling as we have never felt. One moment we have feelings of desperation and the next of wonderment and joy – it is either one or the other. It isn't a normal time at all, and we are constantly aware that any day the men will be called away and that it could be the last time we are together.

John's diary

Friday 29th March 1940

News received we will be leaving for France in two days' time.

 *Rita's diary*

Sunday 31st March 1940

Our day of parting, and it is time for me to say goodbye to John, not knowing if I will ever see him again.

I stayed with him as long as I possibly could; church together, followed by a ceremonial march. Both in tears, we left each other on Sand Hill.

John's diary

Sunday 31st March 1940

Major addressed the troops. Tremendous farewell at Melksham. We all marched out of town and disappeared.

My dearest darling wife,

You have gone and I am sitting in the mess very miserable. The men are all in the canteen having a last good beer up. It is blowing like hell outside. I only hope it will subside for our crossing tomorrow or else we shall all be very ill.

I do hope you have not had too trying a time driving home. It was terrible seeing you drive away, but we have had a good time together here, haven't we? And we now know that we shall always be two. It is a bloody business is this war, but we are really very lucky to be married and to love each other so much.

Cheerio, darling.

I <u>do</u> love you,

Your John

John's diary

Monday 1st April 1940

Depart Southampton on SS Tynwald; land at Le Havre.
Men docked onto cattle trucks, standing room only for the journey.
Officers entrain to the front at Bolbec.

Tuesday 2nd April 1940

Arrive at Saint-Aubin-de-Crétot, a typical little French village.

> *216/63 (WR) Med. Regt. R.A.*
> *British Expeditionary Force*
> *3-4-40*

My very darling wife,

I know you will be glad to know that I am quite well and getting on fine. There are only a couple of farms where we are but there is plenty of real sticky mud. It has rained all morning, but this afternoon is beautiful sunshine and quite warm.

We live in a large house which is quite comfortable. The chief drawback is that it has no toilet. The boys erected a tin hut in the field, but a good wind has soon put paid to that. I have had some fun trying to buy food and stuff for the mess.

I will try and write you a little each day but as we are on the move it is rather difficult. I wish you could be here. I am sure you would enjoy the quaint places around, as well of course having a royal time with me.

I love you and love you,
Your John

Thursday 4ᵗʰ April 1940
Saint-Aubin-de-Crétot

> *216/63ʳᵈ (WR) Med Regt RA*
> *British Expeditionary Force*
> *4-4-40*

My dearest love,

We are now on another busy day as we are off again early tomorrow morning. We look like travelling for the next two or three days stopping at night at little hamlets. When we eventually reach our destination, I hope we shall have time to settle down. The men have had a pretty easy time since they have been here and seem to have spent their time writing as many letters as possible. Nearly every one of them has to be blue-pencilled and some of the fellows say they are writing for the benefit of the Censoring Officer.

The country around us is very bleak, flat and uninteresting, but I don't expect we shall stay here for any length of time; perhaps two or three weeks. It has been raining nearly all day and the mud is just grand. Many of the trucks get stuck, and we just sink in over our boots.

Friday 5ᵗʰ: We have moved today some 60 miles to a little village – Allery. We have been billeted out in various houses. I got a very good one with a feather bed: spotlessly clean and very comfortable. I had a shave and a light sleep. George and the batman came over and madam, a pleasant old lady, brought us in some hot vin blanc *with a slice of lemon. We had a very good lunch at the local hotel, and I was looking forward to a really good night's rest after two very sketchy nights. But no, one of our guns broke down on the road about 50 miles back and I was detailed at about 7.30.P.M. to go back to them with food and stop overnight. I cursed the stars and set off. The driver did well keeping up* to about 55 mph but after about 6 miles the tractor broke down through petrol stoppage, just like the night when we were returning from Bristol. We got it going again but we had a fine time finding our way in the dark. The torch you gave me was just grand as I could focus it onto the signposts without having to get out and I only lost my way once.

Saturday 6th: This morning we were awakened by a local farmer who brought us wood for a fire, some bread and butter, and hot coffee. He served in the last war of which he was very proud and demonstrated that he was wounded in the head, biffin and gut. He was very voluble and kept shaking us all by the hand whilst explaining that should they be invaded again, he would surrender.

We all walked to the local where we had a wash and stood the old boy for a drink. We were relieved at 11 o'clock and I then had to get the tractor and men to the second destination 120 miles away without a map. We got there at 6 o'clock in the evening having gone round in circles for the last two miles.

Sunday 7th: This morning I have been to a very pretty church, but Mass was not quite the same as in England. There were no pews, only chairs, and these were twisted round so that you could kneel on the seat and lean on the chair-back. One of our lads told me this evening that he went into church when it was dark, sat down and, when the light went on, found himself sitting with his back to the altar.

My ears are burning very much tonight so I guess you must be thinking of me. I keep thinking of you all day and only wish I could get back to you again. But never mind, it may be sooner than we expect, who knows? And what a day!

Goodnight, darling. I love you more and more.

John

P.S. How's this for a long letter?

John's diary

Friday 12th April 1940
Courcelles-lès-Lens

216/63rd (WR) Med Regt RA
British Expeditionary Force
12-4-40

My dearest beloved wife,

I have been very busy lately with the Officers' Mess and this is the first opportunity I have had for writing. Unfortunately, some members of the mess wish to run it like a madhouse. I have insisted on keeping a full account of everything so that people are only charged with what they have. This is not at all popular with some of the heavy drinkers, and I have had to watch things so carefully that I have hardly had a moment to take a drink myself.

I have been having quite an easy time other than messing, and have had several visits to the neighbouring town with the Liaison Officer. In our moves we have passed through several of the battlefields fought over in the last war. The villages are mostly quite new, having been entirely rebuilt. The surrounding country is very flat and bleak. However, in summer I can imagine it will look quite pretty when the crops are growing.

We have passed a number of war cemeteries. They are not altogether a cheerful sight, but are rather imposing and beautifully kept. In case you may be getting a little nervous as to my whereabouts, I can tell you I am perfectly safe and just as safe after our next move which comes off in a few days.

And now to answer your dear letter which I received on Wednesday. Your letter is not censored in any way so you can say just what you like.

I will try to answer your numerous questions:

1. I am very well; bowels working beautifully, and I look in the pink.

2. Description of travel etc. already given.

3. Attaché case keys if not in the draw of my desk must be lost. Regarding passionate letters in draw: what's mine is yours, so do read them if you like. I have not yet received any more but will send them on to you when I do.

4. I am sleeping with my sleeping bag on a proper bed at the moment. It is very comfortable and beautifully warm.

You know you must not go worrying about me. I am quite all right; I always am. Still, I should like a little head-stroking. That would be just grand.

Poor old chicken; I know how you must feel. I too feel dreadfully lonely at times, especially in the evenings when I have no dear little wife to go home to. Still, things could be a lot worse, and the war is beginning to open up a bit now so perhaps it won't be such a long affair after all. The Navy seems to have done some good work in the Baltic. I do wish we could get some troops into Norway to cut off the Germans and trap them.

Thank you very much for putting my name in the book at St. Mary's Church. With all these prayers I certainly can't come to any harm.

Heaps and heaps of love to you, my precious one. Cheer up, we are still the two lucky ones.

Ever your loving husband,

John

16-4-40

My darling wife,

How very sweet of you to write each day. Thank you for the chocolate enclosed with your parcel. Chocolate out here is not good, so it was much appreciated.

Everything here was got ready for a move the other day. It has all died down now and I think we shall be here until Hitler makes an advance with his army into another neutral country. He has had rather a setback in Norway, don't you think? If we are going to turn him out of there, there will be some pretty hard fighting. By the way, I am not in Norway and not likely to be because the principal is never to move an army away from one strategical point to another.

I had a bit of luck today. The Colonel came snooping round and I happened to be busy taking Charlie troop. He seemed quite pleased and buzzed off.

Goodnight, my darling. Take great care of yourself.

All my love to you,

John

18-4-40

My very darling wife,

Just received your letter today. They seem to take about six days to get here. I am surprised that you don't seem to have received any of mine. I hope they have not got stuck at the censor. Anyway, there are plenty on the way to you, dear. I certainly think of you a great deal and often feel rather wife-sick. I do quite a lot of censoring, and when I read some of the letters saying how the men miss their wives and sweeties, I rather feel like telling them that there is at least one officer who feels as they do.

The mess now has a gramophone with about six records. I am thinking we shall get a little tired of them before the war is over.

The work here is not strenuous, and I am getting fatter; George says tubby. There is no hope of the top button of my battle dress trousers being used.

Cheerio, my darling. I love you,
Your John

19-4-40

Dearest darling,

The best part of the day for me is about teatime, when the envelopes with the green ink arrive and are passed to me. The others are very amused, but I think they are really a little jealous. Bedtime is about 10 o'clock, so between 10 and 10:30 p.m. the real thinking begins. There is another session in the morning at 7 o'clock. Have you noticed that yet, darling?

Last night we decided to visit the next village and stopped on the way at Regimental Headquarters, near to where the Colonel lives. When he heard we were there he insisted on having us in and of course there we stuck. However, it was one of the most amusing evenings I have had since we have been here. We had bought a bottle of cherry brandy so we entered the Colonel's presence with bottle in hand. He was very amused and welcomed us. We had some wine and then the Colonel (who was quite merry) gave us some Indian army songs and insisted on our singing the chorus. He got up and acted about with his arms, and then came the order 'sing' and we all sang. But just at the critical moment, Humpty disappeared under the table, his chair having collapsed.

The Colonel insisted on our having a prairie oyster. The eggs were brought in, and he thoroughly enjoyed himself cracking a dozen of them and getting the yoke out without the white. He was in a lovely mess when he had finished. Of course, the idea is to swallow the whole lot at once, but it wants some doing. The result is terrific; I felt as if I was going to lay an egg. We eventually got away with our bottle of cherry brandy, which we drank when we got home. This proved fatal because we woke up this morning feeling very groggy. George has not eaten all day.

I am just going to bed now, darling, where I can think of my missus and how much I love her.

Goodnight, precious,

John

20-04-40

My poor darling,

Just got your letter of 15th and you still have not received any letters. I have been sending them off each day and can only think that they have got lost. I do hope you get some soon. I am getting all yours and they are just perfect.

It is beautiful today. Real hot sun and it looks as if Spring is here with a vengeance. All the bushes and trees are sprouting. It is amazing the difference the sun makes to the men. They seem to cheer up at once and their letters are full of spring fever.

I must dash away now darling. Will write again tomorrow.

Cheeribye chicken.

Your loving,

John

My dearest darling wife,

We went to the local town on Saturday afternoon, did our shopping and went to the NAAFI picture house to see 'Charming Ladies'. It was not too good.

I saw some very nice gloves I should like you to have but would like to know your size first. I know it is a dear little hand but although I know how dear I don't know how small. Will you let me know please darling.

We had dinner at a restaurant. I had oysters but was not very successful in choosing the next course. Choucroute Garni has far too much garlic in it. Anyway, we finished up with a Pineapple Kirsch which was very tasty. I wish you could be here to sample the heors d'eauvres (I can't spell the dam thing). They are terrific and only cost 7 francs.

I have received a grand parcel from home. I can tell you have had one or two suggestions to make. We have been tucking into it this evening and opened a champagne for the purpose. Champagne is not really so wonderful. An English lime juice and soda is far more thirst quenching. The only snag is that it costs more. Funny, isn't it?

Goodnight my very precious one.

Your own,

John.

My very own darling,

I have just returned having had my bath and have got your letter telling me all about your shopping expedition. You need not worry darling I think you have done jolly well, and it is worth £90 to know that you have enjoyed yourself.

The bedroom suite sounds very attractive, and I certainly like walnut. I hope the bed is a good one, after all is <u>the</u> most important piece of the lot, don't you agree.

It is very nice to have all the furniture; the only disappointment is that we can't yet use it. But never mind perhaps it won't be so long before we can. Let's hope so darling.

Heaps and heaps of love darling.

Your loving husband,

John

25-4-40

My poor old missus,

You are a funny old thing to worry so much about your purchases for our future home. I hope my last letter set your mind at rest. Anyway, you certainly seem to have got bitten by the buying bug this time. I will try and give you my feelings about buying the dining room suite. It is rather difficult of course because I am not there to know all about it. Firstly, I have not the slightest doubt that it is very nice and is a real bargain. Also, I have no hesitation whatever in leaving the choosing of it entirely to you because I know our tastes are very similar and we have often talked about the style we should like. I should love to be with you and to help you to choose it, but I am afraid that cannot be.

What I feel against the proposition is that there will be practically a houseful of furniture stored away for some time without anybody getting any benefit from it. You know my feelings about this war: they have not changed, in spite of Norway. I only wish they would, and I am not really a pessimist. Also, we do not know what kind of house we shall be able to have. It seems to me we shall be buying a house to fit the furniture instead of the furniture to fit the house. Anyway, I leave it entirely to you; if you think it is worth the risk, you get it. You will probably laugh at me later, anyway. You always do.

Gee, I wish I could be there; it makes me feel more wife-sick than ever. Now don't worry any more about me being an old stoggy. Be guided by your womanly intuition but not fascinated with the art of buying and the itching palm (Shakespeare).

Good night, darling. All my love, you precious thing.

Your loving husband,

John

John's diary

Saturday 27th April 1940

Auchy-les-Mines

216/63rd (WR) Med Regt RA
British Expeditionary Force
29-4-40

My darling wife,

Now to deal with your questions:

1. I have some woollen mittens, and shall not be requiring any more at any rate until next winter. Please thank Mrs Jobbins for her kind offer;

2. I certainly do like the bed you would like purchase. I think it is just grand. All I want to do now is to get this war over as soon as possible and get inside with you;

3. Yes, I think you are a marvel. It all looks grand, and I am just longing to be with you and settle down with it all. So, you had better stop the war pretty soon.

Good night, my love,

Your John

My darling,

We arrived on Sunday afternoon in very good style. I was riding a motorbike in charge of the centre section of the convoy. This town (or village) is larger than the one we have left and is older. It consists of cottages on each side of a main road that also acts as a conduit for open drainage. The people are very hospitable and will do anything for us. I am billeted in a house where I have a double bed to myself. The old girl and her daughter (a comely wench) get us hot water and coffee each morning. We have the use of their parlour, and they turn on the English news for us to hear at 6 o'clock, if we are in. The old boy goes off to his land; the son is serving in the French Army.

Cheerio, my love.

Your ever loving husband,

John

2-5-40

My dearest beloved,

Just got your letter. Yes, I would just love to thank you in my special way; I am sure it is good for you. Try and bear up, darling. I get awful aches myself wanting you so much.

This has been an eventful day. I have now been appointed Wagon Line Officer and hurriedly took over the job this afternoon. The wagon lines are about ten miles away and I shall have my own office there and be able to run the show as I want (I hope).

I am writing this in my old billets where I have changed to attend a battery dinner with the Colonel. Normally I shall feed away at the lines.

All my love, darling.

Ever your loving husband,

John

My beloved,

I am at last able to write and tell you of two very busy days.

I am now in a village (Raimbeaucourt), some 10 miles from the Battery, and I have a billet in a comfortable farmhouse all to myself. I have just had a glass of vin blanc with the family who are very pleasant, and I have a large feather bed in a well-furnished room. How I wish you could be here with me; we could have a grand time. I feel more lonesome than ever when I sleep by myself.

The boys here are a grand lot and I think we shall all get along well. There is, however, a lot of work to do and much to be gingered up. On Friday evening the Colonel came over to dinner. It was certainly a good spread, and the various wines flowed very freely. After dinner, somebody suggested we had a sing song or pay, and that I should start. There was nothing else for it but to recite The Lion and Albert. The Colonel knew it rather better than I did, but between us we got the gist of it. The Colonel was in grand form and gave us a turn for every one of ours. I left the party at about 11:30 to return to my little village but the party went on to about 2 o'clock when everything was more or less finished. I had rather a nasty taste most of the morning through drinking too much Cointreau.

On Saturday I went to a concert with George. The show was very good. Afterwards, the artists came up to the bar and we all had a drink together. There was one of those thought-reading turns where the girl is blindfolded on the stage and a man goes round the audience and is given articles which the good lady identifies. It was extremely clever but a waste of time to me. However, George was most interested, and during our drink suggested to the fellow that it was all a trick. He was not at all pleased and we had another little show on our own to prove that George was wrong. The fellow was a nasty piece of work, and the turn is apparently a favourite among London nightclubs. However, he considerably cheered up when he heard that George came from Wakefield, which was his birthplace. The result is that I can get into any nightclub in London, but I am more than convinced that I won't go.

I must go out now to turn the guard out. I am Orderly Officer all day and every day here.

Goodnight, my love. I do love you such a lot,
Your John

Swan and Edgar Restaurant
Piccadilly
W1
7-5-40

My beloved Mr Snippet,

Well, darling, how are you settling down to your new job? Personally, I'm sure that you're the man for it, dearest. You know all about the lorries' 'innards' etc., and I'm quite sure that you'll manage the drivers equally as well. I should think that you'll be able to derive a lot of satisfaction from having a job that you can run yourself, and imagine that if you do well (and I'm quite certain that you will) you'll be able to keep it.

Isn't it a pity that our troops have come home from Norway? I didn't think they'd leave there; I'm sorry for our loss of prestige.

Goodnight, my very dearest. I love you <u>so</u> much,
Your Rita

My own darlingest Mr Snippet,

I've had a simply splendid letter from you today – lovely and long and 'newsy'. When I read your letters (for which deed I retire to complete privacy so that I can savour them more fully), I feel that I'm with you, and can imagine everything you describe very well. That's when I always thank providence for a good imagination, though sometimes the good imagination goes wrong and gives me bad nights!

I'm <u>very</u> glad, darling, that you're so comfortable in the farmhouse. How do you manage with the language? You'll have to give me French lessons when you come home.

I do wish they wanted a land girl or milkmaid on the farm. I'd come over, do that job by the day and be your wife at night! It annoys me immensely that I could be with you so easily, and yet we each have to be alone. It's so senseless.

Mummie and I are nearly packed ready for our trip to Swanage. I do wish you were coming too.

All my love to my dear, dear Mitty,

Your Rita

John's diary

Wednesday 8th May 1940

Started the day with a German plane flying over, spraying machine gunfire all around the place. We could see the bloody chaps.

Reported incident with coordinates to Headquarters. Response was dismissive and to await further instruction.

The Parade Hotel
Swanage
9-5-40

My own beloved one,

We arrived here quite safely at 5:30 p.m. today, and your darling letter was waiting. It was the first thing I saw, and it was just like an oasis in the desert for me! The rundown was simply beautiful, and the sun shining through the young green leaves of the beech trees made the day seem full of spring.

I came to Swanage when I was a very little girl and I don't remember any of it. It certainly is a very pretty place and would be much prettier still if we could enjoy it together. Never mind, my dearest, we'll have to add it on as a one of our 'joys to come'. Although we won't come to <u>this</u> hotel, I <u>can</u> say! We have to share a rotten little room right at the top. They don't provide any soap at all, scarcely any butter, and I've had to ask four times for this paper, which I was <u>not</u> going to be done out of! It really <u>is</u> a thorough 'take-in', and although we came here for a week, we shall <u>not</u> be staying longer than Tuesday!

I love and adore you.

Your own <u>very</u> loving little wife,

Rita

216/63rd (WR) Med Regt RA
British Expeditionary Force
9-5-40

My dearest darling wife,

All the animals are giving birth in this village. On the farm where I live there are about twenty young ducks and a calf. The birth of a calf is a great event and calls for celebration. Last night, I went round to turn the guard out and could not find them. I followed a streak of light and, in a room, found the Guard and one of my Sergeants round a table drinking café cognac with the family. I was immediately given a drink and informed that our Guard had performed a superhuman effort as midwives. I will have lots to tell you one day.

Goodnight, my darling. I am afraid I am even further away from Paris, but I am just as near to you.

Your John

John's diary

Friday 10ᵗʰ May 1940

03:00: Germany invades Holland and Belgium.

15:00: Three enemy aircraft drop two bombs near Battery.

Air raids all day. Move to covered position and stop and rest in the woods of Waterloo.

The Parade Hotel
Swanage
10-5-40

My darling Mitty,

How are you? Are you safe and sound still, and away from danger? Oh, my precious, if <u>only</u> I could be with you. I wouldn't mind if the bombs were falling everywhere. I feel so cut off from all the news and everything here; I only know that Holland and Belgium have been invaded, and I believe that the part where you are has been bombed. There are no papers or a public wireless in the hotel. I'm trying hard not to worry, but I'd give anything in the world to be near you, my love. I suppose the invasions will be for the best in the end, but if only you weren't there, my dearest one. I shall be so longing to hear from you now, and shan't rest until I do, although now the fun has started, I don't suspect you'll have much time.

How thankful I am that you were made Wagon Line Officer – just in time. It must be your luck holding out still, darling! Let's hope so, anyway! Whatever happens, we'll both go on believing that and just live through it all, knowing how much we love each other, and looking forward to being together for always when it's over.

God bless you, my most precious one. All my love and thoughts are for you,

Your Rita

John's diary

Saturday 11th May 1940

Follow orders for putting in place a gun enfilade on the road into Belgium. Expectation is that Germans will approach from the opposite direction, at which point we will attack and end the war. General consensus in higher ranks is that this will be easy.

11:50: Crossed France-Belgium frontier. Arrive Forêt de Soignes.

On the way into Belgium, we are impressed by the warmth of the reception given to the British troops. After arrival numerous air raid warnings are heard and an enemy air attack is observed over Brussels.

We pass many conscripted Frenchmen wearing their khakis and tin hats, travelling on foot, riding bicycles, and in trucks and carts; anything they can lay their hands on to ensure that they get to the front.

Sunday 12th May 1940

Conference with Colonel. 2 guns have broken track eyes and are left behind, 14 guns move forward, and en route one tractor and gun become ditched.

Monday 13th May 1940

All day, in all kinds of vehicles, refugees move west on the roads out of Brussels.

Batteries move up with gun groups under cover of darkness, and guns occupy positions on lines of fire.

Shelter in a barn for the night.

Tuesday 14th May 1940

Awake to find occupied rat tunnels under the hay where we slept.

23:00: Gas attack on Western Front.

The Parade Hotel
Swanage
15-5-40

My dearest husband,

How are you getting on now, darling? I just live and long for news of you, but so far, the postman is no good! I keep on having more and more shocks every day with the news, but am still sure the tide will turn for us. Perhaps Hitler is throwing in his whole box of tricks at once and we shall be able to go at him when he's finished! My poor precious, I do so wonder how you are.

We are off home tomorrow, thank goodness! It's so miserable here now with everyone gone, and I am longing to go home as I shall feel a little nearer to you. It's sheer mental agony here for me; no wireless, and no papers, and nothing to do but while away the long hours.

I pray for you every minute of the day, my dearest, and love you until I feel I shall burst.

Your very anxious and loving wife,

Rita

Wednesday 15th May 1940

l'Espinette-Centrale

05:47: Message received that a plane has been seen by two observers to have British markings and to have dropped parachutists.

11:30: Considerable air activity.

16:00: Message received informing that a man dressed as a Belgian soldier has called and asked to see a map as he is lost. He is put under arrest and orders are given for him to be sent to Headquarters, under armed escort.

Bombardment by Allied Artillery continues for several hours.

19:30: Battery report confirmation of falling back of machine gun section and that the enemy are reported to have advanced to within 700/800 yards to their front.

Unit Signal report enemy is breaking through our lines. The Commanding Officer orders the withdrawal of Regimental Headquarters to an alternative rear position about 1 mile back down the road. Move to take place at dusk but it is considered that the exigencies of the situation demand an imminent move.

Orders are given for stationery boxes with security and secret contents to be opened and contents destroyed in a supervised operation. All personnel mount vehicles and trucks and proceed back to the Wagon Lines arriving before midnight where they are marshalled in readiness for orders.

My dearest darling wife,

Now that the fun has started, I know you will be a little worried, but there is no need to worry, my dear. I am quite all right and have every chance of remaining so. I have received another hamper from home which has been very welcome. I am now quite well off for food, and very popular.

We have moved again to some extremely beautiful country. It is like midsummer and the flowers and trees are looking grand. I can imagine you and I having a wonderful time here in peacetime. War has not yet altered the beauty but only the mode of living. Each day is filled with new happenings and excitement.

My job as Wagon Line Officer still goes well, and the latest move was carried out all right. I am kept very busy indeed as of course we all are, and I shall be unable to write every day. Also, the postal service is not yet in order, but I will do my best to send you word as often as I can.

This new move of Hitler's, though it is one that we knew he would take sooner or later, was one that I didn't think he would consider for another 12 months. I am beginning to think now that the war won't last very long now; the three years should see it through. The Nazis are going to bang right into it this time and a jolly good job too.

And now, darling, how are you? Write to me as much as you can, won't you? I am still getting plenty of letters and they are just grand.

All my love, darling.

From your loving husband,

John

My most precious darling,

I just couldn't <u>bear</u> another day away, and to my great joy and relief I found your parcel awaiting me. My very dearest, how sweet of you! I can't express what I felt when I saw your dear present, except that I wanted to cry. It's so exactly like you, my love. The scarf is marvellous – what a lovely heavy silk – and the colour is heavenly, and you're quite right about it suiting my hair! It deadens the red in that, and makes it look really quite a nice colour! I shall make them last as long as possible. And as for remembering my perfume, well, I can't think of anything to say, my Mitty. I shall keep both that and the scarf for our next honeymoon, darling, which I am sure we shall have before so very long. I can't say thank you – it's so inadequate for your thought for me in your present circumstances and surroundings – but I'll leave it that <u>you</u> know what I feel inside me. It is marvellous to have your own dear clothes that you've worn, and I shall take them to bed with me and cuddle them all night long.

We had such a beautiful run home today; the country is gorgeous. The fields look as though they've been brushed over with gold, full of buttercups; the chestnut trees are grand, and the May trees are simply lovely. Do you remember the perfume from them on the common and in the park? It's the same this year, dearest. Perhaps next year you'll be here to smell it yourself.

However dark things may seem, I am still keeping our love and faith for our future strong in my heart, and I know you will do the same, my dearest. God will take care of you for me, and after a comparatively short time of this awfulness, we shall be together in peace and joy for the rest of our lives.

Goodnight, my heart. I love you so terribly.

Your own wife,

Rita

John's diary

Thursday 16ᵗʰ May 1940

In action all day.

Batteries move from Wagon Lines to position SW of Brussels.

The route taken is via the outskirts of Brussels where part of the convoy is held up during an air raid. New Headquarters are temporarily established and Batteries locate in hides, undercover of wooded ground.

Barnes

SW13

17-5-40

My own darling,

Things seem to be getting a little brighter, and I'm so glad and proud, because I know that my husband has helped to make them so. Of course, we'll probably have some more setbacks, but I'm sure that it won't be so very long now before we tell old man Hitler just where he gets off.

And now, my dearest, how are you? I never cease thinking of and wondering about you. I feel much better today, now that I'm home again. I'm much calmer, and though of course I still feel terribly worried, it's different somehow. My other worry is that I do hope you still receive my letters fairly well. I presume, from the name on the box of chocolate liqueurs, that you were near Nancy (place, not girl!) though I don't suppose you are now. I wish I could be with you, wherever it is.

We have quite a number of Belgian refugees coming here to live in the empty houses, and they're also being billeted on people who have the room. We saw boatloads of both Dutch and Belgians going into Poole harbour yesterday.

Everyone who sees it <u>loves</u> my scarf! And I love and adore you, my Mitty.

Your very own,

'Little <u>Devil</u>'

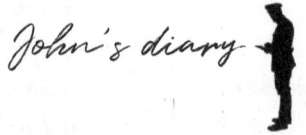

John's diary

Friday 17th May 1940

Considerable air activity.

23:45: Roads running in a NW direction heavily packed with military traffic, causing road jams.

Barnes

SW13

18-5-40

My beloved,

I do hope that you're all right. I've been thinking what a terribly worrying time you must have had, being Wagon Line Officer, and only having a few days to get hold of the ropes before you were truly put to the test. The more I've thought of it the more I realise what an awful time you must have had. I expect you've been too busy for anything, my poor love. I did wonder whether we hadn't heard from you at all on account of all the communications in Belgium being severed, but have come to the conclusion that it's because you just haven't had time. I'm taking 'no news as good news' this end.

I am so longing to see you again, my darling. I take your clothes to bed with me every night and think how simply marvellous it will be when I can hold you as tightly as I do them. I don't get over the lonesomeness of being in bed without you yet. Do you?

I wish I could bite you; I love you so.

Your own,

Rita

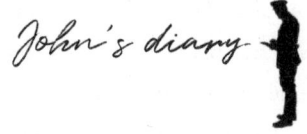

John's diary

Saturday 18ᵗʰ May 1940

08:30: Convoy halts in field. Advance party provides a meal.

16:30: Two guns ditched. Journey resumes.

19:00: We reach Ploegsteert, hide vehicles under cover of trees, and camp for the night. Tournai has been heavily bombed by enemy aircraft and is in flames.

Sunday 19ᵗʰ May 1940

I awake to find a robin perched by where I am sleeping. I think: you lucky little devil, you haven't got to go through all of this. You can just fly off when the ruddy people come along, whereas I've got to get up and fight another day's war.

The unit crosses back into France and en route passes hundreds of refugees. During the journey a German plane makes a forced landing in field bordering the road and the crew are taken prisoner by the Battery. Units proceed to establish Wagon Lines at Auchy. Considerable air activity during morning.

13:15: Headquarters move to rendezvous and proceed to a previously reconnoitred position in small spinney bordering the road. Communication put out.

23:35: Boche reported to have brought up guns and made use of their artillery for first time today. Heavy bombing of nearby town. Bridge reported to have been blown to check German advance.

Monday 20th May 1940

Brilliant moonlit night.

06:10: Report received that a troop has been seen going back down the road. The Commanding Officer halts a subaltern in the rear of the column who states that his Regiment has been shot at by parachutists and that they are withdrawing, although apparently no order has been received to do so. Again, the policy against scams and rumours is emphasised by the Commanding Officer.

06:15: Troop seen returning to its position.

06:35: Battery warned to be prepared to suspect all and everything. A Bren Gun Carrier travelling down the road with a man riding in it dressed as a British Officer, reports that the Cameronians are being pushed back. That man was a spy and is shot as an example.

07:30: Battery ordered to fire 10 rounds per gun on targets chosen during the next hour. The Commanding Officer considers it would be encouraging for the men in front to hear the shells pan over their heads to let them know that the Artillery are doing something. This is recommended owing to the nature of things at the moment.

10:35: The Commanding Officer calls Battery to report a 3-ton wagon with ammo is coming up that needs to go into hiding at a suitable distance from the Battery position. Order instructed to fire 5 rounds per hour, for the next two hours, according to ammo situation.

10:40: Air raid.

12:10: Bombardment on this sector of the front, west of Tournai, carries on throughout the morning.

14:42: Message from Headquarters to report approaching column of infantry and vehicles moving NW along road, and to act immediately.

14:47: Battery ordered to bombard with as many guns as possible.

15:30: Battery ordered to stand by and prepare to bombard Saint Aubert.

17:00: Message from Headquarters reporting since arrival, two cases had occurred of units receiving false orders to withdraw. Orders appear genuine and were given in one case by individual representing himself as a Liaison Officer. One of these men is still at large but the other has been shot.

Headquarters enquire if unit has received any information over its RAF receiving sets and the answer given is negative.

17:50: Commanding Officer gives orders to Batteries for new positions. Sandbags numbering 6000 distributed to Batteries.

18:45: Report received of the capture of two suspect nuns.

20:50: Heavy allied bombardment during last two hours and still continuing.

Barnes
SW13
21-5-40

My dearest darling,

I've been busy transplanting lettuces and sowing marrow seeds this morning, and this afternoon I'm going to tea and supper with your people. Perhaps they will have heard from you – a field postcard? I wonder so much about you, my darling, whether you're getting any proper rest and food, and how you are. I <u>do</u> love you.

I have been feeling so worried that first thing every morning I go to church. There is another parishioner, an elderly black gentleman, with whom I share a sympathetic acknowledging nod of the head. We never speak a word, but this helps me a great deal. Today we exchanged our nods, and I watched as huge tears silently rolled down his cheeks. Oh, my heart did go out to him.

Everyone is expecting England to be invaded any moment now, and there are terrific precautions and troops marching about everywhere.

With all my love and bites and bear hugs and kisses, your <u>very</u> John-sick,

Rita

John's diary

Tuesday 21st May 1940

Créplaine

01:25: Snipers turn out to be a British Anti-Tank detachment who have mistaken our linesman to be German.

09:55: Headquarters order Battery to fire 20 rounds on wood in Calonne.

12:05: Unit Signal Section instructed to withdraw wireless communication.

13:00: Artillery fire, which had been intensive on both sides all morning, quietens down considerably.

New slit trenches to provide air raid protection have been prepared; Signal Section has been engaged on trench and dug out work to accommodate Signal Exchange and Office, and square pits have been dug to accommodate Regimental Headquarters and Counter Battery Officer. Meanwhile, officer personnel occupy and operate from an office truck which has been well sandbagged and camouflaged.

Several cattle in a field adjoining the spinney, belonging to an owner of a nearby farm who had evacuated, are milked by headquarter personnel to relieve animals and provide this commodity for consumption. Eggs are obtained from poultry left on this farm. Sleeping accommodation is in improvised bivouacs constructed against the inner side of the hedge bordering the spinney.

13:37: Line communication to Battery restored.

13:45: Battery given instructions to put two guns in hide into position for firing at Créplaine.

15:30: Soldier found from 16 Field Regiment who has lost his way and is instructed to await until location of his unit is confirmed.

15:53: Commander Corps arrive and report on situation. 214 and 216 batteries are now composed of two troops of only two guns each.

16:33: Report of Boche Observation Balloon.

19:09: Enemy bombing raid in area of Regimental Headquarters.

21:15 Allied artillery fire intensified.

22:30: Commanding Officer calls Battery to inform them their shelling has been effective.

22:55: Very heavy allied bombardment in progress.

23:25: Commanding Officer orders Observation Post to be manned. Concludes by adding, 'Mystify, mislead and dishearten the enemy in your method of fire'.

Barnes
SW13
22-5-40

My darlingest Mr Snippet,

This morning, to my great delight, your father phoned through to say they'd had a letter from you. Oh, darling, what a joy and relief! I feel <u>much </u>better now. And with that good news there is also good news about the fighting. It's all grand! I should imagine that Hitler must have found out that Second Lieutenant Reed is waiting for him, and it's that that's confusing them now!

I'm glad to hear that the wagon line job is going so well. Of course, I'm longing to hear all about everything from you yourself, but until I do get a letter, can now sleep at night.

We were all solemn and serious about you yesterday at Acton. I know your people were <u>very</u> pleased to hear from you. As for me, it's completely changed the complexion of the world!

Heaps and pots of love for my precious,

From your own 'Chicken'

Wednesday 22nd May 1940

03:40: Two Belgium soldiers detained by guard.

04:45: The Belgian soldiers are found to be genuine, and their motorcycles and firearms are returned to them.

07:57: Two guns out of action. One has sunk up to its axles; the other requires air pressure.

08:40: Air raid.

08:50: British Lysander plane observed to be in combat with enemy planes and eventually shot down 600 yards from Regimental Headquarters. Party sent to investigate and report both occupants are dead. Guard put over plane pending arrival of RAF.

11:40: Order received for guns not to fire on Calonne, which is in possession of our infantry.

12:45: No gunfire during last half hour.

13:59: Air Raid.

15:20: Artillery fire in distance.

16:03: Column of enemy infantry and horse cavalry moving on road. Bombard carried out by both Batteries.

16:28: 214 Battery only one gun active.

18:10: Enemy Observation Balloon reported.

18:25: Orders received from Regiment to move back to Gondecourt. Commanding Officer addresses officers of Regimental Headquarters, explaining the situation necessitates further withdrawal on account of weakness and uncertainty of position on our right flank. Position understood to be difficult but not desperate. Battery to remain to cover withdrawal.

My dearest darling husband,

How is the country looking around you now? Still beautiful? Are you <u>very</u> near the Front, darling? Of course though I try not to, I can't help worrying about you. You're my whole world, you know, my Mitty, and that's far too big a thing <u>not</u> to worry about. (I don't mean <u>you're</u> the 'thing', I mean the world.)

You know how I love receiving your letters and field postcards, but I shall of course quite understand that you won't be able to write so much. Don't <u>I</u> wish you could get inside one of your letters! <u>How</u> I want you! I'm sure when I see you, I shall turn into a limpet and cling on to you for all time.

Tonight I've joined the 'League of Health and Beauty' – to make myself as glamorous as possible for my husband's return. It's very good fun, and my morning exercises help me tremendously, so you see, they <u>are</u> some good (tho' these tonight were <u>very</u> strenuous – stiff!).

Goodnight, my most precious darling. I love every tweeny wee bit of you.

Your own,

Rita

John's diary

Thursday 23rd May 1940

Convoy proceeds under cover of darkness to west of Lille, arriving at 05:30 hours.

While unit stands by enemy aircraft make several bombing raids on route to Estaires.

In the early afternoon, the Battery joins the remainder of the Regiment. All vehicles are placed under cover and personnel rest in empty farm.

22:00: Unit moves some 8 miles to a hideout and remains overnight. During this move a tractor and gun of 216 come into collision with a train at a level crossing. Several of the crew are injured but only two seriously. Tractor is turned on its side by engine, detached from its gun and carried 80 yards down the line. Gun is recovered undamaged and taken in tow by spare tractor.

Work all night.

Friday 24th May 1940

Glorious morning.

Terribly tired.

Unit standing by, prepared to move and awaiting orders.

Enemy bombers active again.

Visibility for bombing perfect.

Today is the fourth on which the unit Quartermaster Corps have failed to connect with Ration Supply Column. Petrol has been obtainable, and personnel have partially been fed on iron ration. The frontier position is being held by French, British and Belgium troops. French troops are pressing northwards with success.

No casualties yet.

Barnes

SW13

24-5-40

My own beloved husband,

Today is Empire Day and the King's broadcast has just finished. (I always feel nervous for his stuttering.) Did you have the opportunity to listen, darling? I must say that he did extremely well – the best I've ever heard.

Miss Helsby (the suffragette) has hoisted a huge Union Jack out of her window. She's intensely patriotic, and thinks all our forces are so marvellous that she can't understand how anyone can ever get depressed over the war.

We have the official news that the Germans are in possession of Boulogne, but I'm not in the least worried. I'm sure our Navy will have something to say!

I <u>do</u> hope, my dearest darling, that you're still quite happy and safe. I love you and pray for you every moment. I <u>do</u> so love you so terribly, my precious.

Your own 'little missus'

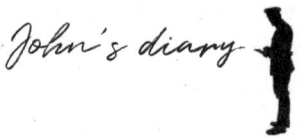

Saturday 25th May 1940

A good night's sleep.

11:00: About 20 enemy bombers are circling our position.

11:30: Second air raid, 12 enemy bombers observed.

12:05: Third air raid, bombs dropped in immediate vicinity.

13:40: Fourth air raid.

Major locates his gun position from the previous war. Trenches still in place, all in fairly good condition. The ground pocketed with a mass of holes.

216/63rd (WR) Med Regt RA
British Expeditionary Force
25-5-40

My dearest darling,

We are now having a couple of days' rest after some strenuous activity. There has been no post for about five days, and I am just longing to get some of your letters, which always cheer me up. I hope they catch us up soon.

We have travelled two or three hundred miles and been in action on many occasions. We were some of the first troops to cross the frontier where we had a terrific reception; the people really thought we were their saviours. We have had plenty of excitement and the men have been just overjoyed.

Fortunately, we have had no casualties (I think we move too quickly for the Jerries to get a line on us). The higher authorities are very pleased with our shooting and are taking good care that we do not get into trouble. If we don't get anything worse, we shall be all right.

The worst things are the air raids. Several of the towns have been bombed. Jerry comes over in waves and the bombs just rain down. The result is really terrible. We of course are always well out in the country. I do hope you never see these bombings, let alone be in them; they just fill you with disgust.

Another sight which is appalling and pitiful are the refugees; thousands and thousands of them all loaded up on anything that will move on wheels with what belongings they can gather together. They all drift slowly down.

John's diary

Sunday 26th May 1940

04:30: A British bomber is brought down by allied anti-aircraft fire, crashing on the road by Battery position. All crew killed and machine a total loss.

08:10: No shooting until ordered. French report to have relieved Belgium troops north of Menin at 04:00 today.

10:50: Message instructing Batteries to forward bearings of any German Observation Balloons sighted. No lines of communication laid from Regimental Headquarters.

13:15: Report that contact has been gained on right front at Ypres-Comines Canal – still held by own troops.

14:00: Air Raid.

18:07: Order received to fire 40 rounds on nearby wooded area at once and shot to be reported.

18:13: Order received to fire 20 rounds on Zandvoorde.

18:20: Signals report difficulty.

19:15: Battery unable to fire owing to presence of enemy bombers overhead.

21:42: Flashes reported from hostile Batteries.

Barnes

SW13

26-5-40

My very dearest Bless-you,

I've had such a full and busy time today. First of all, it is the National Day of Prayer – I expect you've heard about it? Mummie and I went to St Mary's for the 11 o'clock service, and prayed ever so hard for a speedy victory, though that always comes second to my prayers for your safe and speedy return. If numbers of prayers have anything to do with it, we ought to win very soon!

I've never, in all my life, seen so many people in that church. They just streamed in unendingly, and even the gallery was packed out, too (and you know it's quite a big church). I'm sure – certain – that it will help us all enormously, and I only hope that when our Victory Day comes, all those people will be just as ready to go to church and thank God for it. It just shows how many people really believe in the power of prayers – you know I'm one!

Well, my dearest, I wonder whether you felt me praying so hard for you. And another thing I wanted to know was, are you able to keep to our 'thinking times', morning and night now, dear? I am able to of course, and shall always do it whilst you're away from me, even if you can't always manage it.

I do love you so terrifically, my darling, and I want you more and more every day that passes. My heart aches dreadfully when I think of how lovely everything was when we were together, and how sweet you always were to me, and I pray that soon we'll be happy together again. I don't honestly think that it can go on for so very long, at this intensity, do you? I was very cheered by your shortened views of the duration!

Goodnight, my dearest love. I adore you. With all my love,

Your 'Cabbage'

John's diary

Monday 27th May 1940

Adjutant addressed personnel of Regimental Headquarters, stating that orders had been received for the British Expeditionary Force to evacuate from Flanders and northern France, and to reorganise and reform in England. The move is necessitated to prevent us from being surrounded and cut off, which is now at imminent risk owing to capitulation of the Belgians under the head of King Leopold. The evacuation scheme is the result of the co-operation between British and French High Commands and has the latter's full approval. Unit is to move through the evening and minimum personnel to man the remaining guns, with the remainder to follow in about 72 hours. Unit transport is to be employed for the move; stores and equipment to be smashed and ditched except personnel kit and small arms, and two days' rations to be drawn evenly by every man.

Navy is understood to be capable of coping with 30,000 men per day for transport to UK. Remainder of day to be spent in destroying stores and equipment in preparation for the move. The reaction of the men to this move may be generally expressed as one of mixed feelings:

pleasure at the prospect of returning to the UK, but disappointed in that they have not come to real grips with the enemy nor are they for the present able to carry the fight to the Hun.

20:12: 216 Battery withdraw and are unlikely to be able to reoccupy owing to heavy shelling.

During the march to the coast, the appalling loss in equipment becomes more and more evident and, as we travel, remaining inhabitants come out of their homes to deride us.

The Battery is then in action and firing overhead and across the convoy. I lead my convoy on a motorcycle but owing to the considerable numbers involved, the roads are heavily congested, and progress is extremely slow. It is unlikely that more than ten miles are covered in the first two hours on account of continual hold-ups and roadblocks. Over on the right skyline, gunfire flashes; lights and star shells are observed. Just before dawn, a stationary convoy of ambulances, drawn up on the left-hand side of the road, are passed, and a short distance further on enemy shells fall within a few hundred yards of the convoy. No damage resulting. The next village has been shelled and the convoy passes through without incident.

Barnes
SW13
27-5-40

My own darlingest darling,

I received your field postcard at teatime today and am so very, very pleased with it. It's sweet of you to send it, and I do appreciate it, dear; it helps <u>such</u> a lot.

I am still hoping and praying that you're not having too bad a time, my dearest. My ears burn quite a lot these days, and I know it's always my Mr Snippet thinking of me. I'm still serenely confident (inside) that everything will be quite all right for us, even if things don't always seem as bright as they might. I'm never discouraged about anything people may say, and am certain we shall win through, as we always do in the end!

I adore you,

Your own wife

John's diary

Tuesday 28ᵗʰ May 1940

Travel all night. At dawn a little more than half the journey has been completed owing to heavy traffic congestion and lights having been forbidden to all vehicles.

05:00: As dawn breaks, the convoy is able to quicken its pace and observation of rules for spacing of vehicles in operation are in modified form. Progress from this time is comparatively good and in one direction on the horizon a large pall of smoke is observed, rising hundreds of feet into the air. Some 17 kilometres from Dunkirk unit transport is parked in a field on the left side of the road where already there are parked hundreds of vehicles of all types. Here, all British Expeditionary Force transport is being parked and it is understood that it is to be destroyed later. Orders are given to remove gun sights.

This is the limit to which most transport is permitted to approach Dunkirk and from this point personnel in small detachments proceed. I am requested to lead a detachment and continue on motorbike. The roads are over flat low-lying land, and occasional showers of rain are welcome on this monotonous march. At various points on the road, it is evident that dyke sluices have been opened as the fields below road level are beginning to flood in preparation for the defence of Dunkirk. Two short halts are made at intervals in the march and, on approaching Dunkirk, the route taken is through the northern outskirts to locate the bastillion, where further orders are given to follow the stream of men proceeding to the points of embarkation.

In traversing the suburbs, it is necessary to take cover from enemy air raids about a score of times. The remainder of the main body is sadly split up, and Battery parties are separated, but eventually the march to the beach is safely accomplished. On reaching the shore, we flock onto the beach, where on the light, golden sands above high watermark, we are easily conspicuous for aerial machine gun targets. The beach is immediately cleared, and all ranks marshalled on the promenade. From this, a distance of one mile is covered in single file, under cover of the sea wall and along the jetty until they board the waiting ships, which vary from destroyers to much smaller types of craft. Several destroyers are in position in the bay and, on the approach of many aircraft, put up an accurate anti-aircraft fire. Marines are placed at strategic points, marshalling and assisting men along the promenade sea wall and jetty. The organisation and behaviour of the naval and marine forces is admirable.

I report to the naval command post and am requested to proceed on motorbike to investigate the possibility of personnel embarkation from the mole, 3 or 4 miles distance away. I follow a route via the back of the sand dunes and through the wrecked town of Dunkirk; bombed to hell. Oil tanks are ablaze, and some routes are blocked by the extensive devastation. Though bomb-damaged, the mole remains accessible by ships and for embarkation of personnel. I report this back to the Command Post at which point I am ordered to use this route to evacuate myself. I return to the mole (leaving the motorbike on the sands) and start a long wait.

23:00: I board a steam-driven minesweeper, HMS Lydd. Once aboard, I go below deck to the Officer's Mess and fall asleep.

Some time, in the middle of the night, I am awoken by gunfire aboard and go up on deck to investigate. The ship is being attacked and is exchanging gunfire with two vessels, one of which appears to be a German torpedo boat. The torpedo is hit and begins to sink, firing back and killing our gunner, whilst we ram the other.

As we proceed through the gloom of the night, we see a destroyer which has been hit, split into two sections, and sinking. Personnel are in the water, clinging to the upturned hulls. We coast around the ship, picking out of the water as many of the men as we can, most of them in a pretty bad way and covered in oil. We lug them aboard until we just can't get any more on. In all, we only manage to rescue 20 of the 700 men. We calm the survivors, settling down again for the night and chugging away until we get to Margate.

Barnes
SW13
28-5-40

My own beloved husband,

I would give anything to know how, and where, you are. I have had the news of Belgium's surrender, and feel completely numbed, apart from the one thought that you might not be there. Surely it could not hurt anyone for the wives to know whether their husbands are in France or Belgium, and it might save us hours of anguish. I am sure that whatever comes now, I could not pass through a greater hell than this. I haven't of course parted with any degree of confidence in our victory, and nothing matters any longer but that you are safe and well. If only I could do something, anything, to help you, my darling. I can only pray, and let you know that I am beside you in spirit and mind, and am still sure that with my husband's and the other men's magnificent efforts, we <u>cannot</u> fail. I am so very proud of you. If only I could be with you, the bullets and bombs would be a welcome change to this helpless agony of mind.

I know you will let me know how you are, and <u>please,</u> <u>please</u> tell me if it's France or Belgium my dearest; it would relieve my mind tremendously. I am with you, loving you hard all of the time, my precious love,

Your Rita

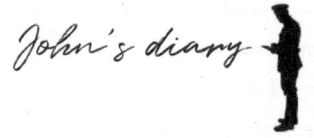

Wednesday 29th May 1940

We dock at Margate pier. It is a beautiful sunny day in England. The reception committee come aboard and enquire as to whether personnel are infested ('lousy'). Once cleared, we are allowed to disembark to entrain for Gloucester, halts being made at different town and village stations at which a plentiful supply of sandwiches, chocolate, fruit, tea and beer for the men is provided by the locals without charge, and where we are welcomed like heroes. At Gloucester we proceed to a rest camp and immediate steps are taken to obtain authority for British Expeditionary Force men to proceed on 48 hours' leave. I find the local Officers' Mess at the Hare and Hounds Hotel and get some rest. I still have my revolver with me, and as is my usual practice, place it under my pillow. After many weeks out in the open I sleep between clean sheets. All I want is peace.

Barnes

SW13

29-5-40

My very dearest dear,

I grow more and more proud of you with every passing hour. With every 'news' that is broadcast, such grand tributes are paid to the magnificent valour and courage of our British Expeditionary Forces, and knowing you as well as I do, I know that you are foremost amongst them to display such an example to your men. I am still holding onto our belief in your luck and am sure that you will get out of that Belgian catastrophe all right. There's no need to tell you how I watch and wait for news, though I know that it will be most unlikely to come from <u>you</u>, just yet. You are surrounded by my love and prayers always, my darling, and perhaps they will help to shield you from danger.

I do hope you will still be receiving these letters, my love; just to let you know how much I'm loving you!

All my love,

Your Rita

Hare and Hounds Hotel
Gloucestershire
30-5-40

My dearest darling wife,

I do hope you received my telegram yesterday saying that I had arrived back in England safe and well. I tried to phone you last night, but after waiting an hour and a half I was tired and went to bed.

Darling, it is marvellous being back in England again. I am at a rest camp and the hotel is the Officers' Mess. There are about five hundred men here and another five hundred are expected. They are all mixed up and the job is to sort them all out.

We had a really exciting time, some of it terrible, but I am none the worse, and after a clean up and a good rest I think you would recognise me again. I do hope you are well and have not upset yourself worrying.

The last letter I received from you was about 10 days ago. I have written and sent field postcards whenever possible, but I understand no mail has reached England for at least a fortnight. You poor kid, you must have been anxious. Anyway, we both knew everything would be all right, didn't we? That was a great consolation to me. I can't begin to tell you what we have been through. I can do that so much better when we are together. I have lost nearly all my kit in getting away, but that is a small thing. It is just grand to be back.

Your loving husband,

John

 *Rita's diary*

Friday 31st May 1940

Drove down to Tetbury – saw my love again. Can't believe he's really here.

John's diary

Saturday 1st June 1940

Inspection by Queen Mary. She seemed quite concerned as to whether I had had enough sleep and food.

 *Rita's diary*

Monday 17th June 1940

France surrenders. Now we're in for it!

Tuesday 18th June 1940

Fear of imminent invasion. Priority for all personnel to defend the south coast of England. 300,000 troops have returned with what they were wearing, but with little equipment or armament. 63rd Regiment are to reassemble and split into small sections, each with an officer.

I and my troop are posted to Melksham with what armour they can give us, to 'do our best'. All personnel have been issued with handspikes, consisting of a piece of gas piping with a bayonet soldered onto the end. Drills are to focus on the use of these and the use of Molotov cocktails as anti-tank missiles.

Saturday 6th July 1940

Rita very unwell today. Medical Officer unsure as to whether she has German measles. I am given a few days' leave to get her home to Barnes. Pull in at Midhurst.

Sunday 7th July 1940

Doctor to Rita. Can't move her.

Tuesday 9th July 1940

Rita has curious fit. Temperature 102.

Sunday 14th July 1940

Overnight Rita becomes delirious, and her skin reddened. I manage to get her into the car and drive her back to Barnes. Upon seeing her, Rita's mother is extremely worried, and Mr Heekes, the local doctor, is called. Diagnosis of scarlet fever.

Monday 15th July 1940

Rita is very weak and is admitted to Isolation Hospital, Mortlake, London. I am only permitted to speak to her through a glass window.

Tuesday 6th August 1940

New posting. Troop stationed on the beach with a museum-released gun, mounted on a platform facing out to sea with the aim of defending Bridport.

Sunday 11th August 1940

Witness extensive dogfights over Portland and the English Channel and multiple aircraft being shot down, piling off and diving into the sea. German pilots shoot down English parachutists as they bail from their planes. Fishermen sent out to sea to look for survivors. Some survivors found. German personnel are not returned to harbour.

I see the Colonel and Major for lunch.

Sunday 25th August 1940

Go down to Lee-on-Solent. Troop is armed with Sten and machine guns, rifles and a mobile submarine deck gun, requisitioned from a museum, mounted onto a truck, with 30 to 40 rounds of ammunition. Orders are given for mobile gun to be seen in different locations with the aim of convincing the Germans that there are multiple guns in this location. Each manoeuvre must include travelling through town centres for everybody to see.

Tuesday 27th August 1940

Stationed at HMS Daedalus, Lee-on-Solent, with troop to prevent German paratroopers landing on the aerodrome.

Long air raid.

My dearest love,

At last, I'm able to write to you myself! It has seemed such ages without my doing so, and very annoying. I <u>have</u> appreciated your letters every day. I looked forward to them as the high spot of each day!

I arrived home today about lunchtime. Was I glad to get out! As a matter of fact, on Monday I was so fed up that I told the doctor I'd come out on my own responsibility, so here I am!

It's marvellous to be 'free' again. I feel as if I've been in prison doing time! I had to be disinfected before I came out, and they did it very thoroughly! So much so that I couldn't bear the smell of myself, so have just washed my hair, and will have a bath later on. I don't think even you would fancy me like that?!

I feel perfectly well, but owing to the air raids have not had much sleep lately, so am consequently rather tired. Every time the siren went, we had to get <u>under</u> our beds. On Monday night I was there from 9:25 p.m. till 4:30 a.m., and the gunfire was too heavy to allow any sleep. I was then woken at 5:30 a.m. to begin the day! A 'lone raider' dropped a bomb <u>after</u> the all clear the other night, and killed the mother and father of two little girls. Wasn't it a shame? They lived half a mile from us, in <u>walking</u> distance.

Well, my darlingest, I'm just longing to be 'squeezed to death' by you!

I love you all the world,

Your Rita

My beloved husband,

I do wish I could hear something of you – nothing since Tuesday now – it seems such a long time, and now (unless you phone?!) I shan't hear until Monday, as the last post has gone.

Upon returning home, I have discovered that Mummie and our next-door neighbours have come to some sort of arrangement and Mr Jobbins has built an air raid shelter under the two front gardens. It is well stocked with tins of food and water in carriers, consists of a small room, with an air vent coming up out of it, and is lined with a sort of rubber stuff which means that every time a bomb falls nearby we bounce, making it a very interesting experience!

We had a terrific raid last night, and the ack-ack guns were so heavy and continuous that we couldn't sleep. The Isolation Hospital, Mortlake, was bombed and the roof of my room there fell in. My bed might have saved me, but I feel the first of my nine lives has gone!

I love you more every minute, and do so hope that on your next birthday we'll be able to celebrate together.

Your very own,

Rita

My darling Mitty,

I wish tomorrow morning would come quickly and bring me a letter from you.

Everyone seems completely astonished that I should look as well as I do. I don't know what they expected, because resting so much, all I've done is to grow fat and lazy. Mr Heekes is <u>very</u> pleased with me, and says my heart is perfect once again. He told me <u>he</u> thought it would be months, not weeks, and he certainly never expected to see me up and about so soon. So you see, your nursing (as I told him!) helped terrifically.

I have a rash under my chin, which has been there for ages. I have to apply hot fomentations and every night paint it with iodine. Well, I made myself look beautiful with it last night, and did it burn! I was hopping about everywhere not knowing what to do with it. Tonight, I'm just 'smearing' it, not painting! I earnestly pray that if a bomb gets me, it won't be an incendiary one.

All my love and thoughts,

Your Rita

Lee-on-Solent
5-9-40

My dearest angel wife,

By the time you get this letter the great day will have arrived, and we shall have been married for one year. There can be no doubt that we have both made it a great success. I love you more than ever and more than I ever thought possible. Let us hope that before very long we shall be together, and live as normal happy married people should live.

Heaps and heaps of love, darling. Only a few more hours now.

Ever your loving husband,

John

Barnes
SW13
9-9-40

My very dearest Mr Snippet,

I expect by now you'll be busy looking after your guns again. How did you find things when you arrived?

It seems ages already since I saw you, and our weekend is like a lovely dream. I feel absolutely lost without you; it's an awfully lonesome feeling! I think you're a darling, and I love you and love you.

Since I've been home today Adolf hasn't paid us a visit, so I suppose he's saving it all up for tonight! I'm not looking forward to a whole night in the 'underground'.

All my love and thoughts all the time,

Your Rita

P.S. Since writing this, we've had a simply terrific air raid; bombs everywhere. Never heard such a row in my life!

10-9-40

My dearest dear,

Since I've been home the whole time seems to have been a nightmare! All that we hear all day is the sound of sirens, gunfire and bombs! Yesterday teatime and all last night was simply terrific, and yet the papers hardly mention it.

Much to my disgust, Mummie insists that I spend the whole night in the dugout. She says that whilst I'm in her care I'm to do as she says, and when I come to you, I'm to do as you say. What I want to know is, where is all this freedom we're fighting for?! Anyway, we were stuck down there from 8:40 p.m. until 6 this morning – six of the Jobbins' and three of us, and at about 2 a.m. Geoffrey arrived too. You can just imagine ten bodies strewn about the floor and squashed in like sardines. I couldn't even turn on my side! Of course, Mr and Mrs Jobbins, Mummie and Geoffrey held a concert (a quartet in snores) and the air got thicker and thicker!

I was up viewing the landscape at 2:00 a.m. when Geoffrey came in. He'd come up from Brighton, and says that though part of Victoria Station has been damaged, the trains seem to be running all right. He'd had a most thrilling journey: fires at Victoria, Kensington, and Earls Court, so big that we could see the scarlet glow in the sky from here.

I love you till I'm nearly bursting!

Your own 'Chicken'

11-9-40

My dearest darling,

I hope you've been receiving my letters; all the posts have gone wrong, and I expect that's why I haven't had any news from you so far. I'm writing this in the dugout this afternoon during another raid. Nowadays you never know whether it's going to be another onslaught, or just a 'mild' attack, so if we hear a goodly number of enemy planes overhead, we come down here. Do I hate it?!

Last night we had some terrific thuds again and, when we came up, the sky was in one tremendous red glow, much worse than even the night before. Covent Garden is almost reduced to debris, and Queen's Gate has numerous unexploded bombs lying about, and nobody is allowed near.

I'm longing to get to you again, my precious. Hurry up Friday! It'll be scrummy again!

I love you all the world,

Your own Rita

11-9-40

My very dearest one,

I do hope things are getting settled for you, and you're not quite so rushed off your feet. Are the guns firing properly now?

How are the raids? We are 'enjoying' our seventh today and are now ensconced for the night. Oh dear, last night was simply <u>terrible</u>! Hell let loose! I didn't get more than twenty minutes' sleep all night. They are definitely worse, and Mummie's snoring is too! Thank the Lord there's only two more nights to go. I couldn't stand a lot of this; I'd be <u>so</u> bad tempered and tired!

I'm so longing to see my Mitty again.

I love you and love you,

Your own missus

12-9-40

My dearest darling husband,

Last night's new methods of persistent and heavy anti-aircraft fire may be very good but, ye gods, <u>what</u> a din! It's quite impossible to go to sleep at all of course, and I expect we shall have it all and every night in future. The anti-aircraft guns at the Ranelagh grounds blasted away all night, and the whole place around here had large pieces of shrapnel on the roads. We also had several incendiary bombs last night.

Mrs Jobbins and the three girls have found it a bit hot to be comfortable in this district now, so have all gone away to

Gloucestershire. I expect they all had a good night's rest last night, the lucky things; I'm afraid we're getting tired, and I have lost all my 'sunburn beauty'. However, with only Mr Jobbins and Lucien (the son), and Mummie, Sarah-Jane and I, we were able to stretch our legs out more last night.

Our poor London! It's quite heartbreaking when you meet people and they tell of the latest destructions. From what I can make out, it's in a truly pitiful condition already, and there's lots more to come, I fear.

All my love,

Your missus

17-9-40

My darling love,

As you see by the address, I am once more spending the night in 'paradise'. I had quite a good journey, considering all things, and arrived home at 1:45 p.m. Mummie was <u>very</u> pleased to see me, as you may imagine! She had been terribly worried, and wept tears of joy over me. They've been having an awful time here over the weekend, worse than ever if possible, and tonight has started off quite hectically again. I'm fearfully husband-sick already!

The phone seems to be completely out of working order, and I haven't been able to get through to anyone. I'll try tomorrow morning again. London has been knocked about a great deal more over the weekend, and traffic is still disorganised. You can't go far now without seeing the effects of bombs; there have been some very big ones in Barnes over the weekend. Some people here have had their water cistern burst by the constant and terrific explosion of the anti-aircraft guns, so that gives you an idea of what the noise is like. I shall look forward to some good nights at the end of the week! (With my darlingest too, I hope!).

Goodnight, my precious darling. I do love you and love you all the world,

Your 'Chicken'

HMS Daedalus
Lee-on-Solent
18-9-40

My very dearest darling,

How are you getting on in London, and are you having many sleepless nights? I do hope not. We have had a very quiet time really, though the lads are in action now with some Jerry bombers.

I am getting the troop a bit more into shape now. I have had to give them a choking off today, but I think it has cleared the air. I went down with them yesterday to Hayling Island where they let off some rounds into the sea. They certainly make a good crack. My next task is to get a concrete shelter for the mess. I have been promised a start by the end of the week.

With heaps and heaps of love for my darling wife,
Your John

John's diary

Tuesday 8th October

Shoot out today as Luftwaffe conduct a heavy attack with Messerschmitts, bombing and machine gunning the hell out of Daedalus. We shoot off the rifles but it's impossible, as German pilots shoot down at us, spraying the ground with bullets. HMS Daedalus is almost wrecked.

5th Corps School
Home Forces
2-12-40

My dearest darling,

I had rather a trying journey back. We got to the station before Southampton where the air raid started at 6:30 p.m. They poured shit and derision on us until about 1 o'clock, and the glass in the station roof came down. The beggars came over in relays every five minutes, rather like London I should think, only we were in a train and not a shelter. The blessed thing kept rocking. Eventually we started off at about 3:30 a.m. but only covered about half a mile to Southampton Central to find the track blocked. There were some pretty big fires going by there. We then came back a long way, after much shunting, to catch another train which eventually arrived in Bournemouth at 9:00 a.m. I got here at about 10 and missed the first two lectures. However, after seeing the Major, I was let off as he didn't twig I had been away without a pass.

We are now very busy swotting up for an exam on Thursday. It seems a queer business, as they are putting up the whole paper on

Wednesday evening which is going to be the same as that set on the last course. We all have copies of the paper, so I don't really see the use of it.

Please thank your mother very much for having me over the weekend. I hope her cold is much better.

With heaps of love for my missus,

Your John

1941

Barnes
SW13
1-4-41

My very dearest Mr Snippet,

I've been thinking all day about this day last year, and what a dreadful day it was. I'm feeling very thankful this year that you're not far away.

Mummie has certainly 'turned up trumps' about the baby and is helping us enormously. She has ordered such a beautiful pram, in green and pinky-beige, from Selfridges, and they are keeping it until we want it. We are only just having the baby in time, as from now on everything is to be 'standardised', and it will be awful.

As for our ongoing house purchase, I've not heard from our estate agents, Goodman and Mann yet, so shall leave it now until Friday morning, and then let them know a few things if they haven't the keys still!

I'll write again later. All my love and thoughts, my precious,

From your wife *avec enfant*

Royal Artillery Mess
Sedgehill
Shaftesbury
3-4-41

My dearest darling,

I have been over to the farm this evening. The laundry seems to be there. Eight handkerchiefs in all but some of them are foreigners I am sure. Still, we will keep them. I seem to be very short of handkerchiefs. Can't think where they could all have gone.

I have heard from Mr Piers that completion is due for Friday and the key will be either with the Agents or handed over to him. If you have

not already got it, give him a ring on the phone.

The planes are buzzing over here tonight. I do hope they are not giving you a visit.

Heaps of love darling.

Your John.

Barnes
SW13
10-4-41

My darlingest Mitty,

I went over to our new little house, 'Craiglea', on Monday, and Mummie came with me. It was a great thrill when I first opened <u>our own</u> front door, tho' of course the whole thing was really spoilt by my other half not being with me. However, it'll be a much bigger thrill when <u>we</u> open it on to our home, instead of just an empty house. Yes, Mrs Cole had gone, taking her furniture but leaving her dirt behind her!

The rooms naturally didn't look so large as when they were furnished, and she'd left quite a bit of her dirty old blackout up, but all the same, I loved it and really felt as if it were 'home'. When the remainder of the blackout is down, and it is cleaned out (which I <u>hope</u> to get done before you see it) I'm sure you'll be <u>very</u> pleased with it, darling. It is (or will be when <u>we</u> go in!) a charming little house and the rooms are most beautifully light and airy. I'm sure that between us we can make it look simply lovely; we'll have everyone envying us, you'll see! Mummie was very favourably impressed with the house and told me she thought your father had greatly exaggerated the bad points of the kitchenette! I wonder what our tenants will make of it.

Be careful if you spend the night at Bournemouth, <u>where</u> you spend it! I couldn't possibly spare you to anyone else, even for one night!

My heaps and heaps of love and thoughts.

Hurry up next week,

From your own Rita (plus Mighty Atom!)

16-8-41

My dearest dear,

I'm getting down to a bit of housework and cooking, which I like and makes me feel a bit more useful! I feel a bit stronger every day, tho' the infant gets heavier. It is very much 'full of life' and has taken to tickling me during the night, and I wake myself up with laughing!

We have had an amusing ('tho also somewhat annoying!) little comedy the last day or so. I rang up your people, when I received your last letter, to talk to them about it, and as usual had to talk first to your father, then your mother, and back again to your father. Anyway, your father suggested that they should come over here this weekend, so I said we'd be very pleased. Then your mother came and said she didn't think they'd come, and then back came your father to say they would. Later Thursday night he phoned to say they'd come today at 4:00 p.m. (after first having upset the applecart with Mummie, who answered the phone first, by telling her that she needn't be in as they were coming to see me! Or words to that effect). These families!!! I shall be grey before I'm a mother!

On Friday morning, your mother rang up (when she'd got the old man of the way!) to say they might not come, and anyway they'd phone. I didn't hear, so went out this morning and bought cakes and things. I waited until 3:30 and then rang up to make sure and was informed that they wouldn't be coming! I'm sorry I wasted the money (I might have known your mother would win!!) and I do wish you could come and help to eat them up, darling!

Heaps and heaps of love, my dearest,

Your own missus

My dearest darling,

I hope you've had a good run back, and the Colonel was in good humour. Did he buy you a drink at his club to give you a start?!

I loved seeing you and shall miss you dreadfully tonight. I hated to see you go and wanted to jump on the bus after you! Now I shall count the days to your leave (but am <u>hoping</u> that maybe you'll <u>have</u> to come to town to get the Colonel some more booze before then!?).

Have you by chance still got the key of the shelter in your pocket, my love? I've looked everywhere but can't find it.

I have just been listening to Mr Churchill; what did you think of him? And what did the Colonel have to say?!

I love you and love you all the world,

Your own Rita

26-8-41

My dearest dear,

Thank you so much for sending the key, which I received this morning.

I (and the Atom) are both very well, but your ungrateful offspring is trying to kick my tummy inside out!

We have been very busy and have had a constant stream of visitors all this week (including four to tea!) to inspect the baby's trousseaux and cot. It seems to have got all round Barnes; one person tells another, I suppose, and they all just come and knock on the door! We've had two more presents: a little brass bell with a stork on it, and another pair of bootees. I don't know where to put everything. Our child is famous already!

This morning we've been very busy cutting beans and salting

them for the winter. Have done quite a nice lot, so we should enjoy them during your December leave!

Yesterday I ventured up to Hammersmith to do a spot of shopping. I wanted a pair of household scales and an ironing board and couldn't get either in Barnes. We've bought some proper blackout material for curtains for the bathroom and are now making them! So I'm going to have a bath tonight.

Mummie sends her love, and with all of mine and lots of thoughts,

From your missus

2-9-41

My dearest darling,

What a lovely day for your birthday, darling! I do hope you're able to get out in this lovely sunshine, and also for a drink or 'something' tonight. We'll have to make up for everything on your leave.

I'm enclosing your birthday predictions, which look pretty good, don't you think? (All except the bit about the 'chance of reviving an old romance'.) She'd stand the chance of having her eyes scratched out if I'm around!

The Atom is celebrating its daddy's birthday with kicks and bounds of joy. Let's hope it won't be long before we can celebrate it all together.

Heaps and heaps of love,

Your Rita

Tenterden
Kent
4-9-41

My dearest darling,

Thank you so very much for all your sweet letters this week which

I am afraid I have not had time to answer though plenty of time to read. I got your parcel this morning and am just in need of some stamps and envelopes. Your letter with cheques arrived at the same time. Your calculations are really astounding but I can't find the connection between them and the cheque. Anyway, I have no complaints provided the cheque does not bounce.

Well, all the best, my darling. My love to your mother, and heaps for your dear self,

Your John

Barnes
SW13
9-9-41

My darlingest,

Today Mummie and I went up to Kensington to get odd bits of shopping, and then we took a bus on to the West End and went to see *Lady Hamilton*. Of course, it made splendid material for comparisons between that time and this. The fighting scenes between the fleets were colossal. We also saw that German propaganda film (that we captured from them) of the beginning of the invasion of Russia. I had wanted to see it, but it was rather amusing! It showed solely the German side of it, with no sign of <u>any</u> Russian activity whatsoever!

Well, my precious, take care of yourself,

From your Rita

12-9-41

My dearest darling,

We keep very 'full up', and I'm not getting on with the preparations as quickly as I'd like. I seem to have swollen considerably the last few days, particularly yesterday and today, and it's getting a bit too much of a good thing to always carry around with me! I shall be very glad to have it outside instead of inside; it'll be much more comfortable! Sometimes I feel as if I can hardly breathe and I <u>must</u> burst. I'm sure it's visibly larger, as people now say, "How are John and Jeremy?" very pointedly!

I see the army consider I'm worth a bob a day extra – very good of them!

Well, my love, I'll write again soon. Take care, and <u>don't</u> <u>work</u> <u>too</u> <u>hard</u>.

All my love,

Your own Rita

16-9-41

My dearest darling,

I'm so annoyed! I rushed to get your letter off this evening and when I got to the pillar box, I found they've cut the last post!

Anyway, I went to see Mr Heekes this morning and had the beastly old examination, which has made me feel a little queer today. He is taking me to the hospital for an X-ray on Thursday as he's afraid the baby is in the wrong position and must have it confirmed before he starts pushing it about! Probably that accounts for the intense pressure I've felt lately. Rather a nuisance, isn't it?

We have a Salvage Drive on here tomorrow, so now I'm going to do some turning out!

All my love and thoughts,

Your Rita

17-9-41

My dearest darling,

I have just this minute returned from the hospital and am glad to say that things are not so extreme as Mr Heekes first thought. The Atom, although not in its normal position, is <u>not</u> upside down, and Mr H hopes it may kick its way round without much or any interference. It is also 'fitting' quite nicely so far, and he doesn't think there'll be any need for an operation (hooray!). He thinks he'll have to keep a watchful eye on its growth, and is going to 'let it be' for the next two to three weeks. So you see, your spouse and offspring know how to behave <u>sometimes</u>!

I've been up to Kensington today, darling (as you'll see by the enclosed!) and do hope you'll think I've done right. I've been keeping my eyes skimmed for your wool undies and pyjamas, so that I could tell you where I'd seen the best value and save you time in shopping on your leave. (It's hopeless nowadays, nobody has anything at all in stock.) Anyway, having asked everywhere we've been for wool shorts and told that there are none without exceptions, I saw some in a shop window in Kensington this morning for 9/6 which are by far the lowest I've seen yet.

Everywhere is no to all-wool flannel pyjamas, until Pontings today (as a <u>very</u> great favour, and <u>very</u> secretly from under the counter, hidden away!) brought forth four pairs, size 40, priced 21/- each. They're the only ones they have left; old price and all wool. They <u>may</u> have in a mixture later on, which will be 35/- so I took the opportunity and bought two pairs for you. Would you sign the enclosed white chit and send it off, <u>with</u> the receipt, as I've put it as soon <u>as</u> possible? I just hadn't got 16 coupons to give you! If you think it's worthwhile buying the other pairs, I'll get them for you. Please let me know about them as soon as you can. (I'm inclined to as we shan't get them again for a long, long time after the war.)

I've also been going crackers trapesing round to find a few household things that I must have for the baby's use now and that will be essential at 'Craiglea'. Everywhere is no until I get desperate, and heaven only knows what I'm going to do later on, as saucepans and kettles are out of the question. How I wish I'd got them earlier!

All my love,

Rita

2-10-41

My dearest love,

I'm sure you'll laugh when you next see me! The silhouette is marvellous and walking now is impossible; I just <u>waddle</u> around! The Atom does gymnastics continually, in spite of its close confines! I think it will be beyond my control very soon after it arrives and will need its father's firm handling! I <u>do</u> hope the Atom will arrive when you're with me; it would make all the difference in the world, and I should feel ever so much safer and braver. I feel very much 'on my own' at the moment.

I'm feeling more lonesome than ever for my beloved, and also longing for this 'ordinary' old war to end so that we can be alone together again. I do hope the Atom and I will be able to come and live near you soon, darling. Remember me to all, won't you? And keep all my love for your own dear self,

From your missus

My dearest darling,

I disgraced myself this morning by being most violently sick! So am having to spend the day in bed, as it's left me rather whacked out. I feel very unhappy about it as everyone lets me see what a nuisance I am. I also heard Mummie and Sarah-Jane talking about what a fuss it was all over nothing, and they never fail to rub that in, either. I told the doctor this morning that the household generally seemed to think it was unnecessary, and I believe she said something to Sarah-Jane, as afterwards she came up and had a row with Mummie, who is today also in bed with a cold!

The Atom was most ruffled and indignant with me and has proceeded to kick my poor, sore tummy ever since with the utmost vigour! Actually, it must have upset its equilibrium, and was to a certain extent my fault. I shall be quite all right tomorrow, but <u>how</u> I wanted you this morning! Do <u>please</u> be here when the Atom starts its journeying.

I love you more every day, darlingest,

Your Rita

18-10-41

My dearest darling,

Well, darling, I do hope I don't have to wait much longer than another week before I see my beloved again. I've been feeling very lonesome for you lately. I suppose it's because I don't sleep very well now and lie awake and think all sorts of things until I get worried stiff, and long for you just to be there beside me. It's so comforting not be alone. However, I shall have you soon, I hope, and then not much longer to wait.

Mummie says she wouldn't be surprised if the birth happened whilst you're here, and really neither would I! The last week has made a tremendous difference – in size, shape, <u>and</u> my feelings – and I feel as if it <u>can't</u> go on much longer now! I got so worried about it that I've been packing up my cases ready; I thought it was coming on any minute one or two days last week!

I love you all the world,

Your Rita

Brooklyn Nursing Home
SW15
25-10-41

My dearest love,

You'll be interested to hear that Mummie has now decided that she was just like Rosemary herself when a babe. As long as it pleases her...! Anyway, I think that she (our offspring) is so adorable that there's only one person that she could possibly take after, and when you're not here I keep discovering fresh little likenesses to my belovedest; I think you're both angels.

Your daughter is now hiccupping loudly from her cot (taking after you again!) tho' hers are caused through greediness at tea, instead of Guinness or cucumber!

All my love and a big x from Rosemary,

Your own Rita

Aldington
Kent
27-10-41

My dearest darling,

I hope you are continuing in your good spirits and that Rosemary is not biting too hard. How is the little nipper behaving? Still doing well at both ends I'll bet. I have just sent her birth certificate to Army Records so as to get the additional 1/6.

I got back to Ashford in very good time to find my batman waiting for me at the station with the Major's car. Everybody wanted to know how you were and send their best wishes.

We have been shooting today at Dungeness. Quite a good day.

Let me know of anything you want or that I can do for you.

Heaps of love to both my girls,

John

Brooklyn Nursing Home
SW15
29-10-41

My dearest darling,

Rosemary gets better-looking every day, tho' I'm sorry to relate that her hair is coming out! I'm in great suspense as to whether the new hair that's now growing is going to be as dark, and I think and hope it is. Her eyes get bigger every day too, and so does her appetite! I call her my little suckling pig, which she doesn't resent in the slightest! I'm now positively reeking with milk and wish I could offer my services as wet nurse to someone so that we could reimburse ourselves for expenditures on her! She has been dreadfully noisy lately, and I'm afraid I've a got a bit overtired and nervy through lack of sleep. I hope she'll settle down soon.

Please write soon (if you can!).

Rosemary sends love and has just blown you three bubbles!

I love you all the world,

Your Rita

31-10-41

My dearest dear,

Mummie isn't coming today but has just rung through to say you phoned her last night, and she spoke about the date for the christening. I've just spoken to matron about it, and she says that to go from here to a cold church less than three weeks after the baby has been born would be endangering both our lives, and she's going to tell Mummie so. I'm afraid <u>she</u> won't be very pleased but matron says that's nonsense! Matron also says that going home will be quite enough for me for one week anyway, and if I had any more excitement my milk would probably go, and then there's no getting it back. This would be a dire calamity, as our little love is really thriving on it, and gets bigger and stronger every day; even matron can see it!

I've had quite a number of letters and visitors, and my room is very bright with the flowers that they bring. I had the infant taken out of my room last night, and slept right thro', so shall continue on those lines!

Rosemary blows bubbles beautifully now and gets sweeter every day, and more cuddlesome. I now dress her myself and change her nappies, and today I'm going to introduce her to her little 'pot' for the first time. Both of us are 'doing our stuff' very well at our 'other ends'; me without taking any medication, and of course that all makes my milk much better for her. I'm sure my other name must be Jerusalem, "a land overflowing with milk and honey". (Mummie has brought me a jar of the latter ingredient.) Of course, it's bound to ease up a bit when I start moving around.

I hear our pram has arrived, and I'm dying to see it.

Rosemary sends love and bubbles, and with all my love to you, my precious,

Your Rita

Aldington
Kent
31-10-41

My dearest darling,

I rang up your mother last night and was very sorry to hear you were not so well. You mustn't let the imp keep you awake like that. Your letter, however, sounds very cheerful, so I hope things are not too bad.

I have been meaning to ask you if you had any valuables down the shelter such as my gold watch and your little jewel case. As you probably know, some wine is missing and your mother doesn't know what else

may have gone. I hope there is nothing else, though the wine is bad enough!

Heaps of love, darling,
Your John

Brooklyn Nursing Home
SW15
5-11-41

My dearest darling,

Thank you so much for your letter which I received yesterday. Rosemary and I were beginning to feel that our 'best boy' had forsaken us, as we waited six whole days for a letter! Of course, in here six days are as long as sixty would be, if I were up and doing. I've just had a message that Mummie has phoned through to say you rang her up last night. She didn't come for a week, as she got het up about Rosemary's arrival and had a relaxed throat and bad cold as a result.

I am <u>very</u> bucked that there's some hope of our being near you later on; it really cheered me up a lot. Perhaps if we got near enough, we might be able to see you for a little while every day? I'm <u>very</u> sorry about 'no sleeping out', but it might be as well, or methinks we should have John Jeremy arriving before we mean him to! By the way, I've heard of some very good 'preventives' we can try!

Rosemary is now behaving really very well and is apparently getting better and sleeping longer every night. She has altered tremendously in the last week; I <u>do</u> wish you could see her.

With heaps and heaps of love from us both,

Your Rita

P.S. There is nothing of ours in the shelter – everything is all right.

My darlingest,

I do hope Mummie hasn't worried you by telling you that I look pale and tired, etc.! I was allowed up for the first time yesterday – for tea – and today I've bathed Rosemary myself, as well as doing everything else for her. I have had a 'proper' bath myself. So you see, I'm getting on better now. I'm ashamed to say that I hadn't been feeling as 'chirpy' as I might have (when I wrote and said I was rather overtired and nervy), but have been feeling better the last few days. I shall be <u>very</u> glad when I get out of here, and manage Rosemary by myself to suit my own times. That sounds very ungrateful, I know, and I don't mean it to be but you see, there are not really enough nurses here to see to all the patients, and it means that you just have to wait your turn to be seen to. I hear that Rosemary now sleeps longer every night, so am hoping she'll be 'broken in' before I go home, which as far as I can see will be about the middle of next week. I feel better just to have a change from lying in bed, tho' am very shaky on my 'pins'!

Our offspring is really a <u>very</u> good little bundle, you know, darling, and it was my fault that she got a bit fretful the second week, as I missed you so very much that as I'm feeding, it affected her. Never mind, I'm looking forward to being near you soon, darling; and the 'sea of mud' won't be so murky for <u>you</u>, if you wade through it to see us most days.

Rosemary looks quite different now; her face is smaller but <u>such</u> a sweet little shape! There are three baby girls here now, and our daughter is already well ahead in the matter of looks!

Mummie brought Sarah-Jane and Chicot over yesterday. Chicot <u>was</u> funny – couldn't make out <u>what</u> the baby was! Mummie and Sarah-Jane now ire with each other in singing her praises!!

Do, <u>do</u> wish I could see you, my precious. I'm counting the days!

Lots and lots of Rosemary's love and all of mine,
Your Rita

7-11-41

My darlingest one,

What miserable weather this is. It doesn't give me any chance of going out myself <u>or</u> taking Rosemary, and tho' I took her down the road on Wednesday, she's too much of a bundle for me to carry far! Matron and I weighed her yesterday again, and matron said she was just on 8lbs, tho' it looked to me less than that. Anyway, they're pocket spring scales, and it's quite impossible to see within half pounds! I've had a pamphlet about hiring proper baby scales for a period of 3 months, so have sent off for them. It's much better than taking the babe round to the chemist every week, waking her up to weigh her, then the next day changing all her clothes and taking <u>them</u> round to be weighed!

Rosemary is getting stronger every day, and you'll be pleased to hear her legs are beautifully straight now! She stretches them out so <u>hard</u> and tries to stand up on my lap when I hold her upright! She's still losing her first lot of hair, tho' the new lot is growing nicely. Her eyes are grey-blue, and very bright and large, and altogether she's an angel!

She's had three very important events this week. First of all, I took her 'visiting' to see her two little girlfriends here. I'm sorry to say she was impolite enough to give them each a look of contempt and then turn her interest to everything else in the room! However, I must say I agree with her. Compared with <u>our</u> offspring the other two are very poor specimens, and if you had seen them together you'd have nearly burst with pride, Mr Snippet! I felt frightfully puffed up, and I'm wondering if it's because we're a good deal younger than the other two lots of parents. The second important thing was going out, and the third that she now uses a little 'pot' five times every day. She looks

<u>so</u> funny sitting on it; I'm sure you'll roar with laughter!

I'm dreading going home as I want to have Rosemary all on my own to manage. (I'm <u>determined</u> not to have my milk driven away!) Mummie seems to be having arguments with Sarah-Jane practically every day, and actually had one with the insurance man who came about her claim for the wines from the shelter, etc.! The latter I call <u>very</u> false policy, don't you?

Rosemary sends lots of love, and with all of mine, my love,

Your Rita

Aldington
Kent
9-11-41

My dearest darling,

Is everything all right for you to go home from Brooklyn? And now how is Rosemary? She seems to be doing pretty well.

I am afraid I am not very satisfied about her hair; I want it fair like yours. It is no use her having blue eyes unless she has fair hair, so you will have to do something about that. How is her weight progressing? She must be getting devilishly fat if her head appears to have shrunk.

All the very best, my darling.

Heaps of love to you both,

From John

Brooklyn Nursing Home
SW15
11-11-41

My dearest darling,

Thank you so much for your dear letter I received this morning; I do so love having them. They usually arrive whilst Rosemary is having her mid-morning lunch (10:00 a.m. feed), so we read it together, and think how lucky we are to have you.

Yesterday our daughter was on her very best behaviour all day and was simply adorable. Anyway, I know you'll laugh, darling, but she's honestly growing <u>exactly</u> like you! I'm thrilled to bits about it and keep on looking and looking at her. Matron came in this morning and announced that there could never be the slightest doubt of my fidelity to you, and told Rosemary that she grows hourly more like her father. So, you see all my 'concentrating' on you while she was coming has had its just reward!

You can have a little fair John Jeremy, if you like, but I openly confess I rub olive oil on our daughter's hair every day after her bath to make it darker! She now reminds me (apart from looking like <u>you</u>!) of a perky little cock sparrow. She has very good, healthy colouring, great big eyes that don't miss anything that's going on, and her little tuft of dark curls on top! She looks <u>so</u> cute!

Tomorrow, I hope to introduce her to the great outdoors. I've asked matron about going home, and she strongly advises leaving it until the weekend. She says it'll give me a chance to get much stronger. I'm awfully sorry, darling! Of course, if I'd been coming home to <u>you</u>, I'd have gone out <u>last</u> weekend, but it's very different going to someone else's home.

Rosemary's now yelling for her dinner, so must do my duty!

With heaps and heaps of love from us both, my precious,

Your Rita

Barnes
SW13
20-11-41

My dearest Mr Snippet,

Thank you so much for your letters. I've been trying so hard to write to you this week and do hope you won't think I'm neglecting you! But I just don't seem to have a minute to squeeze a letter into. Also, our wicked young woman has misbehaved herself at night continuously since I brought her home, and I'm now quite dopey all day, and feel as if I'm doing everything in my sleep. I slept in my old room last night, so wasn't quite so close to the yells, which was a little better. However, she's got to learn that we don't have meals during the night, so the only thing is to stick it out. She's a perfect angel during the daytime, and still seems to be doing very well.

Do want to catch the post, dear, so cheeribye for now. Heaps and heaps of love from us both,

Your missus

My dearest darling,

The washing and tackle arrived OK this morning with socks and Christmas pudding. What a combination! Thank you very much, darling, for sending them and I do hope you did not wind yourself running after me on Sunday. The pudding is very good, but so far I have not found any sovereigns.

The demonstration on Monday went off uproariously. Everybody thought it a huge joke and we all had an amusing day. I must have caught a chill in my back through crawling on the ground because in the evening, after a bath, I suddenly got stuck picking some clothes off the floor. It is the same old place in my back, where I cannot bend to touch my toes. I have had a thorough massage and it is now better, though a bit sore. (Have just found a sixpence in the pudding which has not improved the flavour but otherwise useful.)

How is Rosemary getting on? I don't like the idea of her waking up at 4 o'clock in the morning. She will have to alter her ideas over that.

Heaps of love, darling,
Your John

Barnes
SW13
30-11-41

My dearest Mr Snippet,

Having been worn to a frazzle by the nightly bawlings of your daughter, I determined on a different procedure, which (thank the gods and all the little fishes!) has worked so far, and I've had two nights' running of six and a half hours of sleep. If it carries on, I shall be a new woman.

111

I was visited by a child welfare woman, who informed me that a baby must cry for at least two hours every day in order to stimulate its brain. All I can say is that ours ought to positively turn out a genius! Still, on the whole she's really a very good baby (as long as she cries during the day instead of the night) tho' when she cries, she certainly puts her whole heart and soul into it. I think she definitely takes after her paternal parent in capacity of lung power.

Yesterday, Mummie and I went to the Gaumont. Tho' the flicks weren't terribly thrilling, it was a nice change. *The Night of January 16th*, a thriller, so I had a nightmare as usual last night, and dreamt that you'd had a dreadful accident and I couldn't find where you were. I was still rushing frantically round after you when I awoke to Rosemary's operetta.

I've been shopping for a new belt (for the sake of my tummy!) and oh boy, what a figure I possess in it! Venus is the name!! You'll have to take me on the razz to show it off (the figure I mean, not the belt!).

Well, my precious, please come home again very soon. We do miss you! Rosemary sends <u>her</u> love, and with very much love,

From your own missus

Chelmsford
Essex
2-12-41

My dearest darling,

I have been so busy the last few days I have not had time to answer your letter. The Regiment has now moved in and we are just snowed under with paper. To make matters worse, the Colonel insists on taking three or four officers with him each day to visit the Batteries on the coast. It is a complete waste of time and the ones left behind have all the work to do.

I do hope you don't get too tired with Rosemary. Do you put her downstairs at night when she is naughty?

Heaps and heaps of love, darling. I will try to phone one evening.

Your John

Barnes

SW13

10-12-41

My dearest darling,

I've been trying to get a few Xmas presents together and have bought our daughter a nice cuddly little donkey! At the moment I appreciate it more than she does! But toys are getting terribly dear and are almost unobtainable.

Who do you think has spent the day here today? Dear, darling Doreen! Aren't you pleased you weren't here?! Apparently, her marriage is already 'on the rocks', and she thinks her husband is 'a swine'. Mummie and she have had a most soul-satisfying powwow about men and decided that 'all men are devils'. I said I was very pleased with my own devil and wouldn't be without him for anything!

I've got a bit of a cold and sore throat thro' getting up in the night so much, and 'baring my bosom' to the cold, so now wear a 'mask' when I see to Rosemary. She's also very constipated, but is so sweet, and gives me such a wide smile every time she sees me. She really knows me.

Mummie and she send their love, and with all of mine, my precious,

Your Rita

My dearest darling,

We are having a hell of a time here. The old man has been blitzing everywhere. I try and keep out of harm's way but caught a packet last night.

I am now Entertainments Officer amongst other things, and I got up our first dance for the lads last night. The Colonel of course thought this and that, but we went our own way. However, at the last minute, he was invited along. He arrived at the interval when there was nothing doing, and everyone was in the pub. That was wrong, and then when I slipped off for a quick one, he apparently got frightened by a woman and beat it back to the mess and said we had all deserted him.

Are you still as busy, with Rosemary? I hope she is behaving better.

Heaps of love, darling

Your John

CHRISTMAS THOUGHTS
ACROSS THE MILES.

If there's anything that I could do
To bring you Joy to-day,
If there's anything to Wish for you,
I wish it right away;
For Christmas time is Wishing time
And though we're far apart,
I'm wishing you the New Year through
Things deep down in my Heart.

Barnes

SW13

26-12-41

My dearest darling,

It was lovely to hear from you yesterday, and I'm awfully sorry I was in such a rush. There were lots of things I wanted to say to you, however, we were late for church as it was, and the service had started when we arrived. I thought of you all day, and did so wish we could have been together – never mind, perhaps there won't be many more Christmases before we are, now. I got your card, darling, it was sweet.

Rosemary has been a perfect little angel over the holiday. I was so worried and sad at the prospect of having to wean her from me that I didn't write to you again before Xmas, as I'd intended. However, "all's well that ends well", and she is splendid again now, apart from constipation still, but is as contented and happy a babe as it's possible to be. It just shows that Mothers know better than doctors, sometimes! I'm dying to tell him and get one up on him!

Do you think you can manage to get home on or before Jan. 6th. darling? I'd just love you to see Rosemary's Xmas tree, with all her presents on it, and we have to take it down on the 6th – twelfth night.

I'm just living and longing for your leave, my love. Rosemary sends lots of love, and with all of mine.

Your Rita

Little Waltham

27-12-41

My dearest darling,

I was very pleased to hear from you tonight that Rosemary had been a good girl over Christmas. We had a very quiet Christmas here.

I had a local concert party for the lads on Christmas Eve. I knew it would be awful; still, the old man insisted on going and was not impressed. However, the lads enjoyed themselves. On Christmas Day we had a drink at the Sergeants' Mess and then visited the men at dinner and had our dinner in the evening, which was very good. The turkey was a beauty and we all very much over ate ourselves. The Colonel kept very sober and went to bed about 11 o'clock so we were more or less able to enjoy ourselves till 12.

Last night, the Boxing Day dance went off very well. We had record attendance, kept it going till 12 o'clock and managed to keep the old boy away. There was not a drop to drink in the village by closing time so you can imagine the lads were very merry, but thankfully caused no trouble.

Heaps of love, my darling,
Your John

Barnes
SW13
29-12-41

My very dearest dear,

What a lovely surprise to have a letter from you this morning, after your phone call on Saturday! I've been thinking of you so much all over Xmas that it almost seemed as if you were near, tho' after you'd phoned it somehow made me miss you more than ever. To cheer myself up I kept imagining our first Xmas together at 'Craiglea' with our babe; I wonder how soon that will come!

Do you know that on Wednesday we celebrate our ninth anniversary of meeting each other?! It seems longer than that, and I just can't imagine what I did without you!

You're certainly doing all you can to cheer up the boys, and I think you deserve a putty medal! You must make a very good master of ceremonies! The old man ought to be jolly pleased instead of being such a so-and-so!

I'm glad you enjoyed your turkey; we had a duck, which was jolly good, too, and went round to the Holdens for supper both Xmas and Boxing nights and had turkey there, so we did pretty well. I won 4/1/2d. playing pontoon on Boxing Night – quite useful! Rosemary has been a perfect little angel over the holiday.

Well, my precious, Rosemary sends heaps of love and wishes to her daddy, and with all my love and hopes and thoughts,

From your Rita

1942

My dearest darling,

Rosemary continues to surpass herself in good behaviour; as Sarah-Jane says, 'you wouldn't know there is a baby in the house now'. (I do, though!) She sleeps right round till I wake her in the mornings, which I'm afraid is usually at six now! I'd go on sleeping then if it weren't for a warning pain waking me and telling me it's time for the early morning milk delivery! She's <u>such</u> a happy wee thing; beams at all and sundry, and will be starting that on boyfriends as soon as she knows what's what.

Yesterday, being a very nice morning, I took the opportunity of taking her up to Hammersmith so that we can give you a Xmas present. It was her first bus ride, and she was a perfect angel all the time, even smiling nicely at the camera at the required moment! The photographer was charmed, especially as she has a little granddaughter of the same age who, she said, isn't nearly so big or advanced as our offspring.

All my love and heaps from Rosemary,
Your Rita

5-1-42

My dearest love,

Rosemary is still giving me stinks 4 times a day on average, even tho' I'm giving her everything I can think of to constipate her! You can just imagine me holding my nose and scraping away at everything. In the mornings when I go to her she's kicked in it so much that I just pick her up and plonk her in the washbasin; it's even in her toenails! She's full of beams.

Heaps and heaps and <u>heaps</u> of love from Rosemary and your
Rita.

My dearest darling,

I have just had nearly 24 hours in bed and feel fine. The annual business of the injection for typhoid has come round and the Colonel insisted on everyone going to bed afterwards. It really is the best way to get it over quickly.

I had a very amusing evening on Friday. Chelmsford and the local villages are having a Warship Week next month and Little Waltham had a meeting in the local pub. They asked me to attend as they wanted to use one of our billets for a dance. They were a very mixed crowd presided over by the Colonel. I tried to make myself as affable as possible but when the week arrives, I hope I am away somewhere. It will be rather an ordeal.

The Colonel asked me round to lunch today. He is the local brewer and has a great reputation for meanness. He lives in a very fine house and I thought a good lunch would be forthcoming. As it was, I nearly starved on a little steak and kidney pudding. I had a glass of beer, but the climax came after dinner when a decanter of sherry was produced, and the Colonel asked me if I would have half a glass of sherry. Anyway, I poured it out myself.

Heaps of love to you, my darling,
Your John

Barnes

SW13

13-1-42

My dearest Mr Snippet,

Thank you so much for your nice long letter. I had an awful shock upon reading "I've just spent 24 hours in bed" and was most relieved to read the rest of it; I thought you must have had an accident at first! You did make me laugh about your Sunday lunch. I can just imagine you pouring out the sherry! Actually, we don't ask people (that doesn't include you!) nowadays, as it's so difficult to get.

Both Rosemary and I are now indulging in lovely coughs and colds. I'm mad about it, as Rosemary has been a picture of health this cold weather, with lovely pink cheeks and big bright eyes, and now she looks rotten again. I've taken the utmost care of her, as I did want you to see her looking well, and the only thing I can put it down to is Sarah-Jane bringing home a bad cough and spreading germs about. I caught her kissing the baby's hand the other day, and then the baby

123

put it in her mouth, so there's no wonder!

Well, darlingest, I'll do my best to make Rosemary and myself well and beautiful for you for next weekend – we're just longing to see you.

All my love, my precious,

Your Rita

24-1-42

My dearest darling,

Rosemary is still just as delighted with life in general and herself in particular. She's an angel, (like you!). She seems much better regarding her cough and also the 'nosy' business, and sleeps peacefully and regularly between each feed. Just before she got the cold, she discovered that she could make quite loud sounds with her voice, so whenever she's awake she lies in her cot and practises; the results are at times most peculiar!

She is now in the throes of the most exciting discovery: that the funny little things waving about in front of her are her own hands, and they actually can hold things. Oh, she is *so* funny! I'm sure you'll laugh; she's so serious and bent on making her fingers work.

She's just as much a 'piggy', and this morning at the early feed imbibed so much that she drank herself to sleep and looked absolutely tight – big pink cheeks and head lolling about. I don't know where she gets such gluttonous ideas from. Neither of us are pigs, are we?

Your father rang up this morning (I couldn't speak to him as I was in the bath) but he asked Sarah-Jane if 'his son' was up here yet. So she (having run up to tell me first) said you weren't, and that we didn't know when you are coming.

Her wrist is now practically back to normal, and Mr H says she needn't even keep the bandage on. However, she wants to keep it on and make a nice little fuss still! She has reluctantly given up the idea of going 'home to glory' and has decided to live a bit longer!

Rosemary sends lots of love, and with heaps and heaps and <u>heaps</u> from,

Your own Rita

12-2-42

My very dearest,

I'm enclosing your pants (strongly mended if not elegantly!).

It's been <u>so</u> amusing darling – Rosemary evidently shares her daddy's opinion of Mrs Andrews! The last times Mrs A has called, Rosemary has given her one look (and <u>what</u> a look!) and her little lower lip has promptly gone right down, and then we have the most heartbroken sobs! She doesn't do it to anyone else, so I'm sure it's 'like Father, like daughter!' (<u>And</u> mother, come to that!)

We had some bad news yesterday: we heard that my cousin John has been missing for a couple of weeks or so now. He was an army doctor and was on his way overseas when the convoy was attacked. He was so very, very clever and so young.

I love you all the world, my darling,

Your Rita

Little Waltham
24-2-42

My dearest darling,

I now know I am going to Larkhill next week and, when the course ends, propose breaking my journey in London, and if everything is ready, for you to come down here. If everything is OK, can we bring everything down in the car?

I rather visualise the car full of junk, with a bath on the floor and Pee pot tied on the back; six or seven suitcases, with another dozen large

paper parcels and then no room to put Rosemary. Will she require the whole back seat to herself, or can you have her on your knee for the journey? I shall have my valise with me, but at a pinch I could possibly arrange to have it sent on by rail. The pram we shall have to fix to the roof of the car upside down and tied through the windows.

This is all rather regimental, I am afraid, but I would like to know what you think, dear.

Heaps of love, my darling, to you and all.

Ever,

Your John

26-2-42

My dearest darling,

Since speaking to you today, I have been round to the place I have found for you and Rosemary to stay in Little Waltham. Mrs Orr is very nice and an attractive girl; quite young and fair like you. I think you should be quite comfortable there. They are also having a Captain and his wife for a time. However, I think there will be room for all, and I am sure Mrs Captain is also very nice.

We can have quite a nice bedroom and Rosemary can sleep in the nursery. We can borrow their bath, but Mrs Orr is very short of towels, and we would have to bring our own. A woman comes in and does all the housework and cooking, except for evening meals. Food seems fairly plentiful though, and the milk is very good. Terms are 2gn a week and we will need to buy our own food, and electricity for our bedroom. I should think it would be about £4 all told. This is a fair bit, but if you help I think we can manage it. I think it would be a good thing if you wrote to Mrs Orr and made any suggestions you want. I went over on a bike this evening and it took me about eight minutes from the Mess. Not too bad.

Now as to Rosemary's vaccination: it seems a great pity to upset

her during this cold weather. As it is, we can still claim exemption by
obtaining a certificate from the Registrar of Births, Wandsworth and
doing a swear before a Justice of the Peace or Commissioner for Oaths.
There is almost bound to be a solicitor in Barnes who will take a swear.
This might be the best plan, because then we could have her vaccinated
at any time. What do you think?

  Heaps of love, darling,
  Your John

Barnes

SW13

27-2-42

My dearest darling,

I've now 'slept' on the vexed question of Rosemary's vaccination and have come to the conclusion that we really ought to have it done, before she starts teething in grim earnest. Also, she doesn't finish teething until she's two, and the worst danger will be over by then; otherwise there'll be such an awful business getting an extension, or whatever you call it!

I must tell you the latest achievement she has accomplished this week: she has managed, with a tremendous effort, to get her hands to meet in front of her, and is terribly proud. She now clasps her hands together every few minutes, and even goes to sleep 'saying her prayers'. Only last week her arms were so wide apart that I never thought she'd do it! She's also been studying her feet a lot lately and can't make out why they're not quite like her hands. When she sits on her pottie she makes great efforts, with many grunts, to grab her toes! She's sweet. She grows more interesting every day. I <u>do</u> so hope we can be together throughout the summer, when she'll be getting even more amusing.

I must see about buying a nice big trunk! It would be a good thing to have one nowadays for our growing family! By the way, do you think you'll be able to sleep out a bit? You said 'we' had a nice bedroom? Here's hoping, anyway.

Rosemary sends you heaps of love and bubbles, and with all of my love, darling,

Your Rita

6-3-42

My dearest darling,

Yesterday afternoon, in the snow, I took Rosemary to be vaccinated, and she was simply marvellous; not one tear or even a whimper. Of course, I'd nearly made myself ill, worrying about her, in case it hurt and upset her, and so had Mummie, to whom vaccination is simply dreadful! Even Mr Heekes said how good our wee Rosemary was, and I was so relieved when it was all over without any commotion. She had a good night, but I think she's feeling it a little today. By the way, she is growing into such a little chatterbox (takes after me!) and laughs and makes noises nearly all the time she's awake. The doctor was very amused.

I've to take her back in a week's time to see that it's all right. I do hope it doesn't put her back, darling, as she's got on so beautifully just lately, and is really a picture. I do want you to see her like it.

Heaps and heaps and heaps of love from us both,

Your Rita

Little Waltham
12-3-42

My dearest darling,

This morning I have been on a six-mile route march. Not a bad start after a week at Larkhill and two nights off. That, and an extra four miles walking to and from the office, I am a little weary.

I hear from the news today that petrol is going to be cut out altogether after June. We shall just have to use the car for travel only, and it is a very good thing we have got a bit extra in cans. I am sending you three soap coupons which I hope will keep the family clean for a while.

Heaps of love to you both and your mother. Cheerio, my darling, Your John

Barnes

SW13

13-3-42

My dearest darling,

I did enjoy Tuesday night at Oddenino's – thank you so much, my love. Wasn't it a perfectly scrumptious dinner? I keep on thinking of that lovely salmon! Mummie enjoyed herself very much too and has told several people about the dinner and made their mouths water!

Rosemary was so funny yesterday! Mrs Holden came to tea and of course wanted to nurse her, and Rosemary spied the little 'box of tricks' that Mrs Holden has to help her hearing, which she wears on her chest. Rosemary made a dive for it and apparently thought it was a new kind of bottle! She couldn't make it out at all and kept poking at it with great interest when she found there was no food to be had from it!

I hope you have a good weekend, dearest. Rosemary and I send you heaps and heaps of our love,

Your Rita

15-3-42

My dearest love,

This morning I awoke with spring fever and, feeling full of the joys of life, decided to take a day off from nappy washing, etc., and just enjoy Rosemary and myself. However, our daughter had different ideas and at 6:00 a.m., 10:00 a.m. and 2:00 p.m. she presented me with the most terrific efforts she has made yet in big business! My heavens, the perfumes and the messes! Each time every single thing had to be washed out (after being scraped off – ugh!): binders, vests, nappies, nightdresses and blankets. So I've done washing continually all day. So much for my spring fever. S'pose Rosemary had it too! She's been frightfully lively and full of beans all day, so it seems as if it's done her good.

I hope you'll have time to read this ditty, my love!

Rosemary sends heaps and tons of love and bubbles, and with all my love,

Your Rita

24-3-42

My dearest dear,

We've had a busy day today. This morning we had a jaunt up to London to see what there was to see, as it's Warship Week. We quite enjoyed ourselves, what with all the flags and bunting, bands, crowds of people, and the model warship in Trafalgar Square. By the way, Barnes aimed to raise £250,000, and we got £323,179. Not bad, was it?

We've also been out to tea today to Mrs Jaggers, who also had two or three other people, and they were most amusing! We were weak from mirth when we got back. By the way, Mrs Jaggers (who fancies herself as the greatest amateur singer of her day) called yesterday, and upon seeing Rosemary (who was staring fixedly at her) pounced upon her, held her in the air and started tra-la-la-laing at her, at the top of her voice. Rosemary's eyes grew bigger and wider, and her mouth fell open, until she got fed up, and started pulling her little lip down at the corners, ready to make a noise and join in the fray. I laughed inside so much at Mrs Jaggers's hurt expression that I had to go out of the room! I shared Rosemary's feelings exactly about the proceedings.

Rosemary and I send you our heaps and heaps of love, my precious,

Your Rita

2-4-42

My dearest love,

I do hope you have a happy Easter, darling, tho' I expect it will be much the same as any other weekend to you, as it will to us. I tried to take a photo of Rosemary today. She looks absolutely adorable dressed in a fluffy pale yellow outfit; looks just like an Easter chicken!

Just to make <u>sure</u> for next week's leave, I think I'd better buy a chastity belt, lock it up and throw away the key – that is if it isn't too late!!

Heaps and heaps of love,

From your Rita

17-4-42

My dearest darling,

I've been having an awful time this week with Rosemary when visitors have called. I really don't know what on earth I can do with her; it's very worrying. Of course it's inherited from me I suppose, as I was exactly the same.

Yesterday when Mrs Andrews came, she was quite all right until Mrs A. picked her up and nursed her, and then she bawled and bawled until she got into a terrible state. She was beside herself. Nothing and nobody could comfort her until I took her up to bed and fed her. On Monday too, two of my girlfriends brought their small daughters round, and Rosemary was brought in, took one look at the assembly and yelled the house down. The other babies tried to touch her and play with her, but she only got more frantic, until Sarah-Jane took her away. It makes things so difficult, and everyone gets upset because they think she doesn't like them. She certainly seems better with some people than others.

I must close, darlingest, as I've such heaps to do.

We both send you tons of love,

Your Rita

10-7-42

My dearest darling,

I meant to write to you last night but had so many odd jobs to do that I didn't have time, so am writing this in bed, having just given Rosemary her early feed. It's raining and looks as if it's been doing so most of the night, and I do hope it clears up for your scheme.

I'm so glad, darling, that you're getting on so well and are happy. I wonder when your promotion will be confirmed. I'm just dying to put <u>Capt.</u> E.J. Reed on the envelope already!

The weaning is still going on, and of course causing <u>me</u> more and more discomfort, and I shall be relieved when it's over. Rosemary only has two feeds from me now, and is putting on weight rapidly, tho' she has <u>three</u> big businesses every day, all over <u>everything</u>. Is it a job?! She is saucing everyone and is full of "Dad-dad-dad" and "Mum-mum-ma", and I'm sure sends you pots of love and kisses.

All my love,
Your Rita

15-7-42

My darlingest one,

Your small daughter is, I must tell you, a complete and utter porker. You'll have to make a lot of money to assuage <u>her</u> appetite, alone! I shall <u>have</u> to have a rise to meet the demand, I'm afraid. The other day her lunch consisted of a <u>whole</u> fresh herring, mashed up with butter, a quarter of a tapioca pudding, a rusk, fruit pulp and a beaker <u>full</u> of Trufood! She has a whole cake as well as a rusk at teatime now, and I really think I shall have to start giving her some porridge or cereal as well as her Trufood at 10:00 a.m. Her tummy sticks out so much that she resembles my shape last year; sometimes she looks as if it's twins! As for energy! Heavens preserve me this time <u>next</u> year with her.

Do hope the scheme and the shoot go off well, darling. I expect you'll head the list at the latter!

All my love, darling,

Your Rita

21-7-42

My dearest love,

The weather has changed, and what a welcome change it is. I'm sure everyone is 'sunshine starved' – I feel it! Rosemary lies in her pram all day in the garden without a stitch on, not even a napkin! Yesterday afternoon I had a fine do with her. She did a big business all over everything, and of course as the nappies were only placed <u>under</u> her, it ran and ran! She then carefully wiped Belinda Blue in it and proceeded to smear it all over herself! When I arrived, she was covered, hair and face as well. I just dumped the whole lot in the bath, Belinda included.

She's just gone off to sleep this afternoon, and I'm going to lay in wait with her potty. I give her a little sunbath in the 'altogether' first thing in the mornings, and her tummy is a delicate pink. Sarah-Jane is full of disgust and says I am teaching her to like being naked, and it's indecent!

Rosemary and I are longing to see you again. Every morning, I pat the pillow beside me and say, "Where's our dear daddy?" and she pokes her little head out and peers round to see if you're there! She sends you lots of love and 'noises'.

I'm hoping to hear from you soon, my precious. I love you and love you all the world,

Your own Rita

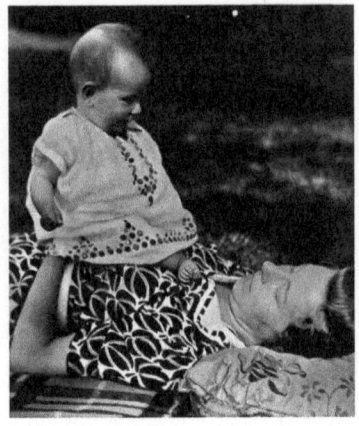

1-8-42

My dearest darling Mr Snippet,

I'm glad you got back quite well, tho' you must have felt very tired yesterday. We queued up for a bus for <u>ages</u> and eventually managed to get on. A girl gave up her seat to Mummie, after I'd enquired after her foot in a loud voice!

We amused ourselves by watching the people coming out of the Piccadilly Hotel and waiting for taxis. The commissionaire got quite frantic (and so did the people!) and was rushing about, up and down and across Piccadilly till he looked quite exhausted! The few taxis that <u>were</u> about whizzed past him without taking any notice of him at all!

I expect you're feeling more settled down now, darling. I hope so. It's always rotten going back, isn't it? I missed you so dreadfully on Thursday night that I just couldn't sleep, and tossed and turned and wanted my Mitty all night. It was <u>miserable</u>. Thursday night we had a lot of guns and a few planes. Everyone thinks we shall be heavily bombed here again before long, so I'm hoping I shall be able to bring Rosemary down near to you soon. I wouldn't keep her up here if we get it badly again. I shall pray hard that you find us a nice place!

The weather has been simply lovely here, and today Rosemary has been lying in the garden wearing only one of her soft nappies! She misses you very much and looks all the way round the bedroom every morning and night, craning and twisting her little neck, and even lifts up the bedclothes your side of the bed and peers underneath! She must think you are an invisible man.

We all send our best love, XXX from Rosemary and all my love and thoughts, my precious,

Your Rita

14-8-42

My dearest darling,

I've just had a bit of a scare with Rosemary! This morning, I pinned on her bib the little coral brooch your mother and father gave her as a christening present, and when I went to take it off to put her feeder on at lunchtime I found that the little bit of coral was missing.

I've turned out her pram and carrycot, and looked everywhere in vain, and am afraid she must have sucked it off. I should think she'd be able to pass it if she <u>has</u> swallowed it!

Cheeribye, my love. Rosemary sends you heaps and heaps of love, and with all of mine,

Your Rita

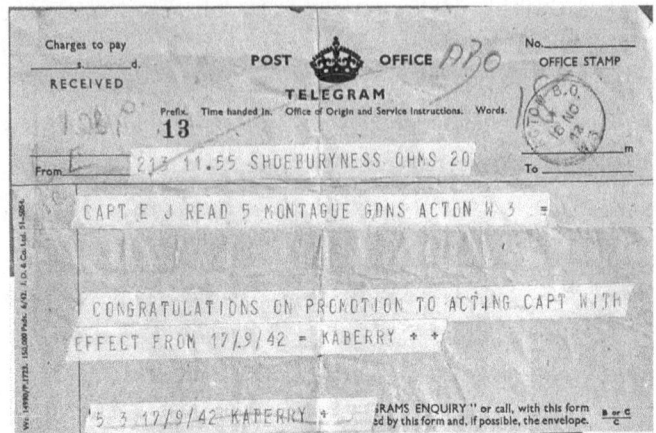

My dearest darling,

Rosemary and I received our letters from you this morning and were very pleased with them respectively. We <u>did</u> have a good birthday celebration for her, didn't we? I'm glad you enjoyed it as much as I, and I'm sure Rosemary did.

The little piggy porker had to pay for her 'internal' enjoyment yesterday. I starved her from lunch yesterday until breakfast today, and then made her 'go slow' with her eating. She seems perfectly all right, tho' not <u>quite</u> as full of life and beams as usual. Still, she stood up to the company today (Mrs Andrews! And matron) very well, and enjoyed her cards and the rest of her parcels. She has had altogether 29 presents, 14 cards and 2 telegrams! My hand aches from the thankyou letters!

Rosemary saw your pyjamas this morning and immediately enquired "Dadda?", so I gave her the two enlargements of you and herself to look at, and she was delighted uttering plenty of "Daddas" and stroking you! She insists that every picture she sees of anyone in uniform is her "da-da-da"! She's very well!

I do miss you, darling, and do hope you'll be home soon.

Rosemary sends heaps of love, and I all of mine, my precious,

Your Rita

29-11-42

My dearest love,

I do hope you keep fit, darling, in your awful 'digs' at the moment. What rotten luck being put there; I don't think they ought to in this cold weather. I wish you'd got a flask of rum with you, my love!

Have you just listened in to Mr Churchill? He doesn't believe in being too optimistic, does he?! I hope to goodness <u>you</u> won't have to fight the Japs, darling! Still, I suppose he has to keep some people calm who might think we've practically won the war!

Am just off to bed, so goodnight, my precious one. Do wish you were here to keep me warm.

Rosemary sends lots of love, and all of mine,

Your Rita

Southend
10-12-42

My dearest darling.

It is damned cold here. The whole Regiment is now down here which is really much better, though most of the chaps are cribbing at having to have a Regimental Mess with the Commanding Officer. The mess is in the hotel, which is quite near the gas works on the esplanade. It is not as luxurious as the Elms, but one great advantage is that it is not furnished, and therefore we get field allowance again.

Everybody has been working terribly hard whilst we have been away, or so we are told. There has been an administration week during which nearly all the books have been rewritten, and the day we got back the Brigadier made an inspection which is always a bloody business.

It looks as if we shall be here at any rate until the end of January when we go to the plain for some shooting.

Heaps and heaps of love, my darling, to you and Rosemary.
Your John

Barnes

SW13

13-12-42

My dearest darling Mr Snippet,

I was so glad to have your letter (and the much needed soap coupons!) which didn't arrive until yesterday. I'd been getting rather worried in case you were going off abroad in the very near future, so felt relieved when I'd read it, although I suppose it's got to come sometime! Do you know why the Regiment has been collected in one place?

Today, Rosemary and I brought the holly home and a plant of white heather for her to give Mummie for Christmas. She looked so sweet in her little scarlet coat and white bonnet and gloves, with the holly heaped up in front of her on the pram. Everyone remarked that she looked most 'seasonable'!

Do hope you'll be able to get up for the day over Christmas still. I'm so looking forward to it. We have got a turkey and Christmas pudding, and yesterday I bought a little Christmas tree and went to Woolworth's and to buy a few things for it. I do wish you were here to help me decorate it for Rosemary on Christmas Eve. Never mind, perhaps next year, or at any rate the year after, we'll be able to do it together!

Rosemary is getting more and more energetic and now refuses to sit down when <u>she</u> wants to walk! I shall be very thankful if you <u>can</u> teach her to walk on her own. She sends you lots and lots of love, and I send you all of mine, my darling,

Your Rita

1943

My dearest darling,

Nothing seems to have been done in preparation for the gun drill scheme, and of course we collected plenty of cans. Some of the men had the straps on their webbing removed. The old man blew up over all this and said Troop Commanders were not doing their job, but we have two officers down with mumps now as well as some with very bad colds. I really wish I never had the bloody job.

We came back for tea, after which there was a miniature range, and I did a bloody good shoot, and then after dinner we had gun drill games at which I was prominent again. However, in a fortnight's time I reckon I shall have paid for my sins and my luck may change.

I am finishing this letter and will then have a bath and so to a cold bed. I do miss coming home to you, even if only for the night.

I do love you and miss you lots,
Your John

Barnes

SW13

5-2-43

My dearest darling,

I've just received your letter and am so very sorry you're having such a rotten time, darling. It is awful but try to bear up; I imagine that the Colonel is getting worse and worse. I'll say some extra little prayers for you that everything will go well. If it doesn't you can remember my motto: Time and hour run thro' the roughest day!

The beloved Mrs Andrews came to tea on Monday. (At least, she came round at 4:00 p.m., insisted that she hadn't come to tea, and ended up eating all the cakes.) She doesn't like the way Rosemary's hair is done, so every time I left the room, she altered it – darned sauce!

I've taken over the principal cooking here now. I <u>must</u> get some experience from somewhere before I start giving my own family indigestion! Actually, it's gone quite well so far, and I thoroughly enjoy myself.

After lunch yesterday I was going to take your daughter for a walk, so put her on her pottie, in which she obliged with big business. I took her off, put it the other side of the chair, covered it up and left her alone for about two mins. When I returned, she had wriggled over to it, taken the cover off, stuck her hands in, literally <u>covered</u> herself and face, and was also making a meal of it. She joyfully offered me some too!

Rosemary 'talks' about you, and I think about you, all day long. We both send heaps and heaps of love to you, my precious, especially,

Your Rita

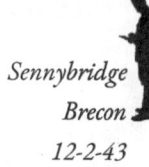

My dearest darling,

I was very amused to hear of Rosemary's escapade. She sounds to have really enjoyed herself. You will have to put such things out of temptation's way now.

Things have not gone too badly to date, though the weather has been very bad, and the ranges are waterlogged which means that there are very few places where the guns can go, and then only after a very thorough reconnaissance.

On Wednesday my troops started off, and everything went well until we got into action, when down came a storm and blotted out everything. Everybody was soaked and then it cleared. The Colonel seemed very anxious to try us out, so we went out again on Thursday when fortunately we did quite well, and I had two good shoots. The Colonel seems more satisfied, though inclined to be tetchy and irritable.

My love to you all,
Your John

My dearest Mr Snippet,

Yesterday Rosemary paid her first visit to the hairdressers! I only had it 'tidied up but it does look better. The assistants were very tickled, and Rosemary took it all as a matter of course and beamed upon her reflection in the mirror!

I've been having a terrible time this week, chasing fleas! I managed to pick some up from heaven knows where and have been tormented night and day. Yesterday I caught one in the bed, so Mummie washed everything to do with it and (I think and hope) ended their career.

Cheeribye for now, darling; do hope you arrive Thursday night.

Heaps and heaps of love, my precious,

Your Rita

4-3-43

My dearest darling,

It's turned so very wintry and there's a thick frost every morning. The night in the vehicles doesn't sound like my idea of comfortable and I shall be jolly glad to hear you're sleeping with a roof over you again (yes, I know there's a war on!).

Rosemary is now in her grown-up cot. She is so charmed by all the lil' girls painted on it that she spends her time examining each one in turn, over and over again, instead of going to sleep!

We had rather a nasty raid the night before last (two in fact), and I got rather het up dithering about and wondering whether to bring Rosemary down or not. I didn't want to frighten her, but had I known how near it was, I wouldn't have hesitated.

Rosemary and I send you heaps and heaps of love,

Your Rita

My dearest darling,

The weather has been very kind and sometimes at midday really hot. I seem to have been up most nights and out most of the daytime and am feeling a little tired. I got a slight cold after sleeping out and getting covered in frost one night but that has worn off.

I must say it has been quite fun being out during the day. The country around is very nice and I have got my carrier and crew well equipped with cooking stove and a certain amount of food, so we do not starve. The Colonel has been, and is still, extremely fussy. He thinks of the most complicated schemes which never have a chance of working.

I have not seen a newspaper for days so have little idea how the real war is going on. I got interrogated by a BBC reporter the other day. They are making reports as they would in battle. There are also hundreds of red hats, from the Commander in Chief downwards, floating around with white flags, and a good many foreign and dominion big bugs looking on. I heard about the raid on London and was very glad to hear that you were OK though you must have had a rather nervous night.

Your story of Rosemary setting the place on fire is most alarming and I don't quite see how she did it. I hope there is not much damage done.

Heaps of love, my darling, and my love to your mother and Rosemary. Your John

My dearest darling,

I wish I knew where you are and what's happening etc. It seems such ages since I saw or heard from you.

Today we've been up to town. Had lunch at Gennaro's then went to Trafalgar Square to see the sights and help on the war total with our little bits. I put £2 in the Post Office Savings Bank, and we bought 8 stamps to stick on the bombs for Hitler; I stuck Rosemary's right on top of the biggest bomb! I bought her a little flag and she loves it.

After all this I feel somewhat weary and shall be off to bed very shortly. I could just do with my beloved to give me a nice warm cuddle to go to sleep with tonight! I've had a horrid feeling the last few days that there's some bad news in the atmosphere, so hope I'm wrong in my presentiment!

Rosemary gets more and more of a pickle and harder work every day, and it is now quite impossible to keep her from doing herself some injury without her big cot and/or playpen. She started the fire by throwing her pink organdie cot cover on the electric fire, and her bunny on top, despite the fact that I'd put the fire under the bed!

Goodnight, my dearest. We both send heaps and heaps of love, especially,

Your Rita

16-3-43

My dearest Mr Snippet,

Thank you so much for your letter and phone call; I was very pleased to receive both, as you can guess! I'm glad the scheme went so well, and that you're all looking so tough and cave-mannish. Still, I don't like the sound of the Regiment being 'ready', even tho' I know you should be! It makes my heart drop right down to under the soles of my feet, truly.

Well, darling, I wondered whether you'd ring up last night about the 'digs' you've found for us. As I told you in my last letter, it will be very difficult now managing Rosemary without a playpen or cot. The only thing I can suggest is that we hire a playpen, and for night-times we should have another single bed in our room, against a wall, and put a chair or so the other side. She couldn't be left downstairs now in her carrycot. We should have to undress downstairs and creep into bed without a light. The carrycot must be on a bed, or something fairly wide, as she sits up and swings her legs over! I'm afraid she's got to a very difficult stage for our vagabond existence, especially under wartime restrictions!

Rosemary sends lots of love to you, and heaps from,
Your Rita

Southend
21-3-43

My dearest darling,

We have had a very good scheme really and done quite well. The old man apparently had a good chit from the Commander and was told that his Regiment, at any rate, was ready. He seems quite pleased and has gone up to London today and left us in peace.

We are all looking disgustingly healthy. My face is one of the best; absolutely crimson and all peeling as a result of driving days and nights in my open carrier. Most of us trooped into the Queen last night for a bit of relaxation. We must have looked pretty comic with our red faces. However, after a few beers we forgot our self-consciousness and had quite a jolly evening. I came home alone on my bicycle. It certainly was a change after spending over two weeks in the field without even tasting a beer.

I do hope I can see you soon, darling.

Heaps of love,

John

Barnes

SW13

25-3-43

My dearest darling,

Thank you so much for your letter just received. I'm very pleased to hear that it really seems settled that you'll be here tomorrow. I'm longing to see you, and Rosemary will be delighted. She hasn't yet got over the shock of your appearance and disappearance on Sunday, and ever since has repeatedly told me, "Mama, Dadda gone!" She was very sad on Sunday afternoon and when I took her out for a walk, she pointed to every man she saw and said, "<u>My</u> Dadda gone."

Hurry up tomorrow! Till then, heaps of love, my darling,

Your Rita

Shrublands Camp

Claydon

Suffolk

4-4-43

My dearest darling,

The officers of 216 Regt. and I arrived back last night having accomplished the trip in one day, which saved staying a night on route. We only had one day's firing which was not very good and came down on a rugger pitch which put the old man in a bad mood. He said we had gone back two years and all this year's drill and study must be done all over again.

I was at the gun in the morning and fortunately did a fairly good shoot. The afternoon was an improvement, but of course the old man was not satisfied and was as miserable as hell. He really is mad! The next morning, he admitted that the shoots were difficult, but I bet he will start all that gun drill nonsense again.

Desert Victory was on in Ipswich which the Major wanted to see, so we went in after dinner. It was very good indeed and was an account of the early battles made up of shots made by the Army Film and Photographic Unit with some captured German film. You must see it if you have the chance.

Heaps for yourself and Rosemary,
Your John

Good Friday, 23-4-43

My dearest darling,

Last evening, we all went to Shrublands Hall for a concert arranged by the Colonel. It went off very well, though was somewhat late in starting. The hall is a fine place with a long, wide staircase which climbs from it to the lounge. The artists performed in the hall and all the lads were seated on the stairs. There was an old boy who told Suffolk stories in a raw Suffolk accent, a fat woman who sang songs to a banjo, a tenor, and a duo turn consisting of xylophone and accordion. They certainly made the most of their talent. We met them all in the Sorrel Horse after and had some bar with them.

Her ladyship has asked some of the officers round on Sunday for tea and afters. I shall probably be going myself. The Colonel is doing very well and made quite a speech last night. We are doing all we can to keep his interest going. On Monday the Brigadier is coming round to inspect us. As you can imagine a great day is being planned and the whole thing is rehearsed.

Heaps for yourself and Rosemary,
Your John

Barnes
SW13
26-5-43

My dearest Mr Snippet,

Rosemary now makes a practice of shrieking for about a couple of hours during every night. Isn't she a wretch? We've just been for her second inoculation against whooping cough, and she was as good as gold again. Mr Heekes says he's never seen such a wonderfully good child, and made a tremendous fuss of her, cuddling her and giving her sweets (which she promptly dribbled all down her clean white coat in a sticky yellow mess!). He is <u>very</u> pleased with her appearance etc., and thinks I'm a very good mother!?! I wonder!

Rosemary and I are missing you dreadfully, darling. Like you, I find the nights are the worst, and Mummie has this morning swept away my last remaining consolation by taking your <u>nice</u>-smelling(!) pyjamas away to wash, so now I can't even cuddle those in bed! Still, perhaps I'll have you inside them before long; I hope so.

It <u>was</u> a lovely week together at the sea, wasn't it, darling? It just couldn't have been more perfect. Now we shall always have that to look upon it as a sample of 'things to come', and I'm sure it will help us if we get depressed again. Isn't it strange that we should just miss the air raids at Bournemouth <u>and</u> here! They say it was terrible at Bournemouth. Providence has us under its wing, I think and hope!

All my love, my darling, and heaps from Rosemary.

I love you all the world,

Your Rita

29-5-43

My darlingest one,

Rosemary has been spending all and every day in the garden, either in her 'nothings' or her cotton sun suit; she <u>does</u> love it and looks so well. Mrs Andrews came to tea and supper yesterday and was crazy enough to give the child a large boiled sweet. Of course, the poor little dear swallowed it and choked until she was almost purple. I turned her upside down at once and patted her back and managed to get it up again, but afterwards she was dreadfully sick and cried like anything. She went quite deathly white, just as she looked at Shoeburyness when she was sick, so I laid her down on my bed and bathed her face. When she looked better, I left her for a little while, lying quietly, and when I went up again Sarah-Jane had gone in and was playing 'roly-poly', rolling her over and over! I've come to the conclusion that <u>very</u> few people have their fair share of common sense!

This week I seem to have put a lot of my energy into gardening and digging a sandpit for Rosemary at the bottom of the garden. Was it hard work?! It was all filled up with large bricks and was like digging at a wall. However, I've done it and lined it with wood, and it now remains for me to filch some sand from the common each day until I've got enough!

XXX from Rosemary, and all my love, darling,

Your Rita

2-6-43

My dearest Mr Snippet,

Everything is good, so far! Rosemary grows more self-important every day and is really amusing. She's getting on well with her talking now and sends you lots of kisses (she smacks her lips and says, "Dear Dadda!"). On Monday morning I traipsed off to the common with her, and after much digging, managed to bring home a bagful of sand. However, by the time I'd sifted out the stones only half the quantity remained and, worse still, after all my efforts, it isn't the right kind of sand! She got filthy in it, and it blew about in great clouds! So I had to get it all out again, and have ordered some proper sand from the builders.

The garden has repaid Mummie's efforts, and Rosemary has been having spinach from it every day since we came home. She is looking nice and brown, and is full of high spirits, as usual!

We still miss you awfully, and send you our heaps and heaps of love, darling, especially,

Your Rita

Strensall Camp
York
27-6-43

My dearest darling,

I am very much looking forward to seeing you and Rosemary and am enclosing two forms for you to get a cheap fare up on Tuesday. I do

hope you have comfortable journey. I only wish I could come for you, but I am afraid that is not possible as we are so very busy just now. The train you want is the Flying Scotsman at 10 o'clock, arriving 2:11 p.m. Check the departures blackboard. You ought to get there no later than 9:20 a.m. to get a good seat. There is only one stop before York. I will have my batman waiting for you on the platform if I can't get there myself.

You should be able to rest here. There is a nice garden, chickens with baby chicks for Rosemary, and they also keep one cow for their own milk. I said you wouldn't mind having meals with them.

I do hope everything goes well, darling.

Your John

Barnes
SW13
4-8-43

My darlingest,

I've been thinking of you so much today, travelling in all this heat. It was awful leaving you and intolerable in the train. I've <u>never</u> been so hot and stifled in my life, and it was made worse by the corridor being so packed and not being able to move from our seat at all.

The sickness has worsened during the last few days, and now I am hardly free from it during the day, tho' it is worst morning and night. Perhaps it's because I'm a bit upset.

I wrote to your mother but didn't mention the pregnancy! I think perhaps we'd better leave it until your leave, tho' I suppose she'll wonder why I'm still not well!

Rosemary keeps asking where 'poor Dadda' is. And I'm to tell you she's a 'good, good girl' twenty times a day! She and I miss you more than ever every day, and send you all our love,

Especially Rita.

My dearest darling,

I am awfully sorry to hear you are not well. Is it the old waterworks trouble again? I do hope you get better soon darling.

I had an airgraph from George. He is a Captain and has a troop in 3rd Field Regt. R.H.A. As far as I could make out he was at Tripoli and just starting on the last phase. He likes the crowd very much though apparently there is a lot of spit and polish.

The Colonel arrived back here on Friday night and is pushing everything around. He does not like living in a tent, but I am afraid he will have to get to used to it. He is making terrific arrangements to keep us all busy in the evenings.

Well darling I hope you soon feel strong again. Please give my love to your Mother and Rosemary.

Heaps for you darling,
Your John

My dearest one,

Last night Mr Heekes stayed over an hour and was here again this morning by 10:30. He is most kind and sympathetic with me. Today he had to bring an instrument and draw off the contents of my bladder direct; a proceeding I didn't much care for, particularly as it's so damn sore! He's going to let us know the results of his examination as soon as possible.

I passed quite a lot of blood etc. during the night, and Mummie had to phone him at lunchtime as I was having a nasty packet again.

He has given me something for the pain, which takes off its violence but unfortunately leaves me feeling rather rotten. He says I've got thin and seems a bit worried; he says I <u>must</u> now begin to eat as much as I can, for the 'two of us'!

Rosemary seems to be getting into mischief every minute of the day and is very tiring to both Mummie and Sarah-Jane, who seem nearly at their wit's end as to what to do with her. As soon as they put a thing down, she picks it up, trots off with it, and puts it in the most unlikely place. Very amusing at first, but exasperating when you're trying to tidy up or get on with things!

I love you all the world,

Your Rita

Strensall Camp
York
25-8-43

My dearest darling,

You do seem unfortunate. I shall be most anxious to hear that you are better. I do hope it won't be long before the pain stops. It must be very exhausting for you as well as being most painful.

I have been made Troop Commander of the other troop for a change. They think a change of command will do both troops some good. We are out for a night march tomorrow on Strensall Common. It is pretty certain we shall move next month to winter quarters but unfortunately not in a Southerly direction.

I must finish now and wash so that I can go into York to post this. I might go and see Life and Death of Colonel Blinks if I can get in.

Heaps of love to you my darling and to Rosemary.

Cheer up and get well soon,

Your loving John

My dearest darling,

Are you pleased about changing over troops? It seems to me that you all get messed around a bit too much. Do you know where your winter quarters will be? I do feel that whilst the baby is coming, I'd give anything to be able to see you fairly frequently, as I did when Rosemary was on the way. Somehow it seems so very important and comforting to see you.

This latest medicine seems to have done the trick, and I haven't had any acute pain today at all, but it is certainly having other effects as well, and I really feel ill in myself. I ache so abominably that I can hardly bear to turn over in bed, let alone get out of it, and feel so languid and heavy that I don't want to do anything but lie still in the dark all day long. I also feel sick and haven't the slightest appetite for anything, not even a dry biscuit! Mr H came this morning, and is phoning up tonight, so I've asked Mummie to ask him if he can't change my medicine and give me something to buck me up and make me hungry! I don't want Secundus to arrive to a bag of skin and bones, and then not be able to feed it.

Rosemary sends you pots of love, and I love you and love you, my precious,

Your Rita

Strensall Camp
York
26.8.43

My dearest darling,

I hope you got my letter this morning. I rode into York to post it but not a hope of pictures. Forces everywhere so as I had missed my

supper I went and had dinner at The George. Quite a nice meal with roast veal. I sat next to a Grenadier Officer. We got talking and found we had both been to nearly all the same places. Mere, Warminster, Ipswich and York. He is a racehorse trainer and owns a large paddock at Newmarket. We had a few drinks and then I rode home to find I had to get up this morning at six to go to an Umpires conference at Scarborough for this coming exercise.

And now darling are you better? I do hope so. I feel awfully lonely without you and no pots to empty and no Rosemary to scold for wetting knickers. However, I shall get into the swing in a few days. It is always the first few days that are the worst.

Heaps of love darling and do get well soon,
Ever Your John.

Barnes
SW13
27-8-43

My very dearest,

I was very relieved to hear you didn't have to go on the night march so soon after your vaccination, darling; I'm sure it would have made you feel very rotten and it would swell a lot too, with the arm-swinging, etc. I do hope it's taken this time, and that it won't have any ill effects upon you.

I expect that by the time you get this you'll have quite settled down again to army life, after the 'shoot', which I hope has gone well? I do wish I were better and could be near you again; it seems such a waste living like this and missing each other so. I know how rotten it must be for you, going back to that, after leave. I've been thinking about you, and how you never complain, and that I ought to be ashamed of myself. All the same, Secundus and I find it hard-going without you to cheer us on, just now when we need you probably more than at any other time! Still, there's a war to be won!

I am still in bed, tho' I've been downstairs yesterday and today for a little while. I stayed a bit longer today and have overtired myself, according to Mr H (who's just been in again). He has the hospital's report of my case, which is that it is an infection of the kidney.

I have had a curtain lecture and sound ticking-off from Mr H on how not to behave during pregnancy! I seem to have brought all this (and deserve worse) on myself through insufficient care for my condition! In future I am to realise fully that I <u>cannot</u> do the same as before, and must take life very carefully, with lots of rest and good food. (Where the food's coming from is problematical!) I should not carry Rosemary, or travel with her on my own now, and I was quite mad to go to Bournemouth and walk up and down hills. Due to 'my condition(!), doing this has caused me to sprain the muscles in my back and has caused me a good deal more pain on top of the other, etc., etc! So on and so forth. I must admit that I didn't know such care had to be taken.

I do miss you so, especially just now. I could do with lots of love and fuss and cheering up, but only from you!

Especially,

Your Rita

The Wolds
Yorkshire
28-8-43

My dearest darling,

I have got your letter and am very sorry you are having such a rotten time. It seems dreadful to think you are still having those pains. I do hope you pass all this gravel soon. I can imagine you must be getting thin. There is nothing so exhausting as pain; and I only hope it won't have you too weak as to affect the coming event.

I am afraid your mother must be getting fed up with Rosemary. I can only suggest she is put in the playpen with her toys. I think she would be quite happy. What she really wants is a baby brother to play with.

I did not have time to finish this last night before it got dark. I don't expect to get much sleep to-night and tomorrow. It has been raining hard all morning and is pretty cold. It looks like being a really miserable wet day.

I do wish I could do something to help you darling, but I don't really know of anything I can do. I do hope you will be well again soon.

Heaps of love to you,

From Your John

Barnes
SW13
31.8.43

My very dearest,

First and foremost, very, very many happy returns of your 30th Birthday. It's a very special one really, darling, and I do wish we could have celebrated it together, but you know I'll be thinking of you every minute, and we'll do something about it the first opportunity we get! Anyway, just wait until the old war is over, and we'll celebrate all right – every occasion! Perhaps we shan't have so long to wait now.

I haven't of course been able to do any birthday shopping for you, but will hope to have something for you a little later from Rosemary and me. She is getting as bad as I am about you, and now refuses to go to bed unless she's cuddling Dadda (your photo), and it will soon be the worse for wear! It's a good thing I'm going to have some more of you soon, or else I can foresee your two best girls will be squabbling and coming to blows about it!

I'm hoping that really and truly at last I'm over the worst and shall be better soon. It's been rather hectic the last few days; in fact, it seems to have been a nightmare of terrific pain, violent sickness and blinding headaches. Mr Heekes said he was sorry for me, but he'd decided it was too dangerous to give me morphine at this stage of pregnancy.

Mummie and Sarah-Jane are getting very tired of having me in bed, <u>and</u> that pickle, Rosemary, to look after. She just won't stay alone in her playpen now, darling; she insists upon being with people all the time, otherwise she yells long and loudly!

Have a birthday drink on me!

With all my love,

Your Rita

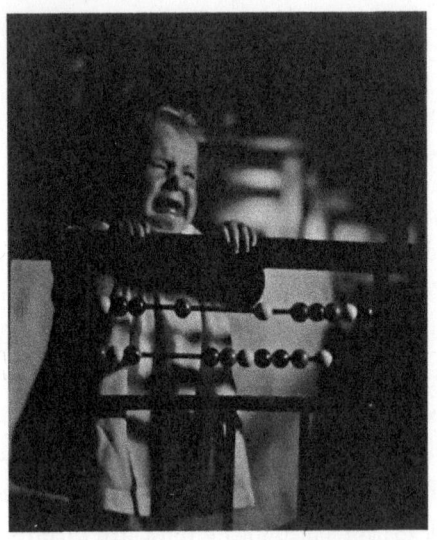

Strensall Camp
York
31-8-43

My dearest darling,

I do hope you will get strong again quickly and not have any more pain. I am always thinking of you and hoping you will soon be better.

We seem to be having our misfortunes now so let's hope we make up for it later on.

The shooting over the weekend was quite good from our Regiment though the shooting from the heavies I was umpiring left a lot to be desired. The weather was really terrible; deluges of rain all the time and at times completely obscuring all visibility. Everyone got very wet, and on top of this the food I got from the heavies was very scanty and poor. Having been out all day, I got back late enough to miss the night march, so I am being a good boy and writing letters by hurricane lamp and a glass of beer. It is quite pleasant to have a bed in a tent again as up till now I have taken what sleep I could in my car.

I will write you all I can, darling, so cheer up and keep smiling.

Heaps and heaps of love, darling.

Ever,

Your John

P.S. It is too dark to write anymore. Sorry I cannot make the fourth page.

Barnes

SW13

2.9.43

My darlingest one,

I have celebrated the day by getting dressed for the first time for nearly a fortnight, and also by going out, so feel as if I've made a big step forward. Our daughter much appreciated it, and beamed upon me without ceasing, patting me every now and again and saying, "Pretty, nice Mama." It was <u>most</u> encouraging! I got up for lunch, rested in the afternoon, and after tea, with the aid of Mummie and the pram, walked round to see a friend's new baby. I did so want to see how Rosemary would react, and it was well worth the effort. She was thrilled to the marrow, and just wouldn't leave the pram, but stood there peering in at it, and talking all sorts of nonsense talk to it. Every now and then she'd come to me, very excitedly talking in a jumble, and I'd hear that the "baba" had moved its "handie," or "baba cry," etc., and then I had to go and see too. The only thing she wasn't quite so keen on was when I nursed it! And directly I gave it back she wouldn't rest until she was on my lap, repeating in triumph, "Wowee (her name for Rosemary!) Mama's baba!" (My friend unfortunately has a large boil on her seat.)

Heaps and heaps of love, my precious,

Your Rita

P.S. Have just received my second 'calling up' form; have got a good reply again, haven't I?!

Strensall Camp
York
3-9-43

My dearest darling,

Thank you so much for your letter, and card from Rosemary. Please give her a chocolate from me and tell her she must be good till I next see her when she can let out her bottled-up energy. I will come and see you as soon as possible but, as I told you, we are on the move. Advance parties are off today, and the Regiment goes early next week.

We are inundated with conferences and schemes. I have hardly seen my new troop and I can only hope to get it going when we have completed the move. There seems no secrecy about it so I can tell you we are going to Scarborough. A very nice place by Yorkshire standards though bound to be wet and cold. The chief snag is that it means a further two hours travelling to get to you, but there it is.

Last night we all went into York for a conference by the AGRA commander. I had some dinner at The George; chicken at last because we got there in good time. We went on to Betty's and there I met Charles who used to be my No. 1. He is in this flying O.P. racket, has got his wings and says it's the finest job out. I keep meeting them and often wish I had taken the plunge. I am afraid it is too late now as they have got more than they want.

Heaps and heaps of love, my darling. Get well and strong soon,
Your John

216/63 Medium Regt RA
Scarborough
York
4-9-43

My dearest darling

I do hope you are better and feeling stronger. I wish I could come down to comfort you but nearly everyone is away, and I am holding the fort. Anything I can do for you my darling let me know.

What do you think of the show in Italy. It seems to be starting all right although we shall not know very much for a few days yet. It looks to me that we shall be here all winter and I shall be able to see Secundus, at any rate, in their first stages. Are you feeling OK in that direction? I suppose the baby is due to start kicking fairly soon.

Heaps of love darling. I love you very much.
Your John

Strensall Camp
York
7-9-43

My dearest darling,

I was glad to hear last evening that you were better. You did not *sound at all well the evening before. I do hope you feel well soon.*

The photographs I suppose are not too bad, but you must agree that my face looks very blotchy and wrinkled. However, I suppose we shall have to pass them. The one with the hat on is probably the best, but I would like you to choose which one you like.

Heaps of love to you, my darling,

Your John

Barnes
SW13
7.9.43

My dearest Mr Snippet,

The photos and your letter came this morning, for which many thanks.

I missed you dreadfully yesterday, and it certainly didn't seem like a wedding anniversary! What with no better half there, the doctor coming, and your lesser half feeling rotten and tired out with sleepless nights and pain, it was certainly no way to spend an anniversary!

I feel quite sorry for the poor Mr Heekes; he's between the devil and the deep and doesn't know what on earth to do with me. Secundus is aggravating all the conditions and stops Mr H from giving me help to stop the pain. My water has gone all queer again, so he's trotted off with another specimen to the hospital, and today he's been in again and taken my blood pressure. He says <u>that</u> and Secundus are, respectively, good and going on well, thank heaven!

The nurse who came from the maternity clinic yesterday said she thought that if the pain went on, the pregnancy would have to be terminated, as it would be so bad for the baby as well as me, and I should probably be unable to deliver. However, Mr Heekes is dead nuts against getting rid of babies, and as for me, I've not gone through all <u>this</u> for nothing! Still, I <u>have</u> gone thin, so much so that the baby is hardly in evidence when I'm dressed, despite that it's supposed to be 4 months on the 9th, and does it roll around some?!

I'm going to drink gallons and pray with all my might and main! Please don't ever forget it in <u>your</u> prayers, Mitty, and I'm sure we shall be able to avoid it. I got through Rosemary's arrival very well and am sure another 'miracle' can happen. I do so want to enjoy my husband and babies, when at last I've got you all together; in fact I'm living for it, tho' several times lately, when the pain has been bad, I've thought how lovely it would be to go to sleep to get away from all the pain and not wake up again.

Rosemary and I send you heaps and heaps of love, my darling, especially,

Your Rita

8.9.43

My dearest one,

Mr Heekes came in yesterday with the latest pathological investigation result which still shows a heavy growth of infection, he's sorry to say. He was very kind (sat next to me on the couch and held my hand and kept patting me!) and talked very nicely. I'm afraid he is quite evidently rather worried about it all; he phoned up Sister and told her that I was really quite ill!! However, I do feel easier today, and can walk about a bit.

Rosemary has been misbehaving lately, and in consequence I've had one or two battles royal with her – one in particular. She's been getting her own way too much whilst I've been in bed and thinks now that if she doesn't want to do something I tell her to, she can just get away with it. She screamed blue murder one day till she was beside herself, because she wouldn't sit on the pot after tea, having not been anywhere since breakfast. I shut her in the drawing room on the pot and left her! We all had bad heads after it, but I won, and she seems to have become more attached to me than ever!

The maternity nurse has managed to find a local day nursery for Rosemary, but Mummie and Sarah-Jane can't manage taking and fetching her every day so it's not going to be possible. Of course, if the worst comes to the worst with me, heaven alone knows how long I shall be away, and I really don't know what to suggest for her now. It is a worry.

All my love,
Your Rita

10.9.43

My dearest Mr Snippet,

Your parcel has just arrived, and what a lovely surprise! I should say the stockings are all right, and as welcome as the flowers in May! I've given Mummie two pairs as she's been awfully good really, and still looks after Rosemary a good bit for me, including bathing her, etc., which I shall be unable to do for a little while yet. She was very pleased with them, but says you must be careful as it's evidently black market stuff. Where did the Major get them, do you know? I bet he did a roaring trade amongst you, anyway!

I have pain continually which makes me feel very weak and depressed, and so dependent upon other people for everything, which you know I hate! I can't even get to the pillar box to post your letters!

I think Albania will be next after Italy, don't you?

Rosemary sends you lots of love, and I send all of mine,

Your Rita

Carlton Hotel
Scarborough
12-9-43

My dearest darling,

We moved out from Strensall yesterday afternoon and got here last evening. The Officers' Mess is a very nice hotel and we each have a bedroom with hot and cold water. The Colonel has a suite to himself and is fairly happy about that, but seems to have one of his depressing fits on. He has already fallen out with the Police here and is tripping everyone. I expect he will have a crack at me next.

You poor thing, you have had a rotten time. I am most terribly sorry and wish I could help you. I would like to come and see you as I know that would help more than anything, but I am most unpopular over leave. Everyone, including the Colonel, are saying I have been away too much. I must go a bit careful, but of course if there is anything urgent, I will come.

Your last letter sounds a little more cheerful and perhaps tomorrow I shall hear that you have passed the worst and are getting better. I do hope so as I can well imagine how awful it must be for you, and your mother must be getting very worried.

I am glad you liked the stockings; they were black market, but just now and then it can't be helped.

Heaps and heaps of love, darling. Keep cheerful; I think you are doing jolly well.

All my love,

John

My dearest darling,

I do hope you are better. I have not had a letter from you this morning, but no doubt will have one tomorrow. We are umpiring a scheme until the weekend, so I shall not be able to write very much. I will try and do what I can though as I know letters must be very welcome to you. How is Rosemary? I hope she is behaving herself and not making too much trouble for your mother.

We are having rather a wet time here. I have had two baths, one today and one yesterday. Rather cold but very nice when I got in. I sent the whole troop bathing this afternoon.

I went to the pictures last evening to see Battle of Stalingrad. *Plenty of atrocity bits to curdle the blood. What do you think of old Musso being kidnapped? The news is certainly interesting these days and will make good reading after the war is over.*

Heaps of love to you, my darling. Do hope to be hearing some good news from you soon.

All my love,
John

Barnes
SW13
13-9-43

My dearest one,

Mr Heekes came again last evening. I really believe he's as delighted as I am that there's no kidney stone in evidence! However, he says the infection itself shows to be very deep. He told me last night that he's had to watch me very carefully, as at any time he might have had to take the baby away. So you see, my love, once more we have lots to be thankful for: no stone, and Secundus still safe in its abode! By the way, Mr H says that pregnancy is by far the most irritant condition for this infection, and says he is afraid that with every child I have it would get worse (only during the pregnancy), so if Secundus's other names are John Jeremy, I think, like you, I shall be satisfied with one of each.

This morning I actually managed, with Mummie's help, to walk round the block. It takes me hours, and I have to rest on route, but I am feeling rather pleased with myself.

Rosemary sends you lots of love, and heaps and heaps,

From your own Rita

P.S. I've had a chat with Mr Heekes and he's promised to keep the bill as low as possible!

Robin Hoods Bay
16-9-43

My dearest darling,

This is supposed to be one of the beauty spots on the Yorkshire coast. It is certainly very quaint, with a very steep road down to the shore after the Clovelly style. It is a popular spot for honeymoons, but like everywhere else up here it has rained nice and steadily and looks miserable.

The exercise has been quite interesting but very wet. I met some old friends and managed to find a pub most evenings to dry the outside and wet the inside. I have used my tent every night so have not been so very uncomfortable. The week after next we go on a fortnight's do, and if the weather is like this, we shall have a pretty grim time.

And now how are you, my dear? I don't quite understand what this infection means and gather that you will always get it when in your present condition. It certainly looks as if two should be your limit and I would not have you go through this again for anything. Two is a pretty useful number; will save me some money, and is bound to be cheaper than six!

Heaps and heaps of love, my darling.

Ever,

Your loving John

My dearest darling,

I'm glad to say I'm going on much better yesterday and today and think I'm more or less "out of the woods" now. I started off on the four-day course of tablets on Monday and by the evening felt so ill and so sick I'd have willingly given up the ghost! Tuesday was worse, and I couldn't keep anything down at all! So Mummie 'phoned Mr. Heekes and told him, and he had mercy upon me and said I was to leave them off at once. He's just been in again and drawn urine off from my bladder, and will let us know the result in a day or so. He seemed pleased with it this morning – it's almost normal now – but, ye gods! Has he left me sore?! If everything's OK this time I can proceed to get strong without any more set-backs, (we hope!)

Yesterday we had a surprise visit from your mother and father. Unfortunately it was at the most inopportune time as it was Sarah-Jane's day out, and Mummie and I had <u>just</u> gone off for our afternoon rests, Mummie tired out after having to go over to Sheen shopping, and yours truly with a head like a sledgehammer, after having cooked the dinner and looked after Rosemary at the same time – a thing I haven't done for weeks! However, after a few kind words (!) – in private, of course – Mummie got some tea whilst I talked to them.

I expect you'll like to have a chat with Mr. Heekes about this 'infection' business when you come up, darling. Then you'll probably understand better.

Secundus is developing rapidly, and I now carry all before me once again! Haven't been out for a week, but people stared hard then! There's no mistaking it now – my streamline has gone!

Rosemary is very good and sends you lots of love, and heaps and heaps from,

Your Rita

18-9-43

My dearest darling,

I had another big disappointment yesterday. I'd no sooner finished your letter saying how much better everything was, than the old pain got steadily worse, and by teatime I was nearly raving again. Oh, darling, it <u>did</u> depress me – I could have cried. After lunch, when I went to the lavatory, I had a terrific pain and suddenly passed a <u>lot</u> of blood. For a moment I was scared stiff for Secundus and then found my senses and realised it wasn't that dark red colour. What I think happened was that in putting the thing into my bladder, Mr, Heekes must have pierced the skin a bit – it's so frightfully tender there.

Everything is much better again this morning than I'd hoped for, after last night, but my urine has gone back to its old dark smoky colour, which denotes the presence of infection. Mr. Heekes is coming today.

Rosemary can now say anything she wants to, and is she a chatterbox? – worse than I ever was!!

Well, my love, heaps and heaps of love, (and from Rosemary)

Your Rita.

My dearest darling,

I was glad to hear Secundus is progressing, but I am afraid must be having rather a rough time. I certainly hope it survives the roughing. You both deserve a life of luxury. I am sure your mother will be getting terribly tired. I will make enquiries about care for Rosemary whenever I can and might hear of something.

Yesterday afternoon I took a cycle ride round the town which I had not seen before. It is a very nice place, and in peacetime obviously caters for holidays with a good time on a large scale. The RAF are in full force and are in all the best places. I went to a RAF dance last evening which was terribly crowded.

I went to church this morning and prayed hard for you, so hope it will do some good. Had a bathe afterwards. Very cold; water never gets a chance to warm up here. I think the old man enjoyed it, but it was a bit forced. This afternoon I did 15 holes on the South Bay Golf Club course. It was very pleasant along the clifftops. I was in better form and won by three holes. I should be getting pretty fit at this rate.

We are off into the wilds again sometime this week for a fortnight's exercise. We get back early October when all the last stages of summer will have gone, and it will be time to settle down to winter.

Please give my love to your mother and thank her for all she is doing.

Heaps of love to you, my darling, and Rosemary,

Your John

24-9-43

My dearest darling,

I am so sorry you did not get a letter this morning. I tried to write yesterday but we had a bit of a blitz and I was not able to get away from the guns and vehicles until 7 o'clock in the evening. I have just received a letter from your mother to say that my mother is trying to fetch Rosemary today. Is Rosemary going to stay with them? I hope everything will be all right. Your Mother says Secundus has moved over which is causing you more pain. You poor thing. I feel an awful wretch to have caused all this for you, but I do hope and pray it won't last for much longer.

I went to the flicks the night before last to see Hit the Ice. Abbott and Costello. Quite amusing. There is a theatre which has variety shows which I think deserves a visit. It should make a relief after living in the trees for ten days.

I will write to you as often as I can darling as I know that letters are the least I can do to cheer you up. And now darling once again I do hope you will be relieved of the pain soon.

Heaps and heaps of love darling.

Your John

In the field
28-9-43

My dearest darling,

How are you? Better, I hope.

I have just had one of the bloodiest nights on record. Up in a slit trench from 6 o'clock last night till 8 o'clock this morning with a howling gale and teaming rain beating down all the time. We were literally soaked. Everything got bogged during the night and generally first-class war conditions have prevailed. We are returning for another do tonight. I have got my tent up and have had some sleep, but the wind is so strong I am expecting the whole lot to be blown away any minute. I must say I don't like conditions in this part of the world one bit.

The division we are now with is a very good one, and strange to say they hold a very good opinion of us. However, we dropped a flanker at

dusk yesterday by setting four wheat fields on fire, causing considerable
damage as well as giving away the whole show. I bet there will be a
silver-mounted one handed out from somewhere.

The news from all fronts still seems good, doesn't it, darling? After
this I think we shall be ready to take on anything.

Heaps of love, my darling. I do hope you are picking up a bit now.

Ever your loving,

John

Barnes
SW13
29.9.43

My dearest darling,

This is just a little note to let you know I'm still in the Land of the Living! Thank you so much for your letters, which just make all the difference, failing seeing you; - what wouldn't I give to be able to do that! I'm afraid Mummie's letters, particularly the first one, were rather incoherent, but she was rushed and worried, and I was too ill to write.

These last ten days in bed have been the worst dose of the lot. At first I couldn't believe the infection had realised Mr Heekes's fears and taken hold of my right side as well. I put it down to the baby lying on a nerve, and refused to give up and go to bed. However, in the end it became such agony that I couldn't even drag my right leg after me, so called in Mr H who put me to bed with a strong dose of morphia. I proceeded to run up a good temperature, so was put on milk solely, with M&B 693 tablets once again, for four or five days, which make me feel terribly depressed. This was when Rosemary had to be quickly sent off to your parents, and Mr H wanted me either to go to Brooklyn Nursing Home or have a nurse here. Mummie refused to have the latter, and said it would be more work to have to troop to and fro to Brooklyn with my washing, and that it would also depress me more. So we have a nurse who comes once a day to give me a blanket bath, antiphlogistine plaster, etc. Mr H comes in twice a day as I have to be kept under constant medical supervision. Of course, the M&Bs made me violently sick again, until in the end I couldn't even keep a drain of milk down, and so was starving. He then had to change the medicine, and I was allowed just a little solid food. I gradually got better again, with no pain, until yesterday, when to our <u>great</u> disappointment, the pain returned on the right side rather badly.

The last two nights have been pretty awful, and today I feel very sick again and the pain is still there. I did so want to write to you, but it has taken me a long time to write this!

Thank you, darling, for understanding how I felt about Rosemary going away; I was heartbroken for days! Secundus is doing extraordinarily well, is the right size and full of life – almost too full at times!

All my love, my darling,

Your Rita

P.S. As soon as the infection has been killed a bit more I shall probably have to have a blood transfusion and/or iron.

216/63 Medium Regt RA
Scarborough
York
6-10-43

My dearest darling,

I have been thinking of you ever since I left you yesterday and have been wondering if you have had as much difficulty in summoning the nurse as you did before we left. I hope not otherwise your bed will be very wet. I do hope you had a comfortable night and that the blood transfusion went off well this morning. Everybody here, without exception, has been asking after you and sends you their best wishes.

I got home soon after six and saw Rosemary put to bed. She had not done a big business for two days, so we gave her some syrup of figs. She is full of fun and life. Nobody seems to like the idea of sending her to the home at Wimbledon, but I don't think either your mother or mine will be able to have her for very long.

I am trying to write you something each day but will have to make a gap this weekend as I am going away for three days on a conference on combined operations. We are going to start cliff scaling, embarking and disembarking. It is going to be cold but should be good fun and we all feel we are getting down to the real thing. I don't think we are likely to be going overseas for some months yet and I have every expectation of seeing Secundus.

I had a good rest last night and am writing more letters tonight. Nearly all officers are in the mess playing cards or reading. Such a scene we never saw under the old boy when everyone crept out and stayed out.

There is talk of my going back to my old troop. I have protested at being buggered about and I hope have put a stop to it.

All my love, darling,

Ever your John

Archer Wing
Royal Hospital
Richmond
7-10-43

Darlingest one,

Just a wee note to let you know that I'm getting better every day. And I do love having your letters. There's so much I want to say to you, and I'd give <u>such</u> a lot to see you again but suppose I must wait! Anyway, I think about you all day long.

Yesterday was the first day free from pain, and last night I slept for 5 ½ hours straight off (with a drug of course), the longest for weeks. I can't sit up yet, and am not allowed visitors except Mummie, but both blood transfusions went off wonderfully well and I feel heaps better than I did.

Mummie complained about my diet and yesterday Mr Heekes raised Cain here about it, so now I'm getting more for our poor, dear Secundus, who is quite lively and "swelling visibly" (Mr H!). I have decided not to be put off our baby by a few other silly people; don't you agree, darling?

I love you all the world,
Your Rita

216/63 Medium Regt RA
Scarborough
York
9-10-43

My dearest darling,

I had a letter from your mother today to say that the blood transfusion was a success. I am so glad, darling. Now perhaps you will really be able to get well and strong again.

I hear you had a shock over the laboratory fees. Well, don't let that upset you. I can afford all the extra fees providing they get you well and strong again. Your mother and my father have spoken to each other and are very generously going to help us out.

We have had the Commanding Officer's inspection this morning. I was not present myself, but I gather things went off quite well and, if anything, we have overdone the bullshit on the guns.

I had the job to classify all the Battery at swimming this morning. We went down to the local baths and those that could swim had to do three lengths. About half got through and the remainder were given tuition. One man refused to go in the water at all, saying he was terrified and would rather go to detention than go in.

Last night I went to the Grand Opera House to see the local variety. Quite an amusing show but a bit raw in parts: such songs sung by a fairy "When my wand begins to droop it's a sign I'm getting old".

I shall expect to hear lots more good news of you, darling.

Heaps of love to you,

Your John

My dearest darling,

I got back last evening and found a letter from your mother who tells me that you are a little stronger and that the tubes may not have to be used after all. That is grand news and I do hope you keep it up. I know how you have been dreading the idea, and if everything will be all right without them you really will have achieved a lot.

We have had a lot of talk today which was chiefly very boring and difficult to follow. The one thing I have appreciated is that the initial landings on the continent will be very difficult and complicated, and it is quite easy to appreciate why we have not yet started the second front.

At the moment I am out with the guns on calibration. We have got them all in a line and have been waiting all morning to fire, but the visibility is not good enough to accurately observe the rounds as they drop. It looks like our being here all day and doing nothing.

Keep up the good work, darling, and let's have you home again and well.

All my love, darling,
Your John

My dearest darling,

Last evening we had a very interesting talk from a Mr Edinger, a newspaper reporter, on the future of France. I had no idea before how much the division of occupied and unoccupied France has really split the country. Apparently, the occupied part is very much belligerent and only awaiting an opportunity to strike, whereas the unoccupied part has collaborated with the Germans and are therefore looked upon as traitors by the occupied territory. He thinks when we go over next time, the difficulty will be to stop the French from fighting, which will be a very different story from last time.

How are you today? I do hope you are continuing to make good progress.

All my love to you, darling,

Your John

20-10-43

My dearest darling,

I have just rung up your mother, darling, and she tells me you have had a very bad night and are feeling very depressed. I am terribly sorry and can just imagine how you must feel. You have done so jolly well and it is very disappointing, but keep going, darling. I am proud of you, my dear. You are doing wonders, and I am absolutely confident you will win in the end. Mr Heekes told me when I was up that you would have these setbacks, so let us hope it is only very temporary and that you will soon get back on the road to improvement.

I have written to Father to find out how they are getting on with Rosemary. Your mother has too much to do to have her, and I doubt whether my people will be able to have her for very long. I am suggesting that she goes to the children's home at Wimbledon which I really think would be the most beneficial to everyone, including Rosemary, who I am sure would make short work of most of the children I saw when I visited there.

I expect, like you, I have been thinking of Rosemary on her second birthday today and imagining her getting all excited with her presents.

Heaps of love, darling, and keep that chin up,

Your John

Archer Wing
Royal Hospital
Richmond

My dearest darling,

Mummie has been, and she tells me, firstly, that your father has phoned and said that it's impossible for either of them or their friends the Bakers to have Rosemary any longer, and Mummie says she can't either (which is quite understandable with having to come over here every day). Mummie, like you, is looking to make arrangements with Wimbledon, of at least five or six weeks. Oh, Mitty, dear, it seems so awful that our little love should be pushed around, with no one wanting her, and I feel myself such an incapable mother, not being able to care for her as I should. I know the home is the best place for her, but it's already three weeks since I saw her, and another five or six to look forward to seems <u>such</u> a long time. Of course, I must admit I still feel too ill for more than a glimpse, and Mummie thinks it would only upset me. Oh, to be altogether in our own home, where we belong!

The other thing is that Mummie warned me that I may not be able to keep the baby yet. If anything happened like that, Mitty, I shouldn't have any stuffing left in me to go on fighting. When I was very ill, my mind went a complete blank of everyone and everything except that I <u>must</u> keep on for the baby to live. Of course when Mummie told me that maybe the tubes needn't be used, it was a nightmare lifted, both on account of my 'funk' and that the baby wouldn't be harmed by them, either.

Already by writing to you I feel better, darlingest; perhaps it'll be all right, after all! The babe has been kicking away every day, and Mr H seems very satisfied with its growth. I've asked the nurses, but they only say as far as they know I'm exceeding all expectations in my recovery! After two days free, I've had a nasty old pain again today –

right side – but Mr H didn't seem at all upset about it this time, and he and three doctors are really jubilant about me. They're quite as thrilled as schoolboys and are really funny!

The last day or so the 'fighting spirit' has flagged a bit, and I've felt terribly, terribly tired after it all. I believe that as soon as I'm out of danger I'm going either to Brooklyn or home, maybe with a nurse, as they say they can't get the diet I need here, and there's been a bust-up about it. There's been talk of third blood transfusion today, but instead I might have injections or even special tablets.

This has taken me ages to write! But I must tell you I think you're the darlingest person in all the world and I love you,

Your Rita

P.S. Unfortunately my tongue has split and cracked with high temperatures, and now it is skinning and there are some ulcers; very difficult to eat, and <u>do</u> I dance when it's painted!

216/63 Medium Regt RA
Scarborough
York
24-10-43

My dearest darling,

I felt awfully bad leaving you while you were feeling so rotten yesterday. I do hope the blood transfusion went off well and that you are feeling stronger. I thought a lot about you and could picture you with all that apparatus around you. If only you can just get steadily better and stronger everything will be all right. It is terribly disappointing when you get these relapses, but they are liable to happen, and we must just hope you will not have any more.

We have been firing this morning; not a very good performance. It was on the anti-tank range and one of my guns scored two hits. The rest

were hopeless. I can see we shall have plenty more practice.

Have you got that nice little nurse with the blue eyes yet? She seemed pleasant and I would not mind being ill with her myself.

Heaps and heaps of love, and keep going.

Ever,

Your John

30-10-43

My dearest darling,

When I rang up your mother last night, I was delighted to hear that after the blood transfusion you were starting to feel better. I knew that fighting spirit of yours was bound to get you through and I am jolly proud of you.

Your mother tells me that the champagne helped you a lot, so of course I have been trying to get you some more. It is very scarce, but I think I have found some which I must get to you somehow. I had an offer of some eggs from a fellow officer in the mess who knew you were ill, so I snapped them up and sent them off to your mother for you. I only hope they do not get broken in the post as it is an offence to buy eggs other than from a shop.

How is Secundus going on? I expect they are feeling much more contented and pleased with life.

The shoot with the air OP on Friday was a flop. The weather has changed again, and we have mist and rain. Visibility was absolutely nil, the mist so thick that it was almost impossible to get the guns into action. We packed up and returned for lunch.

The dance in the evening went off very well and a good time was had by all. I felt much better having had good news of you, and needless to say I behaved myself. There was plenty of drink and quite a number succumbed. Having nothing better to do I acted the good host and took on some of the wallflowers. My first effort turned out to be a schoolgirl who did not drink nor smoke nor do anything except giggle. I was very glad when she had to go home at 10 o'clock. The party finished at 3 o'clock in the morning and we are feeling a bit dim today.

This morning, we have had some practice at loading and disembarking from a mock-up landing craft. Rather amusing, and the men seemed quite enthusiastic about it.

Keep up the good work, darling, and get well just as soon as you can.

All my love,

Your John

My dearest darling,

I have just rung up your mother. She is very worried because one of the doctors has told you that one kidney is damaged. I had not heard about that before, and I am sure it must have distressed you. What I want to know is, how much is it damaged? Because that makes a lot of difference. I have spoken to Doc about it and he says it would mean that you have to take things easy for some time and not drink much beer. I hope he is right, darling.

Well, my dear, I have managed to get a bottle of Dry Royal which is the nearest match to champagne I could find. If it is all right, I will try and get some more, but it is extremely difficult to get. I hope you enjoy it.

What do you think of the Russians' effort on the Dnieper? They are certainly making a grand show. It looks as if the German army will be very shaky next year and should make our job very much easier. Perhaps by Christmas 1944 it will all be over.

If you take plenty of rest and don't have more babes, you should be absolutely strong again and then we can really begin to live.

Heaps and heaps of love, my darling,

Your John

3-11-43

My dearest darling,

I have just spoken to your mother, darling, and I hear the Dry Royal arrived safely, so you have a little in hand. I will try and get you some more, but I am afraid you are drinking faster than the supply.

We had a very interesting talk from the Corps Commander on the North African and Sicilian campaigns. He talked for nearly three hours without referring to a note and just rattled off the names *of obscure wadis and little places. He seemed very optimistic as to the future, but the more we hear about these landings, the more amazing they appear. The preparations and equipment required are stupendous, and that was only on a small beach in Sicily.*

I do hope, darling, you will soon be feeling really better.

Heaps and heaps of love from,

Your John

7-11-43

My dearest darling,

I do hope you are progressing and feeling better. I have been round to the wine merchants today to tell them that you were better as a result of the last bottle of champagne and have got another. Positively the last they have got.

They are urgently calling for blood donors from the army. I had not thought much about it before, but having seen the way it has saved your life I felt very keen to give back what I could, and it was arranged for yesterday afternoon. The other Troop Commander and I volunteered from the Battery and, altogether from the Regiment, there were about 150 of us. We all went to a large hall and laid out on beds twelve at a time. I did not feel too good about it, but did not disgrace myself, though mine took 15 minutes to produce a pint. Some completed theirs in three minutes. The procedure is just like a transfusion in reverse but like you, they got the needle in the wrong part of my arm and the stuff would not flow properly. I felt a bit groggy at the end but soon recovered and today I am back to normal.

The whole thing had a rather amusing sequel. I was laid on the bed and along came a nice little nurse whom I had met a few times at dances in York. She was very pleased to see me and looked after me. It is a touring unit, and they were only in Scarborough for one day, so I arranged to have a drink with her at their hotel and, after talking to the management, got them into the dance at the Royal Hotel. They were dressed in their Red Cross uniforms and were snapped up in a matter of minutes. We all thoroughly enjoyed it and I felt quite pleased with my day's work.

I showed them the pictures of my family which were much admired, and they were very sorry to hear you are so ill. I wish I could ship some of them down to you as they were a jolly crowd. Of course, I have had to answer for it in the mess today, and they are all threatening to write to you about it. So you see, darling, I am confessing to you first.

We had some light automatic shooting yesterday morning on the sands and loosed off thousands of rounds. Very good fun and we certainly learnt a lot about handling Sten guns. I have spent most of this morning wading through masses of paperwork which we are inundated with at the moment.

And now, darling, I do hope you do not have any more setbacks.

All my love, darling,

Ever your loving John

8-11-43

My dearest darling,

I have just telephoned your mother and she has told me what a terrible time you are having. I am terribly sorry, darling. It is very difficult to get to know how you are over the telephone; the three minutes pass so quickly and then they just cut us off. Your mother said she has written to me to give me a full account. I do feel so very sorry for you.

The remainder of the letter, written 11-11-43

This is the letter, darling, which I did not finish in my rush to come up and see you.

I had lunch with Mother and Rosemary, who was very thrilled, *and during which I asked Rosemary if she would like to walk round with me to the garage to put my bike away. She did not say much, but as soon as we had finished, rushed out saying, "I fetch them," returning with her outdoor shoes, and in great haste sitting down on the floor to put them on. Rather cute I thought.*

I do so hope you are keep getting better now and have no more setbacks.

All my love, darling,
Your John

16-11-43

My dearest darling,

Your mother seemed terribly upset tonight when I rang up. I am terribly sorry, darling, to hear you are being given such pain with these examinations. Your mother wants me to come up at once and stop them, but, darling, I don't see how I can do that. Mr Heekes has told me he is doing everything possible to get you well. I can't imagine how painful the procedure is, but it is apparently necessary. Try and bear it a little longer, darling. I still feel confident that you will be all right.

I had about half an hour off this morning so went down to town and arranged for six bottles of champagne to be reserved for you. That ought to brighten you up.

The Commanding Officer is inspecting my troop on Saturday and I am advised to lay on bullshit it its highest form. Everything blazoned and shining. I am afraid that is rather a failing of his and is against my principle, but of course I have no option but to fall in with the policy. I don't like it and it makes me feel 'let's get into action and stop all this nonsense'.

Goodnight, darling, I do hope everything will be all right. You have a great faith, and I have a great faith in you.

Ever your loving John

My dearest darling,

We have been out today learning all about German weapons. We fired quite a number of them and found them to be pretty good. They have a number of most ingenious gadgets and their workmanship is very good, but in some of the more recent it appears to be falling off.

Tomorrow we are going out course shooting. It is a long time since I did a shoot and I have been put on to go first, so anything may happen. It is terribly cold here with snow on the hills. A biting wind and sleet nearly all day so I am not looking forward to laying out in it.

I have just spoken to Mr Heekes. He tells me you are going on all right. I told him he had caused you a lot of pain and he admitted the examination was more difficult than he thought it would be and would consider using an anaesthetic if he had to do it again. I explained how worried your mother was and he thought she was taking an extremely pessimistic view. I hope she doesn't make you pessimistic too, darling. You have a great faith which will want a lot of shaking. I share that faith with you and don't intend to be alarmed.

I have been to some more shops today but can't get any quilted bed jackets. I am told they have been off the market for some time and are considered luxuries. I am afraid I shall have to get you a woollen cloth one. It should be warm but of course will not look as pretty. I am afraid that is just war.

Good night, darling, and may you sleep well.

All my love,

From your John

20-11-43

My very dearest darling,

Many happy returns of your birthday. You have now reached that rife old age of thirty. I am terribly sorry you have to celebrate it in bed in hospital and feeling so rotten. I celebrated mine on Strensall Common which I thought was pretty awful, but little did I think or imagine what we (and I include myself in a very small capacity) would have to endure before your birthday. Anyway, darling, I will celebrate the day hoping and praying that you will soon be returned to me well and strong.

I do wish you would not baffle doctors so much. I hear you have another specialist and that they are going into conference tomorrow. I am always told of these conferences which are to take place, but I never seem to hear of any results. I hope I shall hear some good news this time. I have been to church and heard them say prayers for your recovery.

All my best wishes for your birthday, darling. I love you very much.

Your John

Archer Wing
Royal Hospital
Richmond
20-11-43

My darlingest,

I've just got your letter and you sound so worried that I felt I <u>must</u> try and write you a few lines. I've just been longing to let you know what really has been happening to me, but ever since you returned last time they've not left me alone for more than a day with medical examinations and 'tests', and it has made me very weak again. (I am writing this lying on my back, whilst in the middle of another test, so hope you'll be able to read it!)

Mr Heekes refuses to admit the intense pain he caused me at the cystoscope (bladder) examination, which was a failure anyway because the baby's head was in the way. Sister had to point out how much I was suffering before he'd leave off! I must admit that it seemed to snap the last remnants of my courage and for some days all I wanted was to die and get out of this hideous existence. I'm still sure I couldn't bear it again, but since then have had numerous X-rays, with different dyes injected into my veins to show up the different organs, and also blood and urine tests galore. These don't really give me much pain, darling, only tire and weaken me, but I know they <u>have</u> to be done. They have been almost telling me for certain that the baby will have to go, and I have begged so hard to keep it.

Of course, I'd <u>love</u> to see you, if at all possible. You're an angel to get all the champagne, darling.

All my love,

Your Rita

My very dearest,

By the time you receive this you will have heard the wonderful news. Oh, darling, if <u>only</u> you were here now! I feel so very thankful about it all, but also rather exhausted after the suspense. I had prepared myself to hear that the babe must go and maybe a kidney as well.

Dr Schlossberg, Dr Brown (the specialist) and Mr Heekes all arrived fairly punctually for 9:30 a.m. and of course I had to have another examination (different one this time) which caused a spot of discomfort, but no real pain. Dr Schlossberg also squeezed and poked at my kidneys, which I know will mean a return of the pain in a few hours, but what does that matter! He was very nice indeed, and after going away and the three studying all of the information – X-ray plates and results of tests, etc. – they trooped back again, and Dr Brown settled down for a nice little chat whilst I held my breath!

As you'll already know the baby is to be taken by operation in 9 weeks' time, and there is absolutely no reason (they <u>all</u> assured me) why it should not live and be perfectly healthy and normal in every way. Of course, it will be small, and will need a lot of care for the first month or so. If it were taken away now, I should get better much quicker, but it could not live. Likewise, if they left it the full 9 months it would die inside me during the last month.

Dr Brown said I have a splendid pelvis, perfect for having babies, and that I might even manage an induced labour at 8 months, but Mr Heekes says it's out of the question as it would damage both the baby and me in my weak condition, and to tell you the truth I really feel I could not stand the pain of labour and delivery with instruments after all I've been through. I shan't exactly enjoy the operation of course, but am very much hoping you'll be there to hold my hand and give me the required moral support before, as well as helping me round afterwards. As for me, I have to have another whole lot of fresh tests and examinations before I can leave here, which will take a couple of weeks or so, and then maybe I can go to Brooklyn. As you know, I feel as if I've reached the end of my endurance with them. Mr Heekes says I shall be an invalid all the time until, and a while after, the baby has arrived, but maybe I shall be allowed up for little whiles. He doesn't see why I shouldn't go home for Christmas!

I hope the 'tests' won't mean quite so much starvation as they have lately, as it makes me feel so frightfully weak. The last one was 17 hours without even a sip of water, and was I parched as well as faint. I s'pose in my condition it's nearly equal to a week's fasting in a normal case.

No more babies for 4-5 years at least, and then only if the doctor gives an OK. They asked if you were against using contraceptives, as they understand you are Roman Catholic, so I assured them no, but just that we evidently hadn't found the answer to the problem yet, so they all laughed and said Mr Heekes would put us right!

I think that's the sum and total of the interview, my love, and I feel as if the black cloud hanging over me has gone at last. I don't know what Mummie will think about it all. She may not be coming today as we have been having terrible fogs recently, and last night she and Mr H took nearly two hours to get home.

I'm longing to see you and talk everything over; you're the only one who really understands, and I love you,

Rita

P.S. This epistle has taken nearly a day to write, so give it due importance!

My dearest darling,

I was delighted to have your letter and to hear the good news. You were the first to tell me which is good. I am glad to think that we both had faith and confidence in the result. Now we have to keep it up until the babe arrives and you are well again. I am afraid it is going to be a long nine weeks for you, but now that you know everything should be all right it will be easier for you. I wish I could have come up to see you yesterday, but there it is. This bloody war puts the lid on everything.

Heaps and heaps of love, my darling,

Your John

23-11-43

My dearest darling,

How are you feeling today? I do hope you are feeling stronger and getting better. After your starvation diet you ought to be able to eat a lot and I hope they are giving you plenty of appealing food.

We have been very busy these last few days putting all the lads through an intelligence and aptitude test. They had to answer a lot of written questions and fit patterns together and all sorts of things. Apparently, every man in the British Army is to be graded in this way. So far there is no mention of the officers having to get through it.

We have had our regimental scheme today. I had to take over Battery Commander partway through and rode back with the Commanding Officer in his car. He asked after you, so I was able to give him a full account of our misfortunes. He seemed very sympathetic, but having got that over to him I find I have made rather a bad blob *on the scheme which I have no doubt will be served up on a plate to me tomorrow at the conference. Anyway, it is done now so I will just have to take it as I have done before.*

I am now off to bed, darling, and I hope you are able to sleep. I wish you could come to bed with me; it's just what I am wanting.

Heaps and heaps of love, my darling,

Your John

Archer Wing
Royal Hospital
Richmond
25-11-43

My dearest darling,

I'm so glad you got my last letter in good time; I was just busting for you to know all about it. I am <u>very</u> cross with Mr Heekes for not phoning you or Mummie after, having promised to do so, and shall tell him so this morning. Apparently, he went straight from here to tell Sister at Brooklyn. Had another bumping row with her over me and the hospital, and I suppose forgot all about it! He then went to stay at Capel, to fix up about selling his geese, and is due back today. It's a good sign that he felt he could leave me, isn't it? And also, I have the good news for you that yesterday morning I was actually allowed <u>up</u> for ten minutes and shall probably be allowed up <u>twice</u> today! Of course, it took a bit of agitating on my part(!) but they're all pleased with the result as I had a better night.

They're going to start lessening the strength of the nightly drug now. The specialist said I was to have liquid paraffin, but it made me so violently sick that I had to have it in the form of emulsion, and ye gods, does it keep me busy?! So much so that it tired me out yesterday and Sister has stopped it.

Secundus became highly indignant at events yesterday and paid me out by pretending it was a baby tank on manoeuvres, and was crashing around inside, banging and bumping on all my sorest parts! It started this game again during the night; woke me up and refused to let me sleep again until it had received some admonishment in the form of sharp taps and rubbing!

Did I tell you that when the specialist did the examination, he was very surprised at the size of the babe, and said it's me there's so little of, not the child! Also, the X-ray people told me they had a surprise too when they saw its size in the plates. It's got lots of dark hair, they say, which I expect accounts for my intense bouts of heartburn! Now that it really looks as if Secundus is going to stay with me, there is a terrific rush of preparation starting, and people are offering to knit things.

As you say, darling, it will be a few months before I'm able to take charge of our family, and the care of poor little Rosemary is a constant worry. The only thing I can think of is to put her into the home at Wimbledon, or else advertise our requirements in *Nursery World* for someone who would take her (people do that sort of thing). If only we actually knew of someone! But I can't think of anyone suitably placed during the war. Everyone's either on war work or living with their parents.

I'm dying to see you but hope it won't be in here!

I love you and love you,

Your Rita

216/63 Medium Regt RA
Scarborough
York
26-11-43

My dearest darling,
I got your nice long letter today. It is grand to have letters from you

again, darling. You are making up for the long days of silence. It is wonderful news to know you have been up for a short time. What did it feel like after so long? You must have been very pleased. You must not get overtired again. Take things steadily, it is the only way to get well, and we do not want any setbacks now.

Secundus seems to be getting on well and kicking around. You must get bigger and fatter yourself. The X-ray sounds interesting and if they can tell you what colour hair it has, I should imagine they could tell you its sex as well. (Or perhaps that is not allowed on professional grounds.)

I have just rung up your mother. She sounds quite cheerful these days and much relieved, which is very good and shows you must be better. She told me you were improving, and she is hoping you will be able to go to Brooklyn Nursing Home soon.

I have spoken to Doc about you and told him of the programme. He thinks it is very good and that we are very lucky to get away with it. He very much advises that we should not have any more children, at any rate for some long time. We shall have to be very careful shall we not, darling?

We had the guns down on the sands this morning for gun drill. It was very pleasant and made a very good parade ground.

All my love, darling,

Your John

29-11-43

My dearest darling,

I was very glad to have your letter this morning and to hear that you are getting on so well. You certainly sound to be surpassing yourself and making great strides. Great news, my girl.

I hope you can manage without the champagne because I am terribly afraid I shall not be able to get you another six bottles. I have got two stowed away for you, but the stock which they hoped was coming in has not panned out. You must keep some for the great event because I have no doubt you will be wanting some then now that you have acquired such a taste for it.

We have been playing more gun drill games in the mess. Rather amusing!

Keep up the good work, darling.

All my love,

From your John

Archer Wing

Royal Hospital

Richmond

30-11-43

My dearest darling,

Dr Schlossberg says I must wear a maternity belt every time I get up as the babe is too heavy for me to support by myself whilst I'm so weak, and it will cause the tummy muscles to give way completely. I must say it <u>feels</u> a ton weight! Regarding the sex on the X-ray plates, you can't see it because the babe is curled up into a ball, completely hiding the vital organs! Dr Schlossberg says he thinks it may be a girl as it's so lively and has been so persistent to stay with me, and boys are usually lazier! However, he thinks it's such a miracle that the child and I have survived at all that he wouldn't put anything past us! Whatever it is it will be very wonderful and precious, and my one prayer is that everything will be all right.

All my love, my precious,

Your Rita

Brooklyn Nursing Home
SW15
6-12-43

My dearest darling,

I hear that you rang Mummie last night and heard that the great removal has been made and I am now at the Brooklyn after tremendous conflabs, discussions, pow-wows (Mr Heekes's word) and rows galore! Mr H is apparently still in a fine old mood about it and went off to Capel for the weekend without leaving one instruction regarding my medicine or treatment, which I think was rather mean as I might so easily have had a setback. I shall tell him so when I can get him alone. As it was, I refused to leave the hospital without a bottle of the medicine (without which they say the baby would probably die). As you know, in my obstinate moments I resemble the mule, and I just bounced over all such details such as it was against hospital rules, my last bottle was empty, and the dispensary closed for the weekend etc., etc! Anyway, I got it in the end!

I had a busy time receiving a running deputation of nurses before I left, coming to say goodbye to me. I didn't enjoy the continual lifting about from bed to stretcher, stretcher to ambulance, etc., especially as the men always seemed to push their arms under me right against the poor old kidneys! I ached incredibly all Saturday night and the pain was pretty bad on Sunday. I suppose as Mr H says, I can't expect to get rid of the aches and pains entirely until the babe isn't there any longer.

I have celebrated the day by wearing the new bed jacket and feeling like Lady Muck in it. It's really glorious, and I keep a mirror handy to have a peek at myself every now and again to see how beautiful I am, whilst Secundus is doing its best to remind its mother that one should not feel so vain and frivolous when one has a bulge.

Have just been put back to bed after a most important occasion:

my first meal up for about 13 weeks (quarter of a year!). Feel very full, tired and also slightly tight, having celebrated it with the champagne I'd reserved for the removal here. I think you're awfully clever (and also a love!) to get the champagne.

I do hope the scheme goes well, and also (most fervently!) that you keep well in spite of the intense cold and the flu epidemic.

Heaps and heaps of love,

From your own missus

P.S. Just received your letter, for which many thanks. I'm <u>very</u> glad you got out of that wretched old bivouacking, darling; I should think it's enough to knock off the strongest in this weather!

7-12-43

My darlingest,

I feel like bursting with joy at the news of your leave over Christmas, darling, and if <u>only</u> I can get home and be with all my beloveds for a few days it will simply repay all the long weary weeks, when each day has seemed a month, and feel sure will help me to better bear what's coming.

Of course, I'm longing to see my daughter again. I'm afraid, at times, I get very sad about this separation from her, and rather depressed at the idea of how long it has to be yet. She will be quite different. Still, it's nothing really compared with the separation from <u>you</u>, tho' somehow I never feel as if <u>we</u> are so very far apart.

Oh, <u>how</u> thankful I shall be when it's all over and I can really begin to be properly well. I am so tired of the aches and pains and helplessness, let alone of bed!

I love you heaps and heaps,

Your Rita

My dearest darling,

We are off early tomorrow morning for Redesdale. We are now going to make the whole journey, about 130 miles, in one day. I am having to go on ahead to attend a conference with regard to safety arrangements. So far there is no snow or rain, but we are prepared for the worst. A Regiment which has just come back had thirty-eight accidents due to vehicles coming unstuck on icy roads.

What do you think of the meeting of 'the big three'? It sounds as if Churchill's birthday party was a pretty boozy affair and they all seem to have enjoyed themselves very well. It looks now as if there is going to be a co-ordinated attack from three sides sometime next year. It will be a terrific do, but no doubt will finish off these bloody Germans once and for all.

I have just been to the pictures to see Escape to Danger. *Another Nazi spy film but quite a good one. Next week there is Striptease Lady. I must certainly have a look at that.*

All my love to you. Keep up the good work,
Your John

My dearest darling,

Since arriving here in the dark on Wednesday we have worked long days. The trouble is that everywhere is waterlogged, and the guns just sink and have to be winched out. The first day I had a tractor break down in the mud and had to come out for it after supper. Last night one of my guns ran away downhill and fell in a stream, and today everything was bogged so badly that they never got to the second position and came straight back to camp. Hence my having a few minutes to write to you. My stock has fallen rather than risen I am afraid, but today I did reasonably good shoots against most of the others rather inferior, so perhaps I am back to normal.

I do hope, darling, you are feeling less tired, not having any more pain and that you will be well enough to get home for a few days at Christmas.

I must get off to bed now, darling, as I am up early tomorrow.

Goodnight and heaps of love,

From your John

My dearest darling,

I had a letter from Father just before I left Redesdale to say that Mother was ill and that they had had to take Rosemary to the home at Wimbledon. I am very sorry this has happened, but Mother's doctor has insisted that she can no longer look after Rosemary.

It is very disappointing that Rosemary will not be with us for Christmas. I was looking forward to having her with us again for a little while, but I see no reason why I should not fetch her from the home for a day. Apparently, they only allow visitors once a week for an hour, which I think is sensible as otherwise the children would become very unsettled. I have had a letter this morning from the sister in charge who says Rosemary is very good and happy, and has settled down well. She will apparently make an exception for soldier fathers to visit there, so maybe we shall all be together for a little while. I will try and fix up for Rosemary to come over for Christmas Day, if that will be convenient to your mother.

I have managed to get you three more large bottles of champagne, so I shall have quite a load to bring up with me. I do hope, darling, that you are continuing to get better.

Heaps of love, my darling.

Ever your loving John

My very dearest,

First of all, I must wish you everything you wish yourself for 1944, as that probably covers more than I can think or know of. I wonder what you will do tonight. Anyway, darling, have a drink (one each!) on Rosemary, Secundus and me, and I'll reciprocate (in water!?) to you.

I've missed you dreadfully, especially at night, but have managed all right by myself so far. It was awfully hard saying goodbye to you this time, and I'm afraid I've been fretting a bit and wasn't quite so good yesterday. I expect it was made worse too by parting with our cherub the day before. However, Secundus has been giving me a few hard digs in the ribs and elsewhere, and has made me pull up my socks again, for its sake.

This morning my tummy looks tremendous (even Mummie thinks so!) and Secundus is sticking out in the most queer bumps and angles, which move about as you look at them. I'd love to know what they all are! Mr Heekes is coming at the end of the week to examine me properly. He came last night, and seemed very pleased, but does wish I'd get a bit fatter. I try to do a little more every day and am determined to manage without the operation, if possible. So please go on praying hard that I shall, darling, and that the babe will be perfect when it arrives.

If I have another child with Rosemary's temperament, I shall indeed be lucky, with such a wonderful 'better half' as well! I honestly think you're an absolute marvel of good temper, kindness and consideration and every good thing possible, and I love you more every time I see you.

All my love and thoughts,
Your Rita

216/63 Medium Regt RA
Scarborough
York
31-12-43

My very dearest,

A very happy and momentous New Year to you, darling. Another year, and I have no doubt there will be tremendous changes. We have had our share of trouble this year and I am sure it will be our turn for some success in the next.

I do hope you are feeling better and coping all right at night. Are you able to manage the stairs or are you still resting in the drawing room and getting on and off the old whatnot? I do hope you are able to get out into the fresh air soon. It will be jolly good for you and give you a lot more confidence in yourself.

I doubt if I shall be able to speak to you before the New Year because our phone has gone bust again.

All my love, darling, for the victorious year.

Ever your devoted,

John

1944

My darlingest,

Mr Heekes came yesterday morning. Blood pressure not up to normal, but very pleased apart from that. He then sat down and (with great satisfaction!) informed us that the baby is almost arriving, thereby frightening Mummie out of her wits!

Umpteen people keep calling in to see me, and in the first few moments their eyes invariably go to the bulge, and they give incredulous exclamations of astonishment at its size. It is certainly pretty big now; everyone says it's big for even a normal pregnancy of 7 ½ months. My maternity frock is a great success and, after 4 ½ months, it is grand to be dressed again.

Heaps and heaps of love, my precious,

Your Rita

216/63 Medium Regt RA
Scarborough
York
4-1-44

My dearest darling,

I am very glad everything is going well, though you must keep the blood pressure up if you are going to produce in the very near future. Anyway, darling, I hope you do manage the miracle this month because February looks like being a very busy one for us with schemes and exercises taking up practically the whole time. Now that we have Montgomery back, I expect there will be plenty going on and all previous programmes will be altered.

I do hope, darling, you will continue to make good progress.

Heaps of love to you,
From your John

Barnes
SW13
7-1-44

My dearest darling,

I'm so sorry I haven't written before but I have been having another infection attack, somewhat severe and prolonged this time. I do most fervently hope I shan't have any more, especially when the babe is actually coming. The thought of the two ordeals coming together has confronted me all this week and made an errant coward of me. However, Mr H came yesterday and says nothing can be done until the baby has arrived, when I shall feel a different person (thank goodness!). In the meantime, if I still want the baby, and wish it to have all possible advantages, I've just got to put up with all of this! Which is plain speaking, and there's no use my complaining, but it doesn't stop me from feeling very depressed at realising how terribly weak I am and doubting if I will manage to stand even an hour of labour pains.

Anyway, darling, it's a relief to be able to tell <u>you</u> that I get panicky and scared stiff at times, and to know that you'll understand. After taking some tablets for the pain last night I had the loveliest dream that the war was over, and you'd come home for good. I awoke nearly bursting with excitement, to find that I was clasping the hot water bottle instead of you! What disillusionment!!

I have got the rest of the baby's things ready, just in case of a hurry! tho' I don't <u>think</u> it'll be for a week or so myself. We'll do our best for this month for you, darling.

All my love to you,

Your Rita

My very dearest,

Secundus is kicking hard and making me feel sick. I'm wondering whether it portends anything! Mr H came yesterday and went into full details of exactly what Mummie is to do if labour comes on, despite her obvious distaste for the job! Sarah-Jane walks about in fear and trembling, announcing that <u>she'll</u> die if the baby comes whilst I'm here!

Mr H timed the babe's heartbeats, and that organ seems entirely satisfactory. He announced that the baby was almost <u>falling</u> out! Wish it could! How easy it sounds! I have a faint hope that Dr Christie Brown, who is to deliver Secundus, may be more merciful than Mr H, and to help me out will give me a whiff of liquid chloroform once or twice. Perfectly normal confinements usually are, but old Mr H is very hard-hearted and believes in letting you carry on by yourself until it is vital not to!

<u>What</u> wouldn't I give to have you near me during this very trying period! It must be simply marvellous to have an understanding husband by you, to turn to for comfort and moral support when you need it most. Still, I always try to think that I'm luckier than some, because I do know you understand, and are constantly with me in spirit, if not in the flesh!

We had quite an air raid here the other night; three bombs in the river at the end of the road and two in adjacent roads, <u>none</u> of which have exploded yet, and everyone is still evacuated! I thought <u>one</u> was destined for us and, determined to save Secundus to the last, I dived (as rapidly as circumstances permit!) under the bed. It's a miracle it didn't start everything off!

I've just this minute had a present brought in that's enough to dazzle the eyes! The boy next door has returned from Australia, and has sent me in a parcel of oranges, lemons and grapefruit!!! All fresh fruit. I can hardly believe my eyes!

Heaps and heaps of love. (Maybe I'll see you soon!)

Your Rita

216/63 Medium Regt RA
Scarborough
York
11-1-44

My dearest darling,

I shall certainly be very pleased to hear that everything has gone off well and I hope you manage it soon. The suspense is pretty awful even for me and I am afraid I am getting the real father condition.

I haven't really considered all the names you sent but I feel Cherry ought to be one of them. After all cherries were almost the start of things for us, weren't they, darling? The only thing is our second possible daughter might not quite appreciate the significance.

It is really cold up here now. Snow today and tomorrow, and training is still very difficult with so many jobs going on at once. There is absolutely no indication of future operations and everything is going on perfectly normally to keep everyone guessing.

All my love to you, darling,

Your John

Barnes
SW13
14-1-44

My dearest darling,

Today I have the pleasure of a really awful backache, which is reminding me of the 24 hours before Rosemary started to arrive. The last few days have produced a flood of maternal feelings, and I long to see her more than ever; nature's preparation for another ewe lamb, I suppose! I still live in hopes that soon I will be able to look after our chicks myself.

Mr. Heekes has just been in and examined me again – only externally this time, thank goodness – and seems very well satisfied, especially with the babe. He says it "has plenty of life; a good strong heart-beat, and is quite a decent size, especially considering my condition". He also says it's doing so well inside (!) and getting stronger every day, that he'd like it to stay there a bit longer! The only thing is that it is becoming more and more of a strain upon me, so I need careful watching, and if he had the case, and the infant hadn't arrived during the next fortnight (Heaven help me!) – he'd start by giving me a blood transfusion and then an induction. I hope the latter won't be necessary, as it would require more strength on my part.

I went for a little walk yesterday, about 100 yards down the road and back. It was grand to sniff real fresh air again. When I got back, I realised what a sight I must have looked, as my fur coat was strained across my tummy, with the button sticking out, right in the centre, and underneath the 'mountain' a pair of skinny legs! Still, who cares? One of these days I shall look beautiful (perhaps!?!).

Regarding the girl's names I suggested. I suppose it's of no use mentioning Virginia again. I wondered if you'd like Deidre? And I still do like Cherry! What a blessing we've JJ's name fixed without any bother! I think the babe will be long (and skinny?) this time as its head is right down as far as possible, and yet it still succeeds in kicking me hard under the ribs with its feet, which is a pretty good stretch!

Heaps and heaps of love to you, precious,

Your Rita

216/63 Medium Regt RA
Scarborough
York
17-1-44

My dearest darling,

I was very pleased to hear you last evening. You certainly sounded better and cheerful. I certainly hope you manage things in the next two weeks. Apparently practically the whole of February is taken up with exercises when it will be more difficult to get in touch with me. So do what you can darling, but I am sure everything will be all right.

I have given long consideration to this name business, darling, and I must say I find it very difficult to choose. Cherry should be all right, though somewhat unusual, but the trouble is to get another name that will run easily with it. My efforts are Patricia, Susan, Margaret, June and Francis. What say you? I don't think we would be thanked if we gave the poor girl a name like Deidre. Let me know what you think of these.

Several of us went to see Walt Disney's Saludos Amigos *yesterday. Some wonderful artistic scenes but I did not think it as entertaining as* Snow White.

Heaps of love,
From your John

Barnes
SW13
18.1.44

My dearest,

Yesterday, unfortunately, I started off the day by being very sick, which strained at the old kidneys and the baby, and made me feel rather bad. I've been feeling sick and vomiting ever since. Mr. Heekes is coming in this morning. Sometimes I can't even remember what it was like to have not pain and feel well!

By the way, darling, I <u>must</u> tell you that Mr H told Mummie I was highly intelligent! Isn't it a hoot? He never made a bigger mistake in his life! What he's doing, of course, is to confuse intelligence and common sense; the latter quality I feel I <u>can</u> make claim to, without undue immodesty!

It was grand to be able to talk to you again last night, darling, tho' it makes me want to see you more than ever!

I love you and love you pots,

Your Rita

216/63 Medium Regt RA
Scarborough
York
20-1-44

My dearest darling,

I am very sorry to hear that you have been so sick. It is rotten for you, and I do wish I could do something to help you. I am awaiting every day to hear that I am to come up and see what you have produced. I am still trying for the nappies but no luck. There are very limited supplies about, and the stores can give me no idea when they will arrive. I certainly do hope Dr Christie Brown will be ready. I have received the receipt and I am assured everything is prepared for you.

Heaps of love to you, darling. I love you very much,
Your John

Barnes
SW13
21-1-44

My dearest dear,

Last night Mr Heekes was really in a foul temper again. He says that if <u>he</u> had the case I should be in hospital by now, having treatment and blood transfusions before the induction! Anyway, Dr Christie Brown rang up yesterday, and seemed very surprised to hear that I am so weak and thin and says he can't understand why!? And then Mr H said yesterday that Dr Brown knows all about it. What <u>are</u> you to believe??

The nearer I get to the ordeal ahead, the more I dread it; even the blood transfusions and treatment. I feel so frightfully weak and incapable of standing up to any more severe pain. In fact, I feel a nervous wreck! Before he left last night, even Mr H condescended to be quite sympathetic towards me over my 'trials'!

Regarding your list of names, darling, I like Susan the best. I don't think we can very well name a January-born June; Margaret is so ordinary, and Francis is a boy's name. Sorry you don't like Deirdre, as those Deirdres I've known have all been very nice girls, so I suppose I've got a good impression of it! Anyway, if you dislike it it's no good. Unless you like Shirley (I do), it seems at present to have boiled down to Susan, Cherry and Carole. What do you think?

Cheeribye, my love. Have a nice weekend.

All my love,

Your Rita

216/63 Medium Regt RA
Scarborough
York
23-1-44

My dearest darling,

The Sergeants' mess social last night was quite good, and we all had plenty of beer and some eats. The Sergeants had their lady friends there, but they were a pretty corny crowd and I stuck to the beer as usual. I am afraid I had a bit of a head this morning.

Regarding the names, darling, we can call her Susan. Do you think

Cherry Susan or Susan Cherry Reed sounds the better? I rather think the latter.

Now you must not get depressed. I am sure you are much better and that you will not have very much trouble. I know it must be rotten being away from home, but I feel you should go to the hospital a few days in advance so that you will be absolutely prepared. I am just longing to come up next week to see you and Secundus both doing well.

Heaps of love, my darling,
Your John

Barnes
SW13
23-1-44

My dearest darling,

We went up to 92 Harley Street to see Dr Christie Brown who was just as nice and kind as before, and I am quite sure we are doing the best thing possible by my being under the 'great man's' care. He will not himself attend to me at the confinement, and I cannot have a room all to myself, but will have to share with one other person (the latter is due to war conditions and the fact that every big hospital is under orders to keep so many beds unoccupied for the invasion!). I said I thought I'd be a bit of nuisance to the other person with my continual 'bed-panning', especially in the night, but he said I wasn't to worry, and that he had particularly asked Mr Heekes to pass on the two items of information so as to prepare me for it. Of course, we hadn't heard a word of it!

Well, he seemed to have rather a shock upon seeing me and said at once that I looked more ill and had lost more flesh than when he saw me in November! He gave me a thorough examination – sounded the baby's heart and mine, took my blood pressure, etc. He said the babe is a beauty – strong and vigorous, very good heartbeat – and will, he thinks, be even bigger than Rosemary was!! So that sounds good enough, doesn't it? As to your smaller half, darling, things aren't quite so good. He seems rather perturbed at my general condition and said there's no doubt that I'm an ill woman (what a description!) and is afraid I shall not be a well one for some time!

If everything is fairly satisfactory, he will give me an induction next weekend, so you can 'stand by' for then, darling. The induction may bring labour on immediately or it may take three or four days, tho' he thinks it won't take long in my case. He assures me there will be two resident specialists to see to me, who will be acting exactly according to his instructions. Labour should only take about 10 hours this time (quite long enough!) and I shall be put to sleep (by oxygen and gas) for the actual delivery. He thinks induction is desirable, as the weight of the child must be putting a great deal of pressure on my kidneys, and if it weren't for my 'wonderful' pelvis I shouldn't be able to deliver at all. The aforesaid part of my anatomy is, according to him, the best he's ever come across, and is worthy of being a museum piece! Think I shall have to leave it to one!!

I'll write again before I leave here, darling. Feel terribly tired tonight, but I love you heaps,

Your Rita

216/63 Medium Regt RA
Scarborough
York
25-1-44

My dearest darling,

How are you today? I hope you are keeping up your morale. I feel very sorry for you as I can imagine how you must be feeling just before the great day. I only wish I could be nearer to you to help you over this difficult period, but I am afraid it cannot be. However, I hope to be with you sometime next week when we shall be able to look back on the last few months as a rather grim period in our lives.

I have had a letter from Miss Warner at Wimbledon and Rosemary is much better and taking her tonic. She apparently has quite rosy cheeks again now so she should be more like our Rosemary next time we see her.

I will ring up tomorrow, darling.
All my love to you,
Your John

Barnes
SW13
26-1-44

My dearest dear,

I am hoping that this time next week everything will be over, and that we shall all be feeling much better! I had a very bad day yesterday and got terribly depressed and felt so very, very tired of struggling on, fighting against all the aches and pains. I just haven't the will or the strength to endure much more. I feel like a worn out shell surrounding the new young life, and just want to go to sleep and not wake up till the pain has gone.

I expect the hospital will phone Mummie as soon as it's over, and then she is going to either phone you or send a telegram. I am dreading tomorrow, and the next few days, but am trying to remember my little motto: Time and hour run thro' the roughest day!

Heaps of love, darling,

Your Rita

216/63 Medium Regt RA
Scarborough
York
26-1-44

My dearest darling,

I was very glad I was able to speak to you this evening and wish you all the best before you go up to London. I do hope they get it all over quickly for you as I can imagine you must have a bit of a sinking feeling. I have myself. But once you are there, I expect they will give you all the necessary encouragement. Have you got plenty of champagne to buck you up?

The padre came round to see us this evening. I will ask him to say prayers for you. It certainly proved a great help last time when you were so ill.

I will send this off to the hospital and hope you get it in good time.

Heaps of love, my darling,

Your John

City of London Maternity Hospital
Liverpool Road
N1
28-1-44

My dearest darling,

I simply hated leaving home for hospital yesterday. I tried hard to keep up the morale, but it <u>was</u> difficult! My left ear was burning terrifically just before we left, and I guessed you'd be thinking of us? We arrived about 3:45 p.m., and found they weren't ready for us! However, they gave us a cup of tea, and Mummie unpacked for me and then went home. The doctor (he is young – early 30s I should imagine) seems very efficient, nice and sympathetic. The sister and day nurses also seem very kind tho' the night nurse is a bit of a brute! Of course, <u>all</u> my medicines and tablets, etc. have been changed once again, with the result that my tummy objected thoroughly last night and again this morning. I have been very sick two or three times and slept very little last night.

Dr Christie Brown will be coming tomorrow evening to hear and see full results and decide what and when is to be done to me. Oh, to get the next few days over! Secundus is still frightfully abusive to my insides, and the doctor here says it's a lovely baby too.

Cheeribye for now, my love. Do hope you have good news soon! All my love,
Your Rita

216/63 Medium Regt RA
Scarborough
York
1-2-44

My dearest darling,
I have just spoken to your mother and heard what an awful time

you are having. I am so terribly sorry, darling, and do wish I could do something to help you. Last night your mother told me you had had the induction and that you should do the great deed today, so you can imagine how disappointed I am to hear that you are still having the trouble pains. I do hope you get it over tomorrow and then I can come up to see you and help you to get well again.

We have been out on an exercise today and are going out again tomorrow, but I am afraid I am not taking much interest in army affairs just now. I was thinking of you all the time when we were out today and felt quite happy until we got back and there was no telegram for me.

Well, darling, I am going off to bed now and pray you may be all right tomorrow.

Goodnight, my darling,

Your loving John

2-2-44

My very clever and wonderful wife,

You don't know what a terrific thrill it was to me to hear that you had performed such a marvellous feat. And so, John Jeremy at last is a living being. You certainly manage wonderful things, darling, and I hope you are as pleased as I am.

And now, darling, how are you? I could not make out from what your mother told me exactly how the operation was carried out, but I know you must have had an awful time. The message I got from the hospital was both doing as well as can be expected, but your mother told me that you were very weak and exhausted which I know must be right. Now if you can only get rid of the kidney trouble you will be well pretty quickly. So now we have to pray for the next miracle, and I feel just as confident about that as I did about JJ. I am sure it's now our turn to have good fortune and perhaps before very long the <u>four</u> of us will be *together at 'Craiglea'.*

We must not forget our little princess, Rosemary. I expect she will be very thrilled when she sees her little brother. I wonder when we shall be able to introduce them. It is going to be a great thing for both of them, and to have one of each has been our great ambition. They will be grand company for each other, and now we have both got to pull through the next twelve months so that we can be grand company for them too. I know we will.

I am just going off to bed now, darling, as I feel very tired. Guess it must be the reaction. I do hope you have a good night.

Good night you wonderful and precious thing.

All my love to you, JJ and our Rosemary,

Your John

2-2-44

My dearest darling,

I have just spoken to your mother and am very glad to hear that you are both progressing satisfactorily. Your mother says you are very pleased with JJ and that he is a bright little chap with dark hair and like me. I hear Mother and Father are delighted with him and know they were hoping for a boy, though of course they are charmed with Rosemary. It will be great when we are all together for the first time, won't it, darling?

I expect you are still very groggy, but I guess very pleased with yourself. I am terrifically proud of you, darling. Now I am very anxious to hear any results of the kidney trouble. I do hope Mr Heekes was right when he said you would have no more pain after the babe was born.

Tomorrow we go off on our exercise with the division. It is very wet, so I am not looking forward to it very much. I have now got my open carrier back, which is damned cold and uncomfortable this time of year.

The padre has been in for tea and was very pleased. I have told him we now want help for your recovery.

Everyone here sends their hearty congratulations to you.

Heaps and heaps of love, darling,

Your loving John

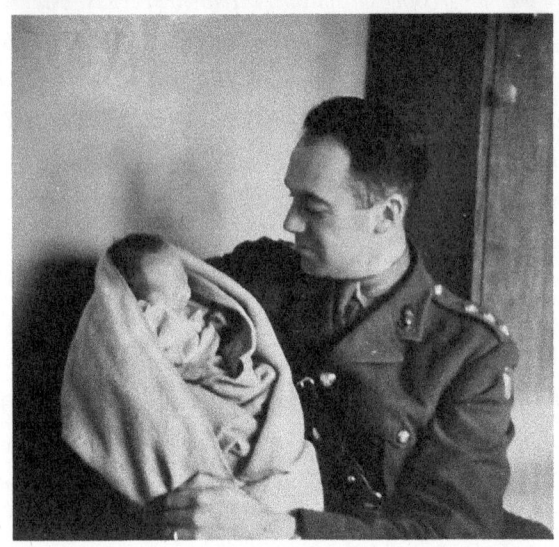

City of London Maternity Hospital
Liverpool Road
N1
8-2-44

My very dearest,

Mummie came to see me this morning and seemed very pleased with herself and life in general. She is going round to see Mr Heekes tonight to have a chat about what's to become of me! She sees a tremendous improvement in both Jeremy and me, and says she thinks it is going to be cruel to part us after all I went through to get him. Of course, I can see it's quite impossible to be all together for a while, and quite realise I must be sensible and accept it. After all, we can't be 'complete' until <u>you're</u> with us for good.

It was <u>so</u> lovely to see you, tho' I hated your having to go. As soon as you come into my near vicinity, all troubles are smoothed out for me, and trials seem just wafted away. I don't know however you manage it all!

If <u>only</u> I could have my other little precious with me! I want to love <u>her</u> such a lot, too. Still, that goes for all my family, and I'm longing for that leave. We really must manage something altogether (the urge is still very much about – how's yours?!)

I love you till I could burst with it. So heaps from all of us,

Your own missus

12-2-44

My dearest darling,

I do hope, darling, the weather isn't too awful for you. We've been having snow here, so I hate to imagine what you're having! It will quite spoil your beautiful gun, too! What do you think of the enclosed snaps, dear? Very good, and those of Rosemary too. She does look so different from how she used to; quite another little person, poor love. It makes me long to have her with me and make her look really happy again.

Well, darlingest, I have some more good news for you! Dr Christie Brown paid me a state call this afternoon, and says he is more amazed by my progress every time he sees me and, patting my cheek as if I were 2!, that I am now positively blooming. He said I am quite the quickest recovery case he's ever had and just can't get over his astonishment. According to Mummie who's seen Mr Heekes, Dr Christie Brown rang up Mr Heekes and rather ticked him off, saying that he thinks I was neglected over my anaemia for too long, and it's only by a miracle that I got through Jeremy's arrival. Mr Heekes is naturally rather put out, tho' is also rather peevish about my marvellous recovery.

Everything is going quite mad this morning, and not a thing has been done for any of us, not even the fires lit. It's jolly cold for Jeremy to come into from the warm nursery. I find it almost impossible to get my medicine given to me regularly, which is a nuisance and won't help as much as it could, but the nurses are so rushed they just don't seem to have time for even their routine jobs. Babies arriving all the time, and to crown it all, triplets this morning!

All being well, I should be going home next weekend for a period of convalescence, and Dr Brown is trying to fix something up for Jeremy (he thinks he can, for a while, until I'm strong enough to care for him). I shall hate having to part with him, and wish we could find someone to help at home.

I'm wondering whether I'll be allowed up today. Mummie came yesterday. She always brings me stacks of food to replenish my ever empty locker. I'm positively starving all day long, and yet do nothing but eat and eat. We only get one meal per week with any suspicion of meat in it, and it certainly isn't a very satisfying diet – I'm not vegetarian!

Well, my precious, take care not to get cold if possible. I know our cherubs both send lots of love, and all of mine,

Your Rita

16-2-44

My dearest darling,

I am now in the midst of my tests and X-rays, etc., and this morning had to wait until 11 o'clock before eating or drinking anything. I got so famished it's given me a splitting headache. Future operations will depend a lot upon the results of these, but we shan't know the results for some time. The pain is <u>almost</u> non-existent now; it's wonderful.

I shall be <u>very</u> glad to go home and get some sleep and decent food. I am feeling the strain rather, especially as I've moved into another patient's room, who snores all night long! However, her husband is fetching her home today and I'm feeling envious once again! It must be <u>most</u> satisfactory to go home in triumph with a new baby and a proud husband to look after you both, and to show the infant to your first-born together. I shall have to go home without even a new baby, as tomorrow he goes off to a nursing home at Stanmore that Dr Christie Brown has found and fixed up for us. Mummie and Sarah-Jane are coming for him, and by request are doing the journey by car all the way. JJ is so wee, and Dr Christie Brown agrees with me that it's best to be on the safe side and not take risks with him.

Cheeribye, my darling, take care.

Heaps and pots of love,

Your Rita

P.S. Jeremy sends his salutations in loud hiccoughs, and I in love.

My dearest darling,

I didn't write again from the hospital as I was feeling rather miserable about parting with Jeremy. Mummie and Sarah-Jane came for him on Thursday, and he looked adorable dressed up in his own clothes. Mummie seems awfully pleased, and proud of him, and in spite of Sarah-Jane's continual assertions that she couldn't possibly love another like Rosemary, as soon as she saw him, she rushed to him exclaiming, "<u>What</u> a little darling!" She nursed him nearly all the way to Stanmore! Mummie is very proud because when I was dressing him (on his tummy), he was raising his little head and arching his back and kicking away already, bless his heart! She tells everyone that he is a fine, strong boy!

It was an awful wrench parting with him and brought back parting with Rosemary all over again too. He's so wee and such a darling. They were very sweet to me at the hospital, and I felt ashamed for giving way, tho' it wasn't for long, in public anyway! I arrived home in time for lunch on Friday, someone else having taken my bed before I was even packed! It's grand to be away from hospital and all the routine; to have freedom and not be woken before 5:00 a.m.! and to have good food and home comforts once again.

Now for the results of the tests, darling. I'm afraid it's not very good news. In spite of all our hopes on account of my general improvement, the kidneys are in exactly the same state as they were before: right one not working at all, and the left has rather a lot of the infection in it still which can flare up again any time. They think that had there been any hope of its working again it would have started as soon as the child was born. The left kidney has grown twice its normal size and is doing all the work, which is a good thing, as if it had not done so I could not have lived.

After raising my hopes, all this news came as rather a depressing blow, and I feel as if instead of just an uphill road to climb with health and strength at the top, all is now blocked up again as far as I can see. I shall never be able to be careless regarding my general health, never be really strong, and there is always the possibility of my one kidney getting badly infected again. I must admit I dread any more physical suffering. I didn't mind for Jeremy, but now it's only for me. Never mind, perhaps <u>another</u> miracle will come to pass! Who knows? I feel as if my experiments as a wife and mother have been failures, and that perhaps after all I was never meant for either.

I love you <u>such</u> a lot, my precious,

Your Rita

21-2-44

My dearest dear,

Well, darling, I'm writing without delay, because last night we had a truly terrible raid here. It was the worst I think <u>I've</u> experienced as regards the number of near misses, and I nearly sent myself silly, worrying over Rosemary. Friday night was pretty terrible, but it was worse here last night. It was over by about 11:00 p.m., so I got Mummie to phone through to the home whilst the all clear was still sounding. She tried for about 20 minutes, including the operator, and just couldn't get any reply or sound at all. You can imagine how I felt, and what sort of night I had, waiting until early this morning to phone again. After trying 4 or 5 times again we at last got through, and thank God they were all right.

Apparently, Rosemary and a small boy there have become very attached to each other, and quite an '*affaire*' is in progress! They spend most of the time talking and playing together, and even after lights out at night they proceed to stand up in their cots and carry on their conversation, meanwhile getting freezing cold and keeping the other babies awake.

It is terrible to see the amount of damage, in Barnes alone, and according to all reports it is right up to Waterloo, and street after street in Earls Court and West Kensington. The fires were terrific, and it is certainly only by the grace of God that <u>we</u> are still alive. We all got under the dining room table (we must have looked funny!) and have now raised the couch so that in future <u>I</u> can go underneath that. I can't walk properly yet of course, so couldn't get down to the shelter.

By the way, Mr Heekes phoned last night to ask after me. He says there is some new treatment for kidneys that he is trying out on another patient and is awaiting results before he sees me! So, my hopes that I can start the old kidney working are raised again.

It's nice to be up and dressed, and grand to have a figure that comes out and goes in at the right places again! I'm quite pleased with it (at present!).

I love you all the world and more,

Your loving missus

23-2-44

My darlingest,

Well, darling, the raids are now coming fast and furiously. Poor little Barnes is in an awful mess, so I hear, although of course it isn't by any means the only place that is. The Civil Defence Service have not finished digging out the bodies from one night's work, and then there is more damage still from the next. It's obvious, I think, that as the climax of the war approaches, the raids will certainly get worse. Mummie is trying to find a place for us all to go to but there has been such a wholesale evacuation from Barnes alone that I don't think we'll stand much chance of finding somewhere.

The Sister at the hospital told me that after my 'do' Dr Christie Brown was still raving about my wonderful pelvis, and gave a lecture on my case, saying that I was that very rare thing: a <u>truly</u> feminine woman to have such a one! I thought perhaps that as you're such a very masculine creature, that makes that part of our relationship such a success – the attraction of the two extremes?!

I hear from Dr C. Brown that Jeremy is doing well and gaining weight, bless him. I <u>do</u> miss our cherubs badly, Mitty! If only I could have <u>you</u> near.

Heaps and heaps of love, my darling,

Your own Rita

216/63 Medium Regt RA
Scarborough
York
5-3-44

My dearest darling,

It was a grand day on Thursday when we were all together for the first time. Rosemary was at her best since she went to the home, although she looked rather miserable when we took her back. She is obviously very well and receiving excellent care and will not take long to settle down at home again. Jeremy looks to be getting on very well and will be getting bigger every day.

I got back on Friday night to find a snowstorm blowing and by morning there was about six inches of snow. The Colonel has put off his inspections for a week owing to the bad conditions.

Please give my love to your mother and heaps for yourself,

Your loving John

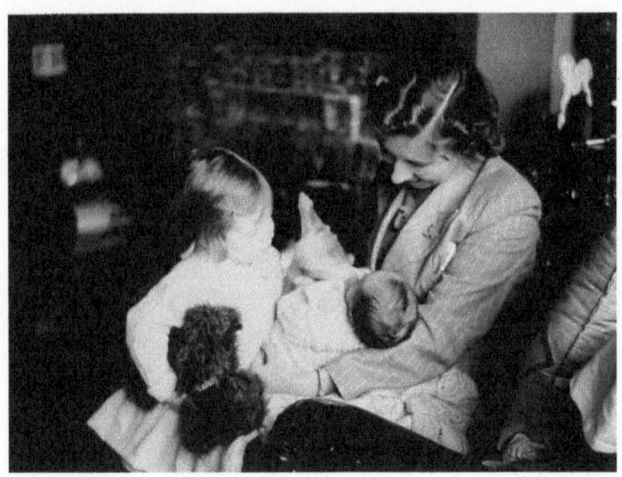

My dearest darling,

I have developed a new complex with this illness, of which I'm ashamed, but can't seem to do anything about: I get scared of the dark when I'm lying awake at night. Last night I was positively shivering with fear as every noise seems certain to be someone in the house, out for burglary or murder, or maybe for both! I expect it's only an attack of nerves but is much worse since I've been home. The obvious cure is to sleep with my husband! but as I unfortunately can't do that, I'll have to try a nerve tonic instead. However, today is very red letter, as this evening Mummie is going to help me have a proper bath – the first for over seven and a half months!

Jeremy has now had four homes and three changes of food in the first five weeks of his life. All these changes must be bad for him, poor little chap! I'd give anything to be able to keep him myself; I seem to miss him more than Rosemary sometimes. I do hope I'm not already developing the 'mother and son' complex so early! but think it's only because I had him 'with' me all during the weary days and got so used to the idea of him being there. Also, he's so wee and so very sweet!

I'm glad you're missing me (if you still are?). It's comforting to know when I'm missing you!

Your Rita

P.S. Am still dirty, as the water was too cold for a bath after all.

16-3-44

My darlingest one,

Dr Christie Brown has told me that I shouldn't be anything like well for at least a year, which is a big disappointment. I've certainly realised lately what slow progress I'm making but thought six months would make a lot of difference to me. He told Mummie that I am still a very ill person and must be very weak. I was glad in a way that he did, as she forgets it and needs a reminder now and again! She admits that she does and says it's because I keep so cheerful! Evidently it doesn't pay!

As it's all going to be such a long business I shan't wait until I'm feeling <u>really</u> strong enough to have the babies – what does a week or so matter in a <u>year</u> (isn't it depressing, Mitty dear?) I couldn't possibly wait even 3 months – and anyway I only fret about not having them. The only thing is that I wondered if I'd wait until the end of March to fetch Rosemary, on account of the bad air-raids we're getting again. You'd be coming home then, and I shouldn't get nearly so worried about her with you here. The raid on Tuesday night was pretty bad, and we went through all of the damage in the West End. The incendiaries were so numerous that every few yards in the roads, especially near Marble Arch, they were either still stuck in or there were black patches where they'd been dug out. Men were working in squads, with lorries packed full of the things.

My nerves are now reacting to the illness, and Dr Christie Brown says I must not try to fight against things, such as my fear at nights, but must keep the light on all night – (Mummie <u>will</u> be pleased!).

Heaps and heaps of love, my darling,

Your Rita

16-5-44

My darlingest one,

I am so very glad you saw Jeremy again, darling. You have relieved my mind; thank you so much. He sounds a perfectly handsome young man (takes after his father, evidently!). All he seems to need now is an upper and lower plate to give that flashing smile! You've made me want to see the little love more than ever, and I'm sure I shall kidnap him when I do. I'm afraid since Rosemary has returned home she has been very fretful and difficult due to having a double tooth coming through.

Rosemary's just said, "Night night, God bless dear Dadda," and blown you kisses.

Heaps and heaps of love, my precious,

From your Rita

15-6-44

My very dearest,

I'm thinking and wondering about you all the time, and how and <u>where</u> you are, etc.! I do hope everything goes well for you, darlingest. The news is excellent, and it's most encouraging that the position is good and safe enough for Mr Churchill to go over, isn't it? I shall be longing to hear how you are and what you're doing.

Your mother and Mrs Baker came to tea yesterday and were delighted with Rosemary and the change in her. Of course, she was showered with presents for which she showed due appreciation, and returned the compliment by pressing cherries on them, most persistently, that she and I had picked in the morning from the garden.

The day is notable in that Rosemary has ascended the stairs all by herself for the first time, in a perpendicular position. She's terribly proud, and we've clapped hands and shouted hip, hip, hooray to celebrate!

Have just spoken to you on the phone, darling. Rosemary is dancing with glee and calling out all that you said – very excited about it! She sends lots of love and is blowing kisses by the score and writing you a 'letter' which I'll enclose.

The news is still good, isn't it? I'm buying a *Daily Telegraph* invasion map to stick on the wall.

I love and love you till I could burst,

Your own missus

A.P.O. England
18-6-44

My dearest darling,

We have not gone yet but are expecting news at any moment.

It was grand seeing you again on Friday evening, if only for an hour. Actually, if it had been longer, we might have got morbid at having to part again. I very much wanted to see Rosemary again and she certainly was in great form and seemed to be thoroughly enjoying life. I hope she did not give you a bad night after being so excited. She is obviously pleased with her mama and also apparently with her Dadda. I am looking forward to the day when all four of us will be together as a family.

I got back in the jeep in good order and the driver was waiting for me as instructed. I put the basket of cherries between us, and we pretty well finished them off on route. He ate a good many more than I did and, as he seemed so fond of them, I gave him what remained. I still have the bag full and the preserves which I am keeping for the crossing.

I went to Didcot yesterday for some more stores and passed through Henley and Wargrave and all those riverside places. The country looked grand and made me long to get on the river again. Perhaps next summer we shall.

Do look after yourself, darling.
Heaps and heaps of love,
From your John

Barnes
SW13
18-6-44

My darlingest one,

As you haven't rung up today or yesterday I'm taking it for granted you've gone to help finish the war in the quickest possible time. I do hope the crossing wasn't too bad? I shall be longing to hear from you, but shan't expect anything until I receive it, as I know you won't have a chance for a bit. In the meantime, I'll write often, tho' I don't want to put too great a strain on the postal transport! (They've asked us on the wireless to use a single sheet for a while.)

It was such a lovely surprise to see you that it took off the 'goodbyes' quite a lot, thanks be! And I'm sure you could see how thrilled both of your best girls were! Wasn't Rosemary excited? What <u>will</u> she be like next time?! She told me yesterday she was so glad to see Dadda, "'Cause he's so sweet!" which I agree with entirely, plus lots more reasons! The big bangs have been incessant day and night, so now Rosemary's cot is by my bed, and we hold hands when the bangs come! We seem to be shooting down a terrific number, so shouldn't think they'll last long. I wish I could take Rosemary away to somewhere safe for a bit, tho' there's nowhere to go!

It being Mummie's birthday, we took Rosemary to church this morning. She was very pleased to go, but in the middle of prayers said loudly, "Haven't we finished <u>yet</u>, Mummie?" We came out soon after!

I love you and love you and don't stop thinking of you for a minute. Rosemary joins in pots of love,

Your own missus

20-6-44

My dearest darling,

I expect you really have gone by now. I should think the crossing was better if you went yesterday; today is simply beautiful, but with a very strong wind. I shall be very thankful to know you're safely there and do hope you're all right.

Rosemary is still very happy, tho' she misses her proper sleep, as I do, and we're both very tired. What on earth would it have been like if the original force had come over?! There is a lot of damage round here, but we're all right so far! Thank goodness Jeremy is in a safe place, tho' I do so miss him.

Rosemary sits in bed and uses the electric light and bell as a telephone to 'speak' to you, every day.

I send you heaps and heaps, and God bless

Your Rita

22-6-44

My dearest darling,

I do hope you're as comfortable as you possibly can be (which I suppose isn't very!). The Straits seem to have been choppy all this week, and I wonder if you've been bothered with the 'flying bomb' at all? They're still just as frequent over here, and I must admit I'm feeling frightfully tired, so tonight am going to bring Rosemary downstairs when the siren goes. I've cleared out the corner by the wireless in the dining room for her carrycot and shall put up the camp bed for myself. Then I shan't spend all night getting into a stew wondering if I should take her down! I get awfully anxious now you're not here. Luckily, she sleeps through most of it, tho' the tremendous blasts always disturb her. She grows more loving and demonstrative every day and is very sweet.

I've found the little pocket dictionary, darling, at last! It's very small and is English-French/French-English. If you'd like it, I'll send it at once.

XXX from Rosemary and Jeremy, and all my love and thoughts, my precious,

Your Rita

24-6-44

My dearest dear,

How are things going with you now? I can't help rushing to the letterbox every time the postman comes. Perhaps I'll be lucky soon. Anyway, darling, I do hope you're not having too hectic a time. The news continues to be most encouraging.

Today is perfect here, with a lovely cooling breeze. It seems so queer to wake up to such lovely mornings after spending almost the entire night lying waiting for a doodlebug to finish you off! I expect you're having much the same experience with other weapons. This last one seems to get worse as you hear more come over and explode just near you! I'd give a lot if I knew of somewhere safe I could take Rosemary and have Jeremy for a while. We've decided that I shall write to various people and ask if there is anywhere outside London we could stay.

Rosemary's still saucy tho' rather tired and sends heaps and heaps of love to Dadda.

I think of you all the time, my precious, and love you all the world, Your Rita

A.P.O. England
26-6-44

My dearest,

We are still playing the waiting game and doing all sorts of schemes for keeping all of the lads amused. I am very fit and leading an open air life in preparation for things to come. The news still seems pretty good but there is no doubt that the weather has been a second enemy to contend with. The fact that we are holding the enemy armour and making small attacks is very good.

I have been doing a bit of sewing to fill in time and have made myself a ration bag which is quite a good effort.

Heaps and heaps of love to you, my darling,
Ever your John

Barnes
SW13
26-6-44

My dearest darling,

How did the crossing go? Did you eat the crystallized fruit? On the wireless they said that one convoy had embarked on the Monday (19th), arrived at the French coast on the Wednesday and couldn't disembark until the following Saturday on account of the very rough seas. I think things are going wonderfully well, especially taking the weather into account, don't you, darling? I'm sure that given the well behaved elements for the big push, we'll be able to get Hitler and co.

really on the run <u>soon</u>.

I went to see the second news reel of the invasion pictures called *Beyond the Beaches* on Saturday. Of course I was very interested, and shall try to see them all, to follow your doings. What a terrible mess France will be in by the time it's all over! You have to actually see it before you can realise it. I do thank God that England wasn't invaded and had to go through all that terrific bombardment. Everything on the screen seemed debris, dust, smoke and flames.

Rosemary and I are still sleeping in the dining room as the doodlebugs are still pretty active. I'm glad you hadn't had any and hope you don't; they're not so funny! Everyone who's able and has somewhere to go to has left. I wish we could. There's been a bit of a dust-up over the shelter next door, so we can't even go down there now.

We've all just this second been under the dining room table, with a doodlebug stopping directly overhead! All OK still!

Rosemary and I send heaps and heaps of love and thoughts,

Especially your Rita

John's diary

Friday 30th June 1944

Sudden orders.

A bloody night. Sleep on road in Southampton.

05:30: Embark LST 126 – a beach landing craft capable of taking tanks, and get the battery of eight guns on board. Loading went off well, but everything must be lashed down. I am Quartering Officer. In charge of accommodation. American boat. Good chaps and food.

11:00: Steam down Solent and set off in convoy.

Sea pretty calm.

22:00: A very nice trip. Arrive off coast – Arromanches, near Ryes.

My very dearest,

I know that you'll be anxious to hear the results! Well, I can't tell you anything for certain yet, except that I saw the specialist before and after the theatre affair, and he was really very encouraging. Before I went up, he said that the last bad report didn't necessarily mean that my right kidney is completely dead, and that he'd do all he possibly could to avoid an operation. Afterwards he said he was very pleased with the whole thing, and was then going into consultation with Mr Heekes. Of course, this may mean just that the job had gone off well, but I'm hoping it means more! I was still doped from the anaesthetic but did manage to ask if the operation would be necessary, and he said he didn't <u>think</u> so. He's a charming man; quite young with a good sense of humour, and most considerate about pain – quite a change from Mr Heekes! The hospital is very nice too – quite the best yet – and apart from being on the top floor with doodlebugs roaring overhead and smashing down all the time, I wouldn't mind staying on! The hospital has been literally bouncing with nearby blasts all night; one of the worst on record, I should think.

I've been in great pain since it was done yesterday afternoon and whilst they doped me at regular intervals throughout the night, wasn't able to sleep at all. However, it's easing off considerably today. I was tremendously relieved when they told me I would certainly have an anaesthetic, you can guess! I have a nice, cheerful little room overlooking Putney.

Rosemary was <u>so</u> sweet. I told her I had a tummy ache and had to go to the doctor-man's house. She was most perturbed, and said, "<u>I'll</u> rub it for you, Mummy; <u>I</u> make you better. Don't you go 'way." I told her I had to, and she said, "That doctor-man won't hurt you,

Mummy, will he? I'll 'mack him if he hurts you," and she smacked and scolded away till she was quite hoarse!

I've been wondering what on earth I can do about her if these raids continue. They're certainly getting worse, and the Germans now promise mass raids. She's beginning to get very frightened, in spite of all I can do to prevent it, and I do think that if we can't get away ourselves, the only right thing is to send her to stay with Jeremy for a while. I shall miss her dreadfully, but she must come first.

We all three send you our heaps and heaps of love,

Especially your missus

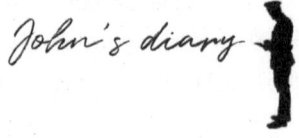

John's diary

Saturday 1ˢᵗ July 1944

Have breakfast and await tide.

12:00: Disembark. Drive off practically dry shod. Not a lot of damage on beach. De-waterproof in cornfield. Villagers on the whole seem very pleased. Some wave but not many. A few look glum. Arrive at Pierrepont to concentrate and re-equip. Meet up with Regiment.

B. W. E. F.
2-7-44

My dearest darling,

Well, as you see we have reached France once more, and the extraordinary address stands for the British Western European Force. We came over in an American boat. The officers thought we were a 'swell lot o' guys'. They did us very well, and as the sea behaved, I ate and slept most of the way. For breakfast we had tinned grapefruit which was a very nice change. I wish I could have saved some for you as I know it is one of your weaknesses.

I am very sorry you have been having such a rotten time with the doodlebugs. They are certainly very unpleasant. We have heard quite a number, but I have not seen one yet. The anti-aircraft guns and fighters are going for them from this side by bombing the projectors and shooting them down over the Channel. I think before very long that we shall have countered their chief trouble.

I went to church this morning in a tiny French village. It was not very damaged and there were a few villagers there. The priest was an army chaplin and seemed a good sort. It is surprising what a number of chaps now want to go to church that as far as I know have never gone before.

We are feeding well and there is no doubt that the whole party is well laid on. We keep getting more and more food thrust on us and all my lockers and boxes are full. My chief trouble is lack of space to carry everything.

Heaps and heaps of love,
From your John

Sunday 2ⁿᵈ July 1944

Attend man in small church at Cainet. Check over all equipment and get ready for action.

Move off to first gun position between Secqueville-en-Bessin and Bretteville-sur-Odon already dug for us. A few shells come over during night, but our artillery is terrific: 900 guns and 1000 anti-tank guns.

Monday 3ʳᵈ July 1944

Move with position at Secqueville-en-Bessin. Complete digging in. Very wet and unpleasant. Get ready for big programme tomorrow. We really have air supremacy, and it seems artillery as well.

Tuesday 4ᵗʰ July 1944

05:00: Programme starts on Carpiquet. We are a bit tense as it is our first. First man out to Operation Post gets lost. I am sent out to find him. Wireless breaks.

Canadians take Carpiquet with heavy fighting on aerodrome.

British Western European Force
4-7-44

My dearest darling,

I had no idea that the doodlebugs were causing so much trouble. They certainly make a terrific noise, and it must be a very anxious moment when the engine stops. I only wish you could get away, but I do think it most important to have your examination completed and then you will know what you can do.

We are not doing too badly here and are pushing plenty of metal across to Jerry. There is not very much coming back, and it is a great relief to have no opposition in the air. It is absolutely different from *last time when the boot was on the other foot. It will be great when the breakthrough comes, and we can start really moving.*

The country here is very like England and it keeps raining very heavily. We are pretty well coated in mud, and the trouble is that when it dries, it turns to dust, and I don't know which is worse.

I have got quite a good little funk hole in a hedge which Watson, my batman, has fitted up with my bed and bare necessities. He is proving quite a useful chap as he was in France before.

I am longing to see you again.

Heaps of love, my darling,

John

Barnes

SW13

4-7-44

My dearest darling,

Well, I've got some lovely, lovely news for you! We've had the report from the specialist and I haven't got to have the kidney removed after all (I'm so excited!). The left kidney is improving, and there are signs of the right one beginning to function. It will take a long time, very long, and I'll always have to take care, but I shall be all right – no semi-invalid business, and I shan't be making you a widower just when we should really be able to enjoy life and each other! It seems like a reprieve to me, and a nightmare lifted.

All our dreams are gradually coming true, my love. Now to be at 'Craiglea' altogether, and the last one will be realised. Perhaps all the trials and troubles we've had before we get there will make us appreciate our happiness so much more, and never let us take each other for granted!

Please God it won't be very long before you're home safely again, with no more partings to look forward to. We seem to be doing awfully well still, and I should think the big push isn't far off now. The Russian front shows just what advances <u>can</u> be made once the Germans start to run.

Rosemary 'telephones' you every morning to send her love.

Cheeribye my lovely. We think and talk about you all the time and send you our love,

Your own loving Missus

John's diary

Wednesday 5th July 1944

Dawn attack on configured aerodrome. Colonel tries to find me an Operation Post at Rauray. Go chasing about frontline hedges. Mined. Terrible stench – dead cattle and half buried Boche, and equipment all over the place. Carry crew first class and we are being fed well. No relief tonight.

Thursday 6th July 1944

07:00: Troubled by mortars. Headquarters in field west of Cheux. Fire 144 rounds by prediction. I don't think it has desired effect.

14:30: Position relieved. We have lost airfield at Carpiquet.

British Western European Force
6-7-44

My dearest darling,

We are now living and sleeping in a six-foot dugout. We are usually out of it during the day and pass the time eating and making tea. The crew are playing up very well and produce all sorts of meals on our little cooker. At the moment we have got pork and vegetables, followed by some steamed pudding, all cooking at once. All the food is in sealed tins and all we do is put them in boiling water. Then we make the water into tea. Water is scarce so we have to economise.

Today it is very hot, and the lads have produced some lemonade powder for a change. We also have tinned sausages and bacon. It sounds an awful waste of tin, but it makes it very easy to carry the food about. We brought quite a lot of extra stuff with us from England such as egg powder and soups which help to thicken up the meal. Our little charging plant for the batteries has to be going nearly all day and makes a bloody awful noise which is only occasionally drowned by gunfire. The wireless is our only means of communication.

At times everything is quiet and peaceful, and it is difficult to imagine that the war around us is real. We are rather reminded of things by the shocking stench which hangs around, chiefly from dead cattle, which no one has time to bury. They swell up to enormous sizes with their legs sticking straight out. Do they stink! The fields and farms are full of them and live ones roaming about without a home. There are quite a number of German tanks near us which have been knocked out. They are nearly all burnt and still have the charred remains of their occupants inside.

I had a bad attack of hay fever yesterday but after dosing myself with whisky last night am pretty well all right today. I have procured some tinted glasses which help a lot.

I have now finished lunch – date pudding. I shall have to have a sleep after that. Sorry to keep harping on about food. We cannot tell you what we are doing until the news is stale enough to be of no use to the enemy. I shall be able to tell you about our landing soon.

All my love to you, darling,
Your John

John's diary

Friday 7ᵗʰ July 1944
Day in. Clean up and maintenance. RAF bomb north of Caen.

251

Terrific show. One shot down. Anti-aircraft fire incessant.

Saturday 8th July 1944

Canadians attack Caen. We expect attack by Boche. Plan is to draw their armour into our area, cut off infantry which will be dealt with by forward troops and destroy armour in killing ground. We dig in 6ft and are not relieved.

Sunday 9th July 1944

A tense night. Relieved early and on return lunch with Regimental Headquarters, and Commanding Officer tells me orders have come from corps to knock down church in Fontenay-le-Pesnel, and I am to do it. Very difficult. Go forward at Cheux. Burnt German tank points up road. Try church. No good.

Barnes
SW13
9-7-44

My darlingest,

I expect you're in on the Caen attack. I listen to every scrap of news, and it's certainly very informative and interesting, tho' it must be hectic for <u>you</u>! Nearly the whole of London seems to have evacuated. We seem to be about the only people with nowhere safer than here.

Rosemary is very funny. She's got very disobedient lately, so we told her that if she didn't mend her ways she'd have to go away and be taught how to behave. She thought this over, and a little later came to me and announced, "Mummy, Rosemary's gone. I'm Margaret!" Ever since, she's insisted that she's Margaret, and the alias certainly seems to make her more obedient, so I'm not disputing it! She told your photo all about it, and also on the 'phone' to you this morning; quite ingenious of her, I thought!

I love you and love you all the world,

Your Rita

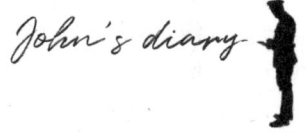

John's diary

Monday 10th July 1944

Establish forward Observation Post in front of Rauray. Right in front line. Very different atmosphere.

14:00: Take on shoot. One or two hits but range too great. Wireless interference stops shoot. Disappointed.

British Western European Force

10-7-44

My dearest darling,

I am delighted to hear the great news that the kidneys are making progress. I always felt that you would be all right, and knowing how virulent you are didn't think you would let it get the better of you. It is really grand news and makes me very happy. I suppose you will be home by now with Rosemary. I expect she missed you and wondered where you were going.

I don't know how the doodlebugs are in London, but I know they are pretty bad. We had quite a lot while I was in the marshalling area awaiting to embark and they do make a terrifying noise. Of course, we are all liable to catch a packet at any time, but I think the chance of not getting hit by a doodle are far more than getting hit by a bomb in the air raids. My advice therefore is naturally for you all to go away, but if you can't I think it would be better to keep Rosemary with you unless her nerves are becoming affected. I was very glad to hear that Jeremy is doing well and putting on so much weight. He must be a very jolly chap by now.

The weather out here continues to be unsettled with hot and wet days. We have done quite a lot since we arrived, have had a number of experiences and seen many sights. To give you some idea of the lighter side of the war, I have at my command put in place a wireless set which blasts out the BBC programmes all day. The other day I was forward, and we were expecting an attack. We dug furiously all day and by evening we were six-foot underground. Practically nothing was visible above ground and there was a definite tension in the air. The local HQ put out a loudspeaker and we heard the news and settled down to the strains of swing music. Quite a novel way to wage war, don't you think?

I am getting somewhat weather-beaten but feel very fit. I took the first real observed shoot the other day – the destruction of a church – but unfortunately it was only partially effective and, after making my report, I have heard nothing more. Everyone was very envious at the time, but I expect we shall all get plenty more opportunities. The battle seems to be going pretty well and spirits are high. It is much more exciting this time, and the lads, especially my own little crew, are right on top and will go and do anything I say. I may say I am not looking for trouble and am naturally cautious, especially when we have so much to learn, and I think they appreciate it.

Now, darling, I hope soon to hear that you have got my letters.

Heaps of love,

Ever your John

Tuesday 11ᵗʰ July 1944

A good day. Do shoot from forward infantry post. Get mortared but everyone too excited to worry. Germans in next field. Summoned to the CAGRA about church: it must be destroyed. Brigadier and I go to Operation Post and he asks me how I can do it. I tell him two mortar guns and 100 rounds, and he gives me the job. Have lunch with Brigadier. Eventually get the party off.

Splendid shoot – third round it blows up. Tower down in 40 rounds. Try to finish off walls. Premature firing on one of the guns. No-one hurt. Have to leave tower with one wall standing.

Barnes

SW13

11-7-44

My dearest darling Mr Snippet,

I do hope you're quite safe and well, and not having too dreadful a time. I <u>shall</u> be so pleased to hear from you, darling. I suspect that now the fighting line is on the move forward you won't have time for writing, so I won't expect much, but shall be glad to have even a field card. The whole war news seems very good, doesn't it? But I do wish the weather would get better.

At present I'm in bed waiting for Mr Heekes who has warned me there's still a long, long way to go. I must eat as much as I can, and rest too. Not so easily done, especially the latter! I can hardly keep my eyes open now, with continual sleepless nights, and I regret to say the responsibility of Rosemary is having a disastrous effect upon my nerves. I'll ask Mr Heekes for a tonic and sleeping tablets today.

Rosemary still says she's 'Margaret' and acts according to whether she's 'R' or 'M'. She's a hoot! We all send tons and tons of love and miss you horribly,

Your own missus

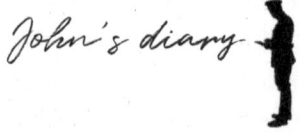

John's diary

Wednesday 12th July 1944

A quiet day and get rest at last. Commanding Officer pleased with shoot but has criticised gun drill. Inspection is made of gun with premature fire. There are lots of explanations but many are malfunctioning.

Barnes
SW13
12-7-44

My very dearest Mr Snippet,

Today is red letter day! I've received <u>two</u> letters from you and could really jump for the joy of it. You sound quite chirpy, darling, despite all of the trials and discomforts you have to put up with, and I guess you feel better still now you have 'broken through' beyond Caen. The whole of France seems to be gradually rising in revolt and I'm really almost beginning to agree with other people that the end isn't so far off after all. Everyone is getting very optimistic that it'll finish this year; some say by the autumn. I wonder! <u>and</u> hope.

Yesterday was a very bad day here in town and at Hinchley Wood too, apparently. I eventually got round Mummie (with Mr Heekes's support when he came) to let me buy a Morrison shelter (£7!) for Rosemary. This took some doing on account of it 'upsetting my home'! However, we've now got it up in the dining room, where the couch was, and Rosemary and I slept in it last night. I now feel Rosemary's safer, and that's what matters.

I'll write again very soon, my precious.

I love you all the world,

Your Rita

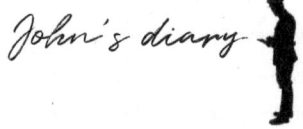

John's diary

Thursday 13th July 1944

Regiment moves from Secqueville to Le Mesnil-Patry taking 25 hits. I lead Battery in. Position mined and terribly dusty almost like a desert.

British Western European Force

13-7-44

My dearest darling,

I can now tell you a bit more about our trip across. We came over in a beach landing craft capable of taking tanks and were at sea for about a day and a half. There was an enormous concentration of shipping off the beaches, as far as the eye could see in both directions. Everything was quiet with no air opposition at all. Apparently, the Jerry planes will not venture over as the anti-aircraft gunfire is so terrific. We saw a sample of it during the night. Most of the beach obstruction had been cleared except for sunken craft and a few burnt out tanks and vehicles. The Americans told me there was a terrific battle on D-Day, but that this part of the beach had been taken by surprise. We collected everyone together, found all present and moved to a hideout to get ready for action.

On the whole, the people we passed seemed very pleased to see us. Most of them waved but some looked very sullen, as if they were just accepting the situation as it was. There are not many people about anywhere in these parts, very different from last time when the roads were flocked with them. The villages behind the lines are filling up with peasants returning to their farms. Where they have been to, we can't imagine. They are all very pleased to get back, even to their shattered homes, and we do all we can to help them.

We went into action the next day, fairly well back, and have supported practically every attack so far, as we can reach great distances with our guns. We had some shelling when we arrived but now it is pretty quiet, and the villagers are returning to the village where the vehicles are. We listen to the news in French each evening which is becoming quite an occasion for a general meeting of the population. My job observing the shooting is by far the best because I go all over the place in my carrier and get to see all sorts of people in different parts of the front.

I saw the bombing of Caen and a most impressive sight it was. There were practically no enemy fighters up, but the anti-aircraft fire was terrific, and the bits just fell around us like rain. It was certainly a clever move, especially as it was generally thought it would have to be taken by a flanking movement. I hope we see the RAF again, but the weather has been, and still is, against it.

The church I told you about last time is no more except for two walls. It became quite a bogey, and I was given charge of a small operation to remove it. All went off well and the Brigadier said it was a good show. My lads were highly delighted, and it has done them a lot of good. Unfortunately, we had a very nasty incident but by a miracle only one chap was very slightly injured. Plenty of Jerry trucks burnt out in the forward areas. The gunners have certainly got on top of them now. The difficulty is to get them out into the open.

Well, darling, that is all the news for now. I have lost my knife, fork and spoon set which all fit together. Can you get me another? Also, if you have any tea and tinned powder milk to spare, I would like some.

Rosemary sounds a funny little soul. I wonder what has made her decide on Margaret.

Heaps of love, darling,

Your John

Friday 14th July 1944

Do recce of new area near Caen. Pick area near Franqueville. German trenches and village flat. Go through Bretteville-l'Orgueilleuse which is coming back into life.

Saturday 15th July 1944

Take digging party to new position. Bad start. Terrible hold up and tank knocks wall down at Brouay which nearly falls on me on battle route. Go on to Carpiquet aerodrome.

Barnes
SW13
15-7-44

My dearest darling Mr Snippet,

I'm so very glad you're keeping fit and so cheerful, but I do wish the weather would behave itself! Today is St Swithin's, and it's raining! If you care to take Sarah-Jane's advice, we're all set for deluges for the next six weeks! It must slow things up for you, as well as being most uncomfortable but, considering all things, we seem to be doing awfully well.

How are your subsequent shoots going? I'm sorry you had to destroy a church, but I know you can't think of that sort of thing in battles for your lives and other people's as well. You'll certainly come back a wise man! Anyway, Mr Snippet, you just go on taking care of yourself as much as ever you can. I want my husband home as soon as possible, and quite whole! I'm sure your natural caution is at its height of usefulness!

Ever since I bought the damned old shelter we've had no London alerts during darkness! Anyway, it was worth it for my peace of mind over Rosemary. I got into such a state of mind that I couldn't relax at all and was straining to listen for them all the time to grab her and rush under the table. I daren't take sleeping tablets in case I didn't hear them, and was on the point of tears all day! I'm just beginning to relax a bit tho' still sleep very badly. We sleep upstairs, and the shelter is all ready with her carrycot in case we have to come down. The effect of knowing it's there is wonderful!

We certainly seem to be getting the better of the flying bombs (touch wood!). I wonder what the next weapon will be. There's the rocket gun, and everyone round here thinks we can expect gas attacks before very long. If we have anything worse than the doodlebugs I shouldn't hesitate to send Rosemary away. She's certainly been upset and if I'm not with her, cries when she hears a warning.

Rosemary is very amusing and cheers me up no end when I'm missing you and Jeremy badly. We talk to your photo a lot, and show you her empty supper plate, etc., etc.! She prays for you and "all the soldiers, 'cause they've got a bad leg." This apparently is sure to make them well! She says, "Jelemy's got a hurt too; he's got his throat in his mouth, and we've got to take it out for him. Poor Jelemy!"

Her latest ambition is to stand on her head, which she endeavours to do by placing a handkerchief carefully on the ground, putting her head on it and sticking one leg up in the air, shouting out for all to come and see. I usually assist her in turning somersaults and she's very pleased and proud!

I do hope the hay fever is keeping off, my love.

Heaps and heaps of love and thoughts,

From your own Rita

My dearest darling,

We are keeping up our incessant showing of metal on the Boche and no doubt will crack him in the end. Our chief trouble at the moment is dust. The vehicles and tanks kick up a continuous cloud which just drifts across the countryside. Apparently, the conditions now are very similar to those in the desert. We are just covered in it the whole time. I am rather afraid of the rain though, because that means an even more unpleasant condition: mud.

Had some more fun today and yesterday. I have certainly got the best job and so far have had most of the luck. I don't think the Colonel can say I am not producing the stuff in action. It is a very different story to the days in Yorkshire.

Heaps of love, darling,
Your John

John's diary

Sunday 16th July 1944

Stationed at Operation Post at Carpiquet for shooting. Great doings on front and smoke of battle obscures target. Big conference in evening on future battle. Firing all night. Another gun premature.

Monday 17th July 1944

Get ready with questions, etc. Report to Regimental Headquarters. Take over tank conference with Brigadier from 1st Coldstream.

Canadians are to clear a way into Caen and make way for guns to pass through to support advance.

22:00: Move off.

Tuesday 18th July 1944

Terrible move. Dust so thick it is impossible to see ground at times. Column loses its way.

03:00: Halt for rest and kip down.

06:00: Terrific air bombardment.

07:15: Clean up and move off. My big plans and targets all plotted.

Go into battle with wireless playing music from London. Wonder how Rita, Rosemary and Jeremy are.

Some shelling of Rat Route. Move to York Bridge Palm Route.

Cross the Orne by pontoon.

No communication.

We go on.

Catch up with the column at Hérouvillette.

Self-propelled gun in action.

Get behind.

Column held up.

More shelling.

Still no communication.

Wireless not good.

Major waves.

Calls me over to his tank.

I go over to him.

I am at his turret.

His wireless isn't working.

Dispatch rider around us is lost.

We tell him to go back.

A large explosion.

I am on my back on the ground.

Heavy shelling.

Right hand feels a bit dead.

Stretchered to Casualty Clearing Station.

Morphia.

Tetanus.

Splint.

Taken to No 88 General Hospital.

Very full.

Everyone working at top speed. Some are being shipped back to England.

Operation.

Panthenol.

Spend night in tent which gets fuller and fuller.

Barnes

SW13

18-7-44

My very dearest,

Today I've received your letter card and I hope that very soon after sending it to me you heard that I had at last received one of yours. Yes, it <u>was</u> a worrying time! I was aching to hear from you that you were all right, and I was going nearly crazy every night over Rosemary as we didn't have a shelter. I also heard that there'd been some flying bombs round Guildford and worried over Jeremy. I felt dreadfully depressed and could willingly have wept every time the postman passed me by! However, directly I heard from you, everything seemed to straighten itself out considerably and now I'm much more cheerful again.

I'm awfully pleased you're doing so well, darling, tho' of course not surprised as I know your capabilities so much better than the Colonel (in every way!) and I knew that once you went into action you'd come out on top. Still, I should think it's very gratifying for you, and quite exciting too. I do wish I could see you and hear all about it. Never mind, perhaps it won't be so very long before I do.

I thought the letter about the landing, etc. most interesting. They didn't lose much time before sending you into action, did they? I'm so glad you've got such a good crowd of men; it must make all the difference. The bombing of enemy positions sounds terrific. The BBC announced another similar big raid last night, which I expect you're in on, too. Monty broadcast again and said it should be over this year. Won't it be wonderful?

Mr Heekes phoned this morning, very chatty, and asked after you again. He is coming round to give me a complete overhaul and examination next week and will then tell me if there's anything further to be done. He's still harping on about no more babies and says he'll discuss it fully then.

As regards flying bombs, it was a very bad night here last night, and Rosemary and I spent the whole night in the Morrison. She loves it and strokes it and says it's good and kind to take care of us. She's a funny wee thing and is still Margaret on occasions.

Cheeribye, my lovey. I love having your cheerful, newsy letters. Take care of yourself for me because I love you so much,

Your Rita

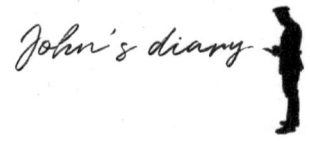

John's diary

Wednesday 19th July 1944

Carried down to sea in relays. Very good.

Move to embarkation – Duke of Rothesay, converted Isle of Man steamer ship.

Off stretcher at last.

Attempt on Hitler's life.

Thursday 20th July 1944

Arrive at Southampton.

Entrained to 2nd Canadian unit at an interim military hospital, Pinewood, Ascot.

Damned good. Splendid crowd with grand food and nurses.

My dearest darling Mr Snippet,

I haven't heard from you since I last wrote, so I hope everything's going on well for you. You've been awfully good, writing frequently, and I'm sure you know how much it's appreciated! It makes all the difference in the world to me.

The news continues to be very good, and the air strategy seems to be working wonders, especially in the bombing of the enemy's forward positions just before an attack. It must be hell to be a German now! Don't you think the latest attack on Hitler's life is a hopeful sign? At first, I thought it might be pure propaganda, but I don't think so, do you? We've just been told that there's some very good news on the wireless, so am going to listen to it at 1 o'clock (it was about the revolt in the German high command).

The train services are very, very bad owing to the flying bombs landing on the railway lines. The last few days and nights have been truly awful as regards the raids, and we're so tired we hardly know what we're doing. I should think these must be the promised mass raids; they're incessant, day and night, and there's no rest at all. They're doing a terrible amount of damage, and there are innumerable people without homes. You can't join any shopping queues without hearing of some fresh person. It's certainly not fit to have a child in, and poor little Rosemary is getting paler every day!

We had the four of us in our Morrison shelter the night before last, and you can guess it's quite impossible to sleep in such a squash! It's only 4 by 6'6". Sarah-Jane wouldn't come in last night and slept under the kitchen table, but I didn't get much sleep with Mummie snoring away, and no room to turn! Still, I wouldn't have her stay in bed.

Are there any Camembert cheeses left in Normandy now?!

Heaps and heaps of love, my precious,

Your Rita

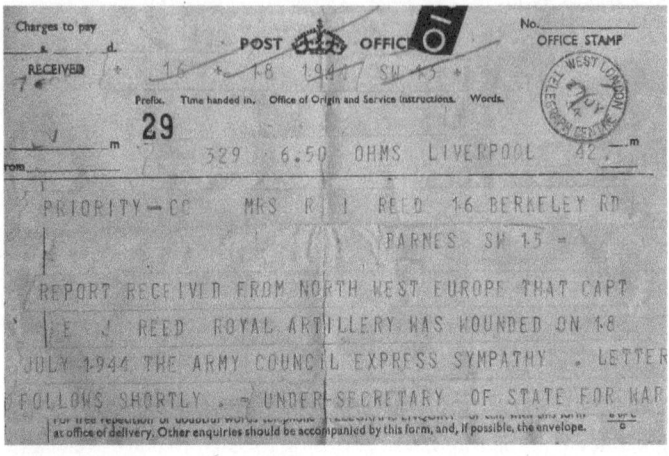

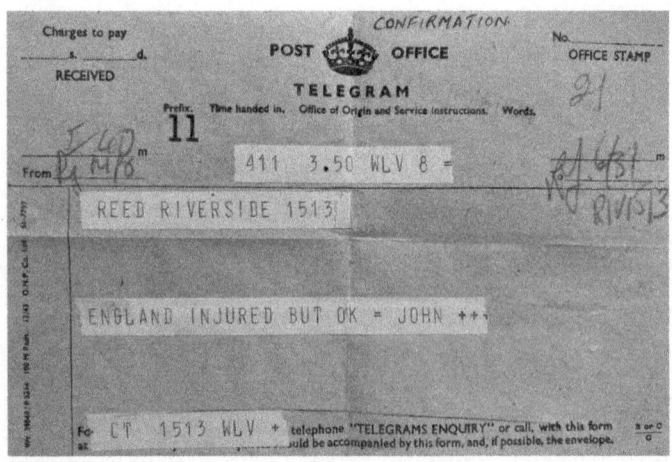

MY DEAREST,

I HOPE MY TELEGRAM THIS MORNING IS NOT WORRYING YOU. THIS IS AN EFFORT TO WRITE WITH MY LEFT HAND. MY RIGHT FOREARM IS BASHED AND I AM DECORATED WITH SHELL SPLINTERS. ONE NEAR E.J. BUT MISSED. I AM VERY LUCKY AS TWO BITS HAVE BLACKENED MY RIGHT EYE, BUT NO MORE. I CAUGHT IT ON TUESDAY IN THE NEW ATTACK EAST OF CAEN. REAL BAD LUCK. I HAD AN OPERATION IN THE FIELD AND ARRIVED HERE LAST NIGHT. THE PLACE IS RUN BY FRENCH CANADIANS AND THEY ARE FIRST CLASS. UNFORTUNATELY, IT IS ONLY AN INTERIM STATION AND WE ARE OFF AGAIN TONIGHT FOR AN UNKNOWN DESTINATION. I HOPE IT IS NOT TOO FAR AS I WANT YOU TO COME AND SEE ME. HOWEVER, LONDON IS OUT OF IT DUE TO BUZZ BOMBS. ONE CAME DOWN NEAR HERE THIS MORNING AND WOKE EVERYBODY UP. I WILL LET YOU KNOW AS SOON AS I AM SETTLED, WHERE I AM, AND WHAT CHANCES THERE ARE OF YOUR SEEING ME. I HAVE NO KIT BUT AM GETTING ON ALL RIGHT WITH HOSPITAL PYJAMAS AND WASHING GEAR.

I DO HOPE YOU ARE BETTER NOW, DARLING, AND FEELING STRONGER. HOW ARE YOUR MOTHER, ROSEMARY AND JEREMY? ALL WELL, I HOPE.

I THINK I AM BOUND TO GET SOME SICK LEAVE AFTER THIS, THOUGH I DON'T WANT TO MISS THE MARCH ON BERLIN.

HEAPS OF LOVE, DARLING,

YOUR JOHN

John's diary

FRIDAY 21ST JULY 1944

ANOTHER GRAND DAY. WISH WE COULD STAY HERE.

21:00: WE ARE ENTRAINED FOR LIVERPOOL. A RESTLESS NIGHT'S JOURNEY.

SATURDAY 22ND JULY 1944

09:00: ARRIVE WHISTON COUNTY HOSPITAL, LIVERPOOL. A DISMAL PLACE AND VERY SLOW. MR OSBORN LOOKS AT ME AND THE SISTER RIPS OFF BANDAGE. COLONEL REID ATTENDS MY EARS.

SUNDAY 23RD JULY 1944

SEVERAL CHAPS FROM ITALY IN WARD HAVE NOT SEEN DOCTOR FOR A WEEK.

MONDAY 24TH JULY 1944

FOOD IS SHOCKING AND THERE IS NO ATTENTION. A MAJOR COMPLAINS BUT NO RESULT.

Barnes

SW13

24-7-44

My dearest darling,

It was such a relief to hear your voice last night, and to know that things aren't too bad for you. I expect you can guess that the two days between your telegram and phone call seemed like two million. It sounds as if we have a great deal to be thankful for, darlingest, tho' I feel very grieved for you that it had to happen; you must be terribly fed up, especially after doing so well and working your 'crew' up to the top of their form. I guess they're hacked off, too. I feel almost as disappointed as you must, tho' of course I shall have peace of mind for the next six weeks and already feel that I can relax a bit. I do hope you don't have bad pain, darling, and you have a nice crowd of chaps with you to pass the time pleasantly.

I phoned up your people immediately to let them know, and they're sending you a letter and some money, so I expect you'll know all their news. They seem to think the whole affair is an excellent thing to have happened, so I'm glad they look at it like that as it will save them a lot of worry. Your father said he was sure you could wangle it to spin things out for longer than six weeks, and seemed rather annoyed when I said you wanted to get back as soon as you could. However, I'm very pleased you feel that way, and I wouldn't be nearly so proud of you if you didn't.

I do so wish you weren't so far away, and I could get over to see you. I do hope it won't be too long; I want to know so much!

Rosemary keeps kissing your photo and giving you sweeties, money and toys (all piled up in front of the photo!) to make your "hurt well".

We all send you tons and tons of our love, and all my thoughts, darling,

Your Rita

John's diary

TUESDAY 25TH JULY 1944

NO DOCTOR SEES US.

X-RAYS TAKEN THREE DAYS AGO HAVE NOT BEEN EXAMINED YET.

My darlingest,

I've just received your letter written at Ascot. I think the letter's a simply marvellous effort; I couldn't do anything like that with my left hand. You're quite ambidextrous! I do hope you're getting on well, darling, and not having any pain. I'm sure the complete rest will do you a lot of good, even if it does become boring. Anyway, darling, I'll do my best to come and stay near you for a while as soon as there's any place for me, but Liverpool is a long way, isn't it? I hear that it has extremely nice surroundings and seaside towns on either side.

Mr Heekes is coming today for a thorough examination and overhaul. Then he'll let me know my future course of action regarding treatment, etc. He's still harping on the sterilisation theme and says he'll discuss it fully with me today. I mentioned it to your father on the phone and he said he couldn't see any need for that sort of thing; all that was needed was willpower from both of us!! I think he must have forgotten! Anyway, personally I just haven't got any of that sort of willpower where you're concerned, and I'm sure it wouldn't be any use relying upon yours!?

Things look as if they'll come to a head pretty quickly now, don't they, darling? Perhaps you'll be well again just in time for that march on Berlin! I really think we have a tremendous lot to be thankful for, lovey; the more I hear of your 'do', the more I think so! It sounds as if the Germans nearly destroyed all need for willpower! And I do thank God your eye will be all right. I presume a shell fell near to you.

I love you and love you all the world,

Your Rita

My dearest,

I hope you're getting on well and the doctor is pleased with you. How do you like life in hospital?

Yesterday I was speaking to a lady who nurses voluntarily at a military hospital, and she told me that as soon as the patient was well on the way to recover, they're nearly always transferred nearer to their homes. Of course, they wouldn't send you to London, but even 100 miles nearer would be most welcome; somewhere where I could get to you easily, anyway. You know how I'd love to be able to look after you myself, darling, but not in London! Anyway, I expect the authorities will decide where you're to go!

Mr Heekes is very sorry to hear about you and sends you all the best. I asked him about coming up to see you as I hadn't been feeling quite so good lately, and he says I <u>must</u> go slowly. He certainly doesn't advise travelling for me just now; not up and back in the same week, etc., it would be too much for me. Re the baby problem, he says the only solutions are either sterilisation or using a form of contraception. He told me of one woman who had been sterilised of her own choice, in the end committing suicide! Doesn't sound too good to me!! Durex is far preferable!

I'm longing to hear something of you or, better still, <u>from</u> you, my darling. I do wish I could be with you.

All my love and thoughts,

Your Rita

John's diary

THURSDAY 27TH JULY 1944

WE HAVE POTATO SLUDGE TWICE A DAY AND ARE TOLD THAT THIS IS WHAT THE LOCALS HAVE TO PUT UP WITH.

My dearest dear,

I phoned up your father last night and he read me extracts from your letter about your wounds. I'm very glad you're going on so well, though I do most fervently hope you won't be well enough to go back until the present phase of the battle is over! I should be scatty by now if you were still in Normandy.

I've hardly left this house since I came back from Putney Hospital as much walking or standing just knocks me out. It's all a darned nuisance, especially with Rosemary to look after, bad travelling, and not being stronger. The conditions are all just about as difficult as they can be. I wish I could just get on a train and come straight to you.

Rosemary is looking forward to seeing you. Mummie has given her the long-clothes baby doll which closes its eyes and cries. She's simply delighted with it and says she's going to bring it to show you. We take it out in the pram every day, and everybody has to admire it. And the <u>times</u> we dress and undress it!! She's really most amusing, and I'm sure will cheer you up no end. She pulls the most expressive grimaces when she's telling you anything and says <u>such</u> funny things.

I'm longing to see you, my darlingest. Perhaps it'll only be a few days more now.

Heaps and heaps of love,

From your own missus

John's diary

SATURDAY 29TH JULY 1944
WE SEND OUR FOOD INTO THE SUPERINTENDENT.

My darlingest,

How are you today? It's a wretched day here, grey and drizzling, and the buzz bombs are taking advantage of it, so I really think you're in a better place! We had a <u>very</u> bad lunch hour yesterday, and quite a nasty night again. As Rosemary says (with great emphasis), "They're devils, Mummie, <u>devils</u>, <u>devils</u>!" There were four very near ones, one after the other, and I hear Earls Court Road caught a direct hit at lunchtime and the casualties were dreadful. I always get a bit frantic about Rosemary when I hear of them.

Yesterday, Rosemary decided that cleanliness is next to godliness, and when the sirens were sounding and I went to get her in from the garden, I found her by the kitchen door, holding Chicot's basin of water over her head! She was <u>soaked</u> and looked like a drowned rat; she said she was washing her hair (I'd just washed mine). I had to take her upstairs, strip all her wet clothes off, and 'rewash' it, during which process I had to rush her up and downstairs <u>four</u> times, hair all dripping wet, because the old buzz bombs were right overhead. She's up to all and every trick there is and is now writing a letter (which I'll enclose). She keeps on saying, "He <u>will</u> be pleased, won't he, Mummie?"

I love you and love you,

Your own missus

29-7-44

My dearest darling,

I hear that you're on extremely short rations at the hospital. I'm very sorry and can fully sympathise as it was the same thing at the City of London. If there's anything that I can get that you'd like, just let me know, darling. The news seems wonderfully promising, doesn't it?

Rosemary still insists that she's 'Margaret'. She tells everyone that's her name, and of course they all believe her if they don't know her real one! Still, 'Margaret' does things for me when 'Rosemary' won't, so I'm not quarrelling with it!

For some time past she's been gravely giving me a tiny portion of everything she has to eat or drink "to keep for Jelemy when he comes home". Now I've told her that before long you'll be coming home too, so I'm under strict orders to keep something of everything for you too. You should neither of you starve, at any rate! Every night when I go to bed now, I find a small person in 'Mummy's big bed', taking up every scrap of room. She climbs out of her cot and into my bed to go to sleep and informs me that I can sleep in her tiny bed when forcibly removed!

I do hope the use of all your fingers is almost back now, my love, and no pain. I shall be so pleased to hear from you again, but don't bother to write.

We all send heaps of love, and so very many people ask after you every day.

Heaps and heaps of love, my precious,

Your own Rita

31-7-44

My dearest darling,

Today I've been into the Red Cross to see if they can help me. They said they will contact the hospital and find out exactly how you are and how long you're likely to remain there. If you're doing well, I'm requested most earnestly not to come, firstly for the travelling, and secondly because you'll be moved to another area as soon as possible. They try to keep the safest areas for the worst cases, apparently. If they think it's necessary (and they'll do what they can) they'll find a billet for me, but don't hold out very much hope, especially with a child. They say all the safe areas are crammed to overflowing (they're telling me!) and the travelling is dreadful, too. So, there we are, my love! Never mind, perhaps you'll be moved soon to where I can come more easily.

Friends have phoned with the most awful tales of journeys. Eileen had to stand every bit of the way there and back to Melton; Millie had the same to and from York, and it was so packed she couldn't even blow her nose! Ken has the same story to and from Harrogate. Mrs Holden can't get home from Coventry, and Stella is still trying to get home from Newcastle after two days of going to the station and waiting! Everyone says you have to start queueing at 6:30 a.m. for the 10:15. a.m. train. They're all worried about me because they say I couldn't possibly stand the crowds and would be collapsing from exhaustion long before I started! I couldn't possibly take Rosemary in those crowds.

Well, darling, it does sound pretty grim, doesn't it? I think there's been the biggest wholesale evacuation from London and the south since the war began, and nearly everyone has gone north, tho' even travelling to Guildford you have to queue and then stand, I hear. So, it looks as if I'll have to wait to see you. If you _are_ discharged from hospital, I'd just love to be with you.

Rosemary picked some flowers (dandelions) for you this morning, with her love.

Tons of love,

Your Rita

3-8-44

My dearest,

I've just had the letter about you from the War Office, from

Liverpool funnily enough, but they don't know where you are, or the nature of your wounds! They say <u>you'll</u> let me know!

I received your letter, and was so very pleased to hear from you, but you don't sound too happy, darling. I do wish I could be with you and help to pass the time a bit more pleasantly! I knew (from my own experiences) how bored you'd get, and probably depressed at times, too. The only thing to help is to set your mind on to counting your blessings; at least, that's what I found.

I'm sorry to hear about the fuss over the food, 'tho perhaps it will be worth it in the end. If there's anything I've got you can have it, you know. Would you like some more cakes, and a jam or mince tart?

Last night we had a perfectly hellish time from the buzz bombs (that's the only word to describe it) and it continued all thro' the morning. A lot of damage has been done around here, and the doors and windows blew in several times. We hardly slept at all and are all very tired today. I can't sleep in the Morrison unfortunately because it sags in the middle so much, and since I've been ill I get the most severe backaches if I don't lie on something hard and straight. I then feel too ill with it all day that I'd rather risk it in my bed upstairs and get a bit of rest. Rosemary sometimes cries when the bangs go off, so I spend a goodly proportion of every night trotting to and from the dining room and my bedroom. We're still trying every means possible to get away.

Rosemary is very pleased with your letter; a remarkable achievement with your left hand, my love. She's carrying it around with her. I expect she'll 'write' to you again tomorrow, but I'm in a hurry to catch the post today. Did I tell you that she's been telling everyone about "my Dadda's got a hurt, bad eye like <u>that</u> – (pulling it down and making it look awful) – and bad arm like <u>that</u>," (nursing it up and slapping the place vigorously). She goes on to explain that, "The shoot, bang, fires did it, so Mummie and I are going to <u>kill</u> them," (with great gusto!).

Cheeribye for now, darling. I think of you all the time.

Heaps and heaps of love,

From your Rita

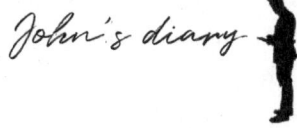 John's diary →

FRIDAY 4TH AUGUST 1944

GO TO SEE COLONEL REID ABOUT MY EARS.

Barnes

SW13

6-8-44

My dearest dear,

I was awfully pleased you rang up last night but do wish we could have more than six minutes; I've always got so much to say to you!

I guess you must be feeling awfully fed up, darling. I wish I could do something for you. I'm afraid your father thinks I'm very soft, and that I encourage you to be dissatisfied because I'm too sympathetic. He says you've got a pipe to smoke and a book to read, and what more can you want? I suppose my hospital experiences are too recent for me and I know only too well how dreadfully boring and monotonous it is.

We went to the Police station this morning to enquire about finding a place to stay in Sussex as we had heard that it is now a banned area. The Police say it <u>is</u> to 'ordinary' folks, but not to mothers with young children who wish to evacuate there and that it's perfectly safe. I'm going to the evacuation centre tomorrow to find out the best way to get Mummie down there too. She'll probably have to get a medical certificate from Mr Heekes; Sarah-Jane will come amongst the 'old' people, I should think. I shall also apply for free travel warrants and billeting allowances. It'll all help towards the cost of rent.

We've further particulars of a friend's bungalow at Elmer Sands, if we can get it! It certainly is a paradise for children and would be marvellous. There are rumours that the Huns are going to use 'something dreadful' on London any day now. I suspect it'll be gas.

All my love, darling,

Your Rita

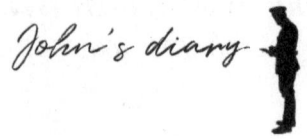

John's diary

TUESDAY 8TH AUGUST 1944

WOMAN COMES FROM THE MINISTRY OF HEALTH TO INSPECT, AND FINDS WE ARE NOT GETTING OUR SHARE OF RATIONS.

WEDNESDAY 9TH AUGUST 1944

COOKING IMPROVING.

Barnes
SW13
9-8-44

My darlingest,

It's another lovely day here, and how I wish you were in pleasanter surrounds so that you could get the full benefit of the sunshine.

Your father phoned last night to know if I'd heard from you, but I hadn't of course. He's now quite decided that the war will be over before you go back! He tickles me no end with the way he decides the events of the universe! And he goes on sublimely doing so after nearly every time being proved wrong. He just doesn't take any notice of <u>that</u>! I do think he's really funny. Six weeks ago, he said the flying bombs were finished, a failure, and we needn't worry about <u>them</u> anymore. Ah, well I suppose it's a nice way to go on if only you can believe yourself, but personally I have greater faith in the knowledge of Mr Churchill.

Rosemary sends lots of love and kisses, and I send all of mine,

Your own missus

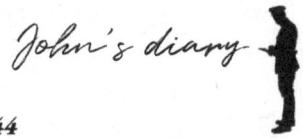

THURSDAY 10TH AUGUST 1944

*RATIONS ARE BETTER AND WE GET MEAT NOW,
ALSO SOME PUDDING.*

Barnes

SW13

10-8-44

My dearest darling,

You still don't say anything about your arm; please let me know how it is when you next write or phone. I <u>am</u> so sorry about the food, darling, and do wish I could do something for you. I should imagine that there would be a shortage of food in the whole district, with so many people evacuated there. We have just managed to buy a huge uncooked ham, and a bit of ox tongue; if I packed some in a tin and sent it by letter post you'd get it the next day. Would you like some, darling? Or I could get a tin of Spam or something similar and send it to you, tho' the other would be nicer. We also have some apples.

I've written to the Red Cross and explained everything and asked them if they will do all that's possible to get you transferred to the south coast as soon as you're convalescent, if not before. Maybe it isn't any good, but it's worth trying!

We all send you tons and tons of love and hope to see you before very long.

I love you all the world,

Your Rita

My darlingest,

I was so glad you phoned last night, I did love it. I'm sorry about the deafness; I didn't know about it before, darling. I can imagine how very irritating it is for you.

The lady next door to 'Craiglea' phoned last night just after you did, with some rather bad news. A flying bomb has fallen about 70 yards away from the house, causing a terrific amount of damage. She says over 50 houses are completely demolished, and very many more uninhabitable. 'Craiglea' had about a quarter of the roof blown off, every window smashed, the front and back doors completely blown out and others unhinged, and part of the ceiling in the back bedroom has fallen. She says other houses have sustained more damage and nearly all their ceilings have fallen in, so she reckons that we have come off pretty lightly. I suppose there are bound to be cracks in the walls which they haven't yet noticed. It happened at 6:00 a.m., and by 9:00 a.m. hordes of workmen had descended upon them. By the end of the day the tiles were back on the roof, all the doors firmly back, and black felt stuff covered all the windows. All the pretty leaded panes have gone, but they retrieved them from the road, and I expect they can be straightened out later on. The tenants were all asleep in the Morrison, and weren't hurt in any way, thank goodness, tho' it must have been a shock.

We had another flying bomb fall very close to us at 7:30 this morning, but only windows (we keep them nearly all open) and doors blown wide open again. I tore downstairs to Rosemary while the thing was making a terrific noise rushing through the air after the engine had stopped. I think the Morrison is very hot and low over her head and she begs me to take her up with me but I simply daren't.

Well, my lovey, we certainly are having our share of everything going in this beastly old war, aren't we? I'll send off the ham and tongue as soon as they're cooked.

Heaps and heaps of love, my darling. I do wish I could see you; maybe I shall!

Your own missus

13-8-44

My dearest darling,

Mummie has received your letter, so now we know a little more about your arm. I gather that all has not gone quite according to plan, as they talk of re-opening the wound.

I've now done everything possible for us to get away, and if nothing comes of it all I shall be satisfied that we're really not meant to! I phoned through to three places at Bognor this morning, but there's simply nothing at all to let anywhere down there.

I sleep terribly badly now, and when Mummie snores I can't sleep at all. The Red Cross said they'd do what they could to get you transferred to the south coast but they couldn't promise anything.

Heaps and heaps of love,

From your Rita

John's diary

SUNDAY 13ᵀᴴ AUGUST 1944

MORNING OPERATION TO SUTURE MY ARM. VERY LITTLE AFTEREFFECTS BUT HAVE MORPHIA TO GIVE ME SLEEP.

Barnes
SW13
13-8-44

My very dearest,

How are you now? I wonder if they've done anything to your arm yet; I do hope it won't give you any pain when they do.

I rang your father and he said the Germans are now saying that they're going to send a bigger and faster flying bomb, and also that they will soon use gas on London. We had a bad night again last night, and this morning at about 7:00 a.m. (as usual!) we had at least five big explosions with only about 2 seconds in between, so that might be something new. We seldom hear the noise before the explosion now; I think they're using more of the gliding type that don't give you any chance of getting into the shelter. Your father also said your mother isn't as good as she was, either. No one is, of course.

Cheeribye, my precious. I love you and love you,

Your Rita

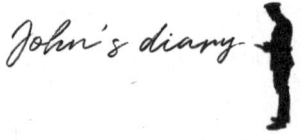

MONDAY 14TH AUGUST 1944

MY ARM HAS 14 STITCHES AND A RUBBER TUBE SEWN INTO IT, TAKING 10CC PENICILLIN A DAY.

Barnes
SW13
14-8-44

My dearest darling,

I wondered if I'd hear from you today, but now the last delivery has passed. I hope they haven't been hurting your arm, darling, and made you feel rotten. It's very hot today; really the last week has been perfect holiday weather. Too hot to work! I do wish they'd sent you by the sea.

We had a very nasty night last night, three or four very close indeed, and lots of windows broken round here, though not ours, thank goodness. I really thought our last had come once in particular, and dived under the bed on several occasions during the night as I couldn't get downstairs in time. They come at a terrific rate now. I hear Putney Hospital got it last night.

How I wish we could get away out of it. There's not the slightest hope of anywhere if the Red Cross falls through.

Heaps and heaps of love,

Your Rita

15-8-44

My dearest darling,

It's good news today of the second landing in France, so that will buck you up, and I sincerely hope shorten the war a good bit too. It seems to be going well, with resistance not too heavy yet. It must be pretty terrible making a landing in this heat.

I suppose we may now expect heavier flying bomb raids, or another 'secret weapon'. The Government Evacuation Scheme is nearly complete, I believe, so evidently they've been trying to get everybody away before this started. I've heard that Barnes may become a compulsory evacuation area. I don't know how true it is, but if I can't get up to Liverpool with Rosemary soon, I shall send her off to Guildford to be with Jeremy. I think they'll have her if they possibly can, and I just couldn't stand the worry of having her here and knowing that I'm not doing all I can to keep her safe. As long as the two cherubs (and you, of course!) are safe I don't care a hang.

Well, my lovey, let's hope we're nearly out of our wood!

Heaps and heaps of love, darling,

Your Rita

My darlingest,

I still haven't heard from the Red Cross, so I suppose they're having difficulty in finding us a place. This morning I went round to the shops as soon as they opened, borrowed a Dalton's Weekly and wrote off to two adverts for furnished places. I'm doing everything I can think of to get away.

Your father has changed his mind about the rocket guns not coming and has now decided that they'll send them filled with gas! I do think that it's quite possible myself, don't you?

Rosemary has written you a letter and I'll enclose it in this. She'll be very excited when she sees you, darling; we're always talking about you and Jeremy. I do long to see you both.

I love you and love you,

Your Rita

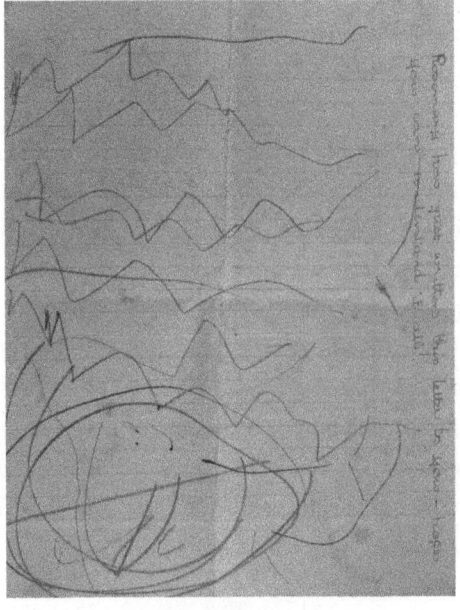

20-8-44

My dearest darling,

Thank you so much for your letter just received, and for the two telephone calls. I'm so sorry we were out the first time and hope it didn't hurt you having to get out of bed twice. It had been pouring here all day, and cleared up at teatime, so I took the opportunity of giving Rosemary some fresh air. I knew you were in bed and didn't think you'd phone. Sarah-Jane never can hear a word!

I went shopping this morning, and there was hardly a soul out; it was completely deserted. I never should have believed there'd be quite such a frantic rush to leave London.

We've had two alerts today with the doodlebugs almost skimming the roof and falling very near – about six or seven of them. The Morrison is a tremendous morale support to me! I think your father's idea (and its lots of other people's too) of doodlebugs carrying gas is quite feasible, as our air supremacy doesn't really count much against them; a great number get through every day and night. However, they know that they'll get it all back with interest if they start, and that might hold them up for a while. Did you see Hitler has placed a priority demand for 60 million gas masks as soon as possible?!

I'm very glad you think your arm really is going to start healing soon. Do you have pain when it's dressed now? What does the doctor say about it?

We all send you lots and lots of love,
Your Rita

County Hospital
Whiston
21-8-44

My dearest darling,
As you can see, I am writing with my right hand. The wound

285

is partly healed but there are some doubts as to whether it will hold together. I have had the tube removed today and I am to start exercising it. I can also get up for a while, so I am going on better. I shall be here another two weeks at least though.

I do hope you are having some rest from bombs. I shall be very glad to hear you have left London. I am just longing to see you. It is cold and wet up here now, and very depressing.

Heaps of love, my darling,

Your John

Barnes

SW13

24-8-44

My dearest,

Isn't the news of Paris and Rumania simply wonderful? It's so stupendous that at first I could hardly believe my ears! I should think the end could be this year now, wouldn't you? I listened in to the overseas BBC editor this morning, and he evidently thinks it'll not be much longer before Hungary either falls or is overrun by Russia and Rumania, and then they'll all join up with the Yugoslavs and Greeks and come on to meet us in France and Italy. It sounds very sweeping to me, but of course it's quite feasible, I suppose!

I took Rosemary to post your letter at 6:10 p.m. yesterday as it had practically stopped raining and there seemed no doodlebugs about just then. She loves to post Dadda's letter herself, and always kisses it most fervently first! We'd just stopped to speak to a friend who came to her gate to call to us, and a wretched doodlebug came buzzing, bang overhead again. The friends bundled us into their dining room and under the table, and the old thing came diving down on us (so it seemed!) and crashed quite near. Mummie was frightfully worried about us.

Take care of yourself, my darling.

Tons and tons of love,

Your Rita

28-8-44

My dearest darling,

I'm very glad your arm is making good progress. How is the deafness?

The news about Paris is splendid, isn't it? I really feel quite optimistic myself today!

If it's a nice day tomorrow and I feel well enough I think Mummie and I are going to see Jeremy. I so want to take Rosemary, but can't see how I can, with her afternoon nap to fit in. Mummie hasn't seen him for five months, and I'm sure won't recognise him now. I saw a perfectly darling baby boy yesterday, and it made me want mine more than ever.

Rosemary has been misbehaving herself badly, and is getting very naughty and disobedient, I'm sorry to say. She's obviously getting too much fuss!

Heaps and heaps of love,

Your Rita

29-8-44

My dearest,

We have found and taken a bungalow at Elmer for one month and shall stay on for longer if we like it and it's still bad here. I've been rushing around trying to get the evacuation papers all fixed up. Now I have to see the food office, get the tickets (free ones!) and see about sending the luggage off in advance. When we get down there, I have to see the Billeting Officer. Isn't it a to-do?!

Rosemary of course is very excited, and can't see any point in waiting another day! She's full of the seaside, and also of her Dadda in hospital, and is going to make sand pies to send you, so that you'll get well quickly and come down to make some more with her on the sands, and "paggle" in the water. It is such a relief to us all to be leaving London.

Having been a perfect little devil the last few days, and nearly driven me to drink, Rosemary has today become an absolute angel. She's very keen to see her Dadda and Jelemy again and talks of you both all day. I've been trying to teach her her ABC with the aid of printed bricks and a book, but it just doesn't sink in at all! When we've got as far as E and I ask her what it is she says, "A puffer-train!"

Tons and tons of love, my darling,

Your own missus.

County Hospital
Whiston
1-9-44

My dearest darling,

I was so glad to have your letter and to hear that you have got fixed up at Elmer. I have put in a request to be transferred to Bognor Regis Memorial Hospital as an outpatient. I shall be able to live out and attend daily for treatment. The arm is rather stiff, but it is being exercised. I had my eyes tested yesterday and they are apparently quite OK.

I have written to the Colonel to ask him to make it easy to put me back. I hear some awful stories about chaps being shoved all over the place when they get to the depot. I should like to be with them now that they are approaching the places we were in in 1940.

How are you now, darling? I hope you are feeling more rested. Let me know as soon as you can when you will be at Elmer, and I will get down as soon as I can. I am longing to see you again.

Give my love to your mother and Rosemary.

Heaps for yourself,

Your John

Barnes

SW13

1-9-44

My darlingest,

I do hope you have as good a birthday as possible tomorrow and are able to get out somewhere. We'll make up for it on your leave, darling.

I went to Guildford yesterday and saw Jeremy. He's the proud possessor of two teeth, nearly two months ahead of when Rosemary got hers, and apparently has beaten all the other babies in the home of about the same age. There seems much rivalry amongst the nurses! He's just on 27 inches long, 20 inches chest measurement, and 11 inches round the thigh! It looks as if the suits I'm making him are outgrown already!

Your parents are coming to tea with us tomorrow, and we shall be thinking of you all of the time and wishing you all sorts of the nicest birthday things! Sarah-Jane sends you her very best wishes, and Rosemary has written you a 'birthday letter' for me to enclose!

Heaps and heaps and heaps of love, my darling,

Your Rita

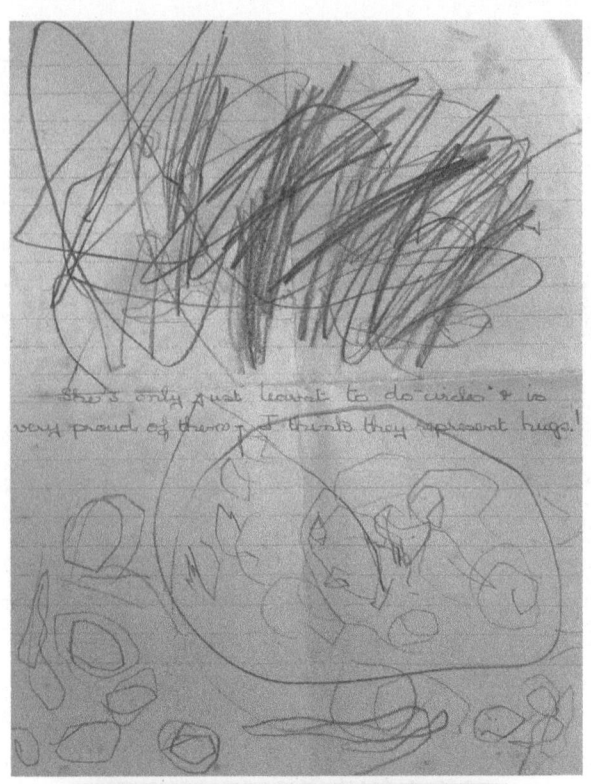

She's only just learnt to do 'circles' & is very proud of them, I think they represent hugs!

My dearest darling,

Thank you so much for your letter and card. Please thank Rosemary and Jeremy for their cards and handkerchiefs. You have quite a task on at birthday time now, don't you? When I kept opening fresh envelopes with cards and what not all from my own family, I tell you, I was quite staggered.

I was very glad you have seen Jeremy and to hear he is doing so well. He will be the apple of his father's eye.

Let me know as soon as you will be going down. I am doing exercises to get my arm working and manage a little more each day. I shall probably be quite fit by the time I see you and it looks as if I shall just get back in time to visit Berlin.

Ever your John

Barnes
SW13
5-9-44

My very dearest,

First of all – many happy returns of today to you, and may this anniversary be the last one we spend apart! As Mr. Armiston said in church on Sunday, "The cycle of the years is now complete", and we've got round to the same day again. We've certainly had enough happen to us in the last five years to satisfy even the most adventurous souls, I think! It hasn't been all good, I know, but we've been blessed most wonderfully and, in the end, have come out right on top of all our woes so far, and I'm sure we shall till we're all together for always. I feel very proud of our effort in the family line, don't you darling?!

– not bad going to have a daughter and son to show for five years "work"! Still, most of all I'm proud of my husband!

I've now got to do the final packing and we'll be ready! The car is coming at 10.30. It's almost as much rush and bustle as five years ago!

By the way, I've just received another (at last!) £10 Emergency Grant for my illness, which will be a help.

Tons and tons of love, my precious,

Your Rita.

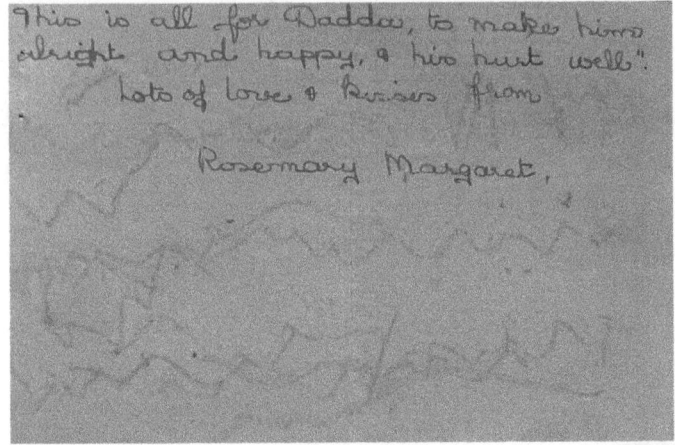

This is all for Dadda, to make him alright and happy, & his hurt well". Lots of love & kisses from

Rosemary Margaret.

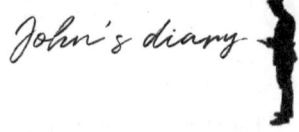

John's diary

Wednesday 6th September 1944

Medical Board Cat D for one month, then review boil on forearm and abscess on wound. Sent to see Mr Osborn who says will nip it.

The Brown Hut,
Elmer Sands
8-9-44

My dearest darling,

I nearly jumped for joy at the prospect of a whole month with you here, but at the same time, darling, I realise what a disappointment it must be for you. Maybe the war will still be on in October, and you might get back just in time for the grand finale. Perhaps then you won't come down a pip after all, tho' if you do it's damned unfair, but there's nothing to be done about it. If Hitler's war is over, I should think you've a chance of being demobbed, so it won't matter anyway then. Whatever happens you've the satisfaction of having done jolly well, darling, and I'm very proud of you.

We arrived down here in state (by car) on Wednesday, in time for lunch, and have ever since been chasing food! We had to go into Chichester yesterday (in torrents of rain) to get our ration books changed before we could buy any eatables. I've never felt so hungry in my life as when I saw the food and couldn't buy! This morning we've been to the village re-registering and buying up everything we could.

We are pleased with the bungalow, which is very comfortable, especially considering what it is. 'The Brown Hut' is an understatement as regards size, but it is made of wood. We have all our meals on the veranda which is filled with glass, faces the sea, and a positive suntrap.

The beach is open, and Rosemary spends all her time there and is very thrilled. I'm just longing for you to be here, darling, and do hope you can come down soon. Rosemary and I have decided we'll be at the station to meet you, and she says she'll wave and run and call out, "Dadda, here I am," and then kiss you hard! I think it'll be a race between us!

Tons and tons of love, my dearest,
Your Rita

John's diary

Thursday 7th September 1944

Operation on arm to clear out poison.

Wait all day and then demand Panthenol.

Friday 8th September 1944

Taking it easy, dressing rather painful.

The Brown Hut,
Elmer Sands
10-9-44

My dearest darling,

I received your letter last night and am so very sorry to hear about your arm, darling. It sounds to me as if they hadn't got all the shrapnel out, and I hope they have now. It is rotten for you, hanging on all this while. Are you having much pain with it? I do hope not. Hospitals have a way of disregarding all signs and symptoms until the worst has happened. I found it the same, and used to get very annoyed with them as so much trouble could be saved if only they took notice. However, they only think you're making a fuss if you point things out, so it's of no use trying.

I walked into the village last night to see if I could find out about the nearest Military Hospital, but there's no Police station here, and I could only find a van-driver from Bognor who said he didn't know about the military hospital here. Anyway, I'll go into Bognor tomorrow morning and call at the hospital, and also see the Red Cross and Citizens Advice Bureau, to see if they can help.

I'm simply longing for you to come down, darling. Yesterday, was the most glorious day here, and I just lay on the beach and roasted. The sea was marvellous, and the water seems quite warm. We're more settled in now, and it really is very comfortable, and not nearly so far from the village as we thought. I do so wish you and Jeremy were here.

We're all on the sands and Rosemary is very busy digging; she does love it, bless her.

Heaps and heaps of love,

Your Rita

John's diary

Monday 11th September 1944

About time we heard some news of going home. I am now fit to travel.

The Brown Hut
Elmer Sands
14-9-44

My very dearest,

I do hope you are all right and no complications have set in after the last operation on your arm. I feel very worried as I haven't heard from you since last week and do hope it's only because you're waiting to give me some definite news, darling.

All these operations are bound to make you feel weak. I think the complete freedom after hospital life will help as much as anything; it did me! If only you could get down here and just rest in the sunshine all day, I'm sure you'd feel better very soon.

It certainly is quiet here; just an ideal place for children. The weather seems to get better every day. Rosemary simply adores the sea and sands and is very busy digging. She's been bathing in the nude this morning, (just what I'd like too!) She does love it, bless her.

I think she can't make out why Dadda doesn't come, when I've promised he will so often. To distract her we go blackberrying and searching for mushrooms in the fields; it's lovely Sussex countryside round here.

I'm afraid my letters take ages to reach you, don't they, darling? I hope you didn't think I'd forgotten you! I'm just longing to see you and feel I really <u>can't</u> wait much longer!

All my love,
Your Rita

John's diary

Monday 18th September 1944
At last, I hear I can go.

Tuesday 19ᵗʰ September 1944

*Ambulance late and breaks down. Catch 9:40 from Lime Street.
Go to Acton.*

The Brown Hut
Elmer Sands
19-9-44

My dearest dear,

Still no news of your arrival, and at times I feel like giving up all hope of it ever coming off! I do wish I could do something, darling, and should think the exasperation the authorities cause is guaranteed to put you back instead of helping you. I wish I could get at them with a hammer!

There's no news here, yet the days seem to fly by. We miss the extra hour's sunshine in the evening, and now have to have supper indoors.

Mummie and I went for our after-supper stroll on the sands last night and were held up by a very important Home Guard who told us we were breaking the law by going on the beach between sunrise and sunset!

We've been hearing terrific gun fire explosions out to sea the last few days.

Well, my love, do write and let me know how you are and if there's any more hope yet.

I love you all the world,

Your Rita

John's diary

Wednesday 20ᵗʰ September 1944

Arrive Bognor.

Thursday 21st September 1944

Report to War Memorial Hospital Bognor.

Saturday 23rd September 1944

Visit a small department and start treatment. They all seem very competent and nice.

Sunday 24th September 1944

Have rest. I find I get pretty tired.

Tuesday 26th September 1944

Rita and I go to fetch Jeremy.

Wednesday 27th September 1944

Trouble because Jeremy cried in the night. He has snuffles but is very fit otherwise.

Friday 29th September 1944

Treatment certainly doing a lot to my arm, and I can now touch the shoulder.

Wednesday 4th October 1944

I now have electric galvanism with arm in saltwater bath. The wrist is still weak and painful. Thumb has no power.

Friday 6th October 1944

Still grand weather. People's last visit to us. Go digging with Rosemary.

Sunday 8ᵗʰ October 1944

Rita feeling rotten.

Monday 9ᵗʰ October 1944

Rita has Doctor Ferrier – bad sickness. May affect kidney.

Tuesday 10ᵗʰ October 1944

Rita worse. Doctor says she ought to be in hospital.

Wednesday 11ᵗʰ October 1944

Doctor arrives and prescribes for Rita.

Thursday 12ᵗʰ October 1944

Mrs Porter and I doing well but Jeremy is too much with Rita ill.

Friday 13ᵗʰ October 1944

Take Jeremy back to Guildford in guard's van. A wet day. Rita very sad.

Tuesday 17ᵗʰ October 1944

Letter from Registrar Whilan to report as instructed. Leave for London in afternoon.

The Brown Hut,
Elmer Sands
17-10-44

My very dear,

We watched and waved to you until you were right out of sight round the bend, and all the afternoon I've been with you (in spirit!). I do so hope you get home early after a quick train journey and have a good supper after a dry and warm-through. I shall pray for a fine day tomorrow for you to get to Whiston, darling.

Well, my love, I shall be longing to have a letter from you, and to hear some news. I do so hope something really good will come out of all this for you; you certainly deserve it, darling, and perhaps the fates or providence will see to it that you get it this time! I shall pray for it.

Rosemary (apropos of Mummie) has just exclaimed in feeling tones, "Mummie, I feel knocked over!" She keeps asking when Dadda is coming in, so I've tried to explain to her where you've gone.

I wanted to thank you so very, very much for all your love and for being so sweet, my darlingest, and best of all for being your own dear self whom I love more and more every day,

Your own Rita

Whiston
19-10-44

My dear Rosemary,

Very many happy returns of your third birthday. I know you will

have a lovely day and I am very sorry I shall not be with you to take you on the sands to make pies. Anyway, I shall be thinking of you and I hope you will go for a ride on your bicycle. I shall be away for a little while but expect to come down and see you again quite soon.

I went to Barnes yesterday and your toys are all well. I saw 'Diana' and she was looking very sad, so I have sent her to you to help you make puddings and pies. She had very few clothes on, so you will have to wrap her up warm. I believe Grandma is sending you some dolls clothes which might do.

I am sorry I could not find you a pretty postcard, but I will draw a few pussy catties to take to bed.

Your loving
Dadda

The Brown Hut
Elmer Sands
21-10-44

My dearest darling,

We've both (Mummie and I) had to go back to bed again, and although we've got up today are feeling really lousy. I've got a bad pain which gets worse the longer I sit up, but I can't leave Rosemary to Sarah-Jane and Mummie, with the latter not well and the former nearly going scatty!

Yesterday Mummie was in bed all day, and I just staggered into the dining room for every meal with Rosemary. I spent the rest of the time in bed. It was a terrible day here – a great gale and torrents of rain lashing down – so we couldn't have done much for Rosemary's birthday anyway. However, Rosemary was very happy all day, and pleased with all her presents. All her 'family' of toys have a snooze in the cot in turn, which is completely successful apart from the fact that it occasionally falls to bits! I'll stick it when we get home. Her birthday cards are a great joy to her, as is a big ABC book, spinning top and skipping rope.

Well, darling, I shall be longing to hear you're coming down again <u>soon</u>.

I love you and love you,

Your Rita

23-10-44

My dearest dear,

I'm pleased to say we are both feeling quite a bit better, and Mummie has today decided that she hasn't got a growth after all (she was certain she had last Friday!). The doctor has just been again, and I am to have a further course of M&B tablets for another fortnight and must take great care, etc., etc. The backache is distinctly uncomfortable, but I'm certainly better.

Today, for Rosemary's birthday treat we took her into Bognor with us, much to her excitement and delight. She shouted out at everything she saw from the top of the bus, to everyone else's amusement, and was thrilled. We had a very good meal at a hotel and she did more than justice to it, and played about with other visitors, whom seemed very friendly. We left directly after lunch and brought her back for her sleep, but the excursion made her very overtired and fretful this evening.

Cheeribye for now, my precious.

Heaps and heaps of love,

Your Rita

26-10-44

My dearest darling,

On Monday night we heard several (or so it sounded) flying bombs going over and one explosion which we heard later was a flying bomb brought down between Wittering and Littlehampton. We still don't know what to do about returning. The papers are giving warnings that Hitler will most likely use gas soon. What do you think? We'd be much better off down here if he does!

Rosemary has been behaving very badly the last few days, in the mornings especially, and we have had to put up with yells and screams, kicks and hits from her to start the day off! I'm sure it's because she's getting spoilt with too much fuss made of her. We found the 'tweeny pussy-catty' on the back of the stamp on her birthday letter and she was very pleased!

I do hope I see you soon, my love. I feel dreadfully lonely and cold at nights!

Heaps and heaps of love,

Your Rita

My dearest dear,

I was so very sorry to hear from your letter that you've got a beastly carbuncle. I know only too well how painful they are. I wish you could get away from that awful place; it seems to make you worse instead of better. I'm afraid it'll take some time to clear up. What absolute idiots the authorities must be; I <u>am</u> sorry you rushed back as quickly as you did, they don't deserve it!

I do hope the papers arrive soon. Perhaps you'll be able to come down here for a bit again, and we'll do our best to get, and keep, well this time!

Rosemary is writing you a letter, full of how sorry she is about your shoulder and how she hopes you'll come back to us soon, and lots of 'drawings'. I've taken her out on her tricycle once or twice, pulling her along with the skipping rope, which she enjoys. I hear that Jeremy is doing well, bless him.

Cheerio, my darling. I wish I could do something to cheer you up.

All my love,
Your Rita

Shrublands Park
Claydon
Ipswich
25-11-44

My dearest darling,

I have arrived once more in this dismal spot and am missing you terribly, especially nights, which get colder and colder. The chaps here seem a very decent crowd but the thought of doing gun drill and practice camp makes me shudder.

I have seen the Commanding Officer who has no instructions for us. There are no vacancies in the Regiment, so we are just hangers-on ready to be drafted anywhere and mucked about. He recommended me to write to the Colonel, though I don't hold out much hope. Drafts have been sent off from here for the Far East and I don't want to get embroiled in one of those. I am afraid what will happen is that I shall just sit down and rot until the end of the war.

I shall keep my eyes open and watch out for any jobs going as it is a very risky thing having no appointment. There are crowds of officers in the same boat all over the country and I suppose we are not wanted unless there are some pretty heavy casualties. By the way, dear, I am back to Lieut.

The first night here I developed into a bit of a drunk in the mess. I suppose they wanted to see how much I could take. Anyway, I came to no harm and my bowels now work better than ever. I should be able to get home to see you next month and of course I will make Christmas if possible.

Now, darling, how are you? It has been lovely being with you for so long though not long enough. Now you must take great care and not get ill again. Rosemary is doing very well, and it was grand to see her and get to know her.

Heaps of love, darling,
Ever your John

Barnes
SW13
28-11-44

My very dear,

First of all, I <u>should</u> like to make a comment on the demoting, but on second thoughts I'd better not as it wouldn't be readable! The mildest description of the system is disgraceful. Everyone I speak to thinks so too. However, darling, we'd better just think of it as quite impersonal and happening to everyone, not just you.

I do hope and pray you get settled into something good shortly. The idea of the Far East fills me with horror; it would be dreadful if that happened. What about air observation if the 63rd falls through, darling? It might be worth trying. I can't say that I want you to go back to the front, dearest, but I do want you to be happy in your job for as long as it lasts. I do wish the old war would end, for so many reasons!

I still can't sleep at night and am missing you just as much, darling. It's awful. Rosemary keeps saying, "I do want my Dadda, Mama," so pathetically! We're looking forward to that leave and Christmas!

Tons and tons, precious,

Your Rita

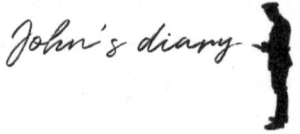

John's diary

30th November 1944

Take draft to 145 Regiment East. Return to London for the night. Rita looking much better. Rosemary in good form and has been to a party.

Barnes
SW13
5-12-44

My dearest darling,

I was so pleased to have your letter last night. Yes, it was simply lovely to have you home again, and I'm longing for the next time. I do hope you'll be home for Christmas, darling, weekends before or after won't be anything like as good, so do try and try, won't you? Wangle it somehow!

I don't know what to say about France, my love, but I do want you to be happy, so I'll leave it in the laps of the gods and trust for the best! Your Father rang up last night and amongst other things informed me you were quite all right where you are, and it'll only be your own fault if you get sent abroad. He just <u>can't</u> understand your point of view, and when I tried to explain it, he almost told me I was urging you on in your madness and <u>he</u> doesn't want you to be killed! Perhaps he seriously thinks that we do!! – it is <u>most</u> irritating trying to talk to that sort of person, I don't know how you keep your temper!

Tons and tons of love, my precious. Do come home soon –
Your Rita
XXX from Rosemary, who <u>does</u> want to see her Dadda!

7-12-44

My dearest dear,

I don't know what to think about the civil affairs job, darling. When I first read your letter my insides did a somersault and landed upside-down at the idea of your going away from us again at the end of 3 months. I must admit I dread it very much, and sometimes feel that I just couldn't put up with another parting and having to carry on my life here without your moral support and being able to see you sometimes. I don't know if you can understand how I feel, darling, but at times I think I shall go to pieces if I have much more of it. Don't you think there <u>is</u> a possibility of a post in England? There must be, (in fact I know there are) administrative jobs here, too, <u>if</u> only you could get one!

I know the experiences would help you a great deal in your 'job', but I think they'd be just as good in England without all the "sordidness" you'd find in Europe. Also, I can't think that you'd stand the same chance of demobilization darling! I presume that it would only lead to posts in occupied Europe, and I can't see that being a very happy or healthy place to live in for the next few years. Of course, I do know that it's easy to <u>talk</u> about a good job in England, but isn't there <u>anything</u> you could apply for here?

307

Do hope it's not too cold this weekend, darling.

I love you and love you,

Your Rita

My very dearest,

I shall be so glad to know you're back again from the Scheme. It's been bitterly cold and rather miserable all over the weekend, and I've thought of you all the time. I do hope it hasn't made your arm ache?

I'm longing to see you again, and also talk over the civil affairs job with you. Thinking it over I've come to the conclusion that it wouldn't be bad as long as you can get your demobilization as quickly as you would in anything else, but I can hardly believe that you would, darling! As regards the possibilities it might open up, I must admit that they seem to be things to avoid rather than to look for, darling! I do want us all to be together just as soon as we can, and for always, but I can't see that happening if you stay out there. I certainly don't think it would be a happy place to live in, especially to bring children up in, and as I feel our duty is to them now that we've produced them I should have to stay here with them. That to me, would be far worse than if you never made any money at all, but we were together. This is all surmise, but I rather gathered from your letter that this is what it would, or might, lead to? Everyone else that I speak to thinks much along the same lines. Mr. Holden says he "wouldn't touch the job with a pitchfork"! – (he's pretty wise and far-seeing). Anyway darling, perhaps I'll see you soon, before you decide?

I'm looking forward to hearing from you, my love; I love you and love you all the world,

Your Rita

1945

Barnes
SW13
3-1-45

My dearest darling,

Your father and mother still think Rosemary is a super child, but also that I've got a handful with her! She tries to wangle dreadfully there, and plays up to Grandma very much, as she always gives into her. (Grandpa isn't quite so easy and sees through her a little more!)

On Tuesday I went over to see Jeremy. Had a nice long chat with the sister who was very sympathetic and helpful. I gave JJ his dinner myself – meat and two veg with gravy, then chocolate pudding! Quite grown up now. He sat in his highchair to have it, and misbehaved violently when he saw the chocolate pudding, lunging forward and sticking both fists right in it and then wiping them over his face in an effort to get it all in his mouth at once! (Evidently follows the family tradition where chocolate is concerned!) He got tired of waiting for the pudding so had a little nap on my lap until it came. He's very well.

Rosemary had been very good and wanted to hear <u>all</u> about 'Jelemy' when I returned. Today, your mother and I took her up to Harrods to see the Zoo there and have lunch. She was very good but got terribly tired.

Heaps and heaps of love, my darling, and Rosemary, Jeremy and your parents send theirs,

From your Rita

142/168 Medium Regt. R.A.
Ipswich
4-1-45

My dearest darling,

I have found quite a nice place for you and Rosemary at

Coddenham, Ipswich. It is an old house and has a garden next to the church. Coddenham is only a small village but is picturesque and you will be able to have a quiet time. The owner, Miss Martin seems a very nice elderly lady. She leaves the running of the house to a housekeeper and her husband a Mr and Mrs Hill. Mrs Hill is apparently temperamental but seemed quite reasonable to me. There is a fair-sized bedroom with two single beds for us. I suggest we sleep in one of them to keep warm. Rosemary can have a camp bed in our room or a proper bed in a room of her own. There is a drawing room downstairs which we can have. Miss Martin has a hot mid-day meal and only a cold supper which should suit us. I have not been into the question of terms but I am going over to tea on Sunday and will broach the subject.

Coddenham is about one and a half miles from the camp over a track and about 6 miles from Ipswich. It is rather cold up here so bring plenty of warm clothes.

I have written to our tenants about our need to move back into 'Craiglea' and am awaiting their response.

Well darling, it will be lovely to have you with me again and I hope you will be comfortable.

Heaps of love,
Your John

7-1-45

My dearest

I am going over this afternoon to see Miss Martin and make the final arrangements for your arrival tomorrow. The one thing I have not been able to get is a pram. We could probably do without one which would make it much easier for you travelling or else have it sent on.

As you will hear from my letter to Father and Mother I am now Adjutant and have been given a troop here. I start tomorrow so will be rather busy and unable to come and meet you at Ipswich. However I will send in my batman Barker with or without a car. He is a short *stocky little fellow and should do all that is necessary.*

I was very glad to hear Jeremy is O.K.

Heaps of love darling to you and Rosemary. Longing to see you tomorrow.

Your John

John's diary

Monday 8th January 1945

142/168 Medium Regt. R.A. Start as Adjutant with my own troop.

 *Rita's diary*

Friday 5th April 1945

Brought Jeremy home today. It is so wonderful to finally have the children together.

My very dearest,

Thank you so much for your very welcome letter just received. I am sorry you had such a rotten journey back, and am glad you had a meal and caught the 7:30.p.m. train otherwise you'd probably have still been in the train at midnight. I hated your leaving us, too, and have been missing you terribly badly ever since.

I've been having a most hectic time here. When I arrived I had to unpack the cot things and put the cot itself together, for Jeremy; - then pull out the camp bed and find bed-clothes, etc, for Rosemary. After that there was the undressing, washing and suppers for both to get, so that when your Father 'phoned at 8.30 I hadn't even started mine! He offered to have Rosemary for Saturday and Sunday, but it's really far less trouble to keep her here. She really is wonderfully helpful with Jeremy and I can safely leave him with her to play together in the mornings. I've been tearing around ever since, and hardly stop for anything.

I saw the doctor, and he asked me about my M&B tablets and said I'd have to have some more, and take the whole lot this time, if I didn't want to be really ill. However, I just can't be sick again with so much to do, so I'll have to wait a bit. Jeremy had a terribly bad first night here, but is recovering marvellously now, and is already very much better.

Cheeribye, my love. The cherubs send heaps of love, and I send all of mine,

Your Rita

Coddenham,
Ipswich
7-4-45

My dearest darling,

I was very glad to have your letter and to know that you are getting on fairly well. I don't like the sound of you having to have another course of M&B's and do hope you don't feel too ill. You must rest all you can. I am glad Rosemary is helping you with Jeremy. Tell her I am very pleased with her and that she is a good girl.

We shall be pretty busy this week packing up ready for a very early start next Friday. We stage Friday night in Doncaster and get to Newcastle the next day. It is very cold up here just now and today is the first sunny day since I have been back. I am feeling very fed up which I bet would not be the case if you were here. Anyway darling I hope it won't be long now before we are together again.

Heaps of love to you and all,
Your John

Barnes
SW13
14-4-45

My dearest darling,

Thank you so much for your letter and 'phone call. I'm sorry I sounded rather aloof, (I suppose I did?!) – Mummie was in the bedroom with me, and that always clamps me down. Also I was worried about the children, and was (and still am) in bed with the most frightful sore throat I've had since Scarlet Fever. Mr Heekes says I have to paint it about every 30 mins. I've hardly been able to breathe or swallow, but think the worst is nearly over and shall try to get up tomorrow morning, because of the children. Rosemary's cold and cough are quite nasty, but "nothing to worry about", and Jeremy's sickness was pure piggyness, caused only through over-eating!

What is Gosforth like? It was so <u>lovely</u> to see you again

I love you and love you –

Your Rita.

P.S. Please excuse scrawl, this is the last of the paper!

18-4-45

My darlingest one,

I am so sorry you're in such a rotten place. Do you think you'll be staying in England now? I don't think VE Day will be for some weeks yet. Last week, your father said it would be all over in a few days, but I expect he's changed his mind once again!

I'm afraid we've all been too ill since I last wrote to do anything at all but get through each day as best we can. I had to have the doctor again because Rosemary had a temp of 100.6, was very unwell and exceedingly fretful, and I felt very grim myself. The doctor said we'd both got a bronchial germ and it could turn to pneumonia if we're not careful.

I'm afraid I can't do anything at all in getting ready to move into 'Craiglea'; I don't know how I get through the days, especially with the children being so troublesome and fretful. (Jeremy's teething!!)

We all send you heaps and heaps of love,

Especially your Rita

P.S. Isn't Mr Roosevelt's death a blow?

24-4-45

My dearest darling,

All last week it was simply frightful: Rosemary proceeded to get worse so I used one of Mr Heekes's old prescriptions, and I <u>think</u>

she's gradually improving. She did nothing but cry, cry, cry, day and night, till we were nearly all balmy. I had to get up (and still do) four or five times every night to her, and am quite exhausted with lack of sleep.

Jeremy has had a chesty cough, which is better again, but I can't move his catarrh. Mummie has been driven nearly mad with Rosemary's grizzling and Jeremy's 'joie de vivre' and has definitely got worse. Sarah-Jane is better. As for myself, I feel about the same.

Our tenants rang me up last Friday to tell me they have bought a house. As far as they know, they should be out by the middle of June. I am highly delighted with the news, and as soon as circumstances here (and my own health) permits, I shall go over and try to fix up with the decorators to do the repairs so that it is ready for us to move into.

I'm sorry you're so very fed up and do hope something definite happens for you soon – either Berlin or demobbing. I'm sure you know which I'd rather!

We all send you heaps of love,

Your Rita

Gosforth
26-4-45

My dearest darling,

You sound to be having a troubled time and I am most sorry for you. It must be very trying to have to get up so often during the night and I pray that you won't make yourself ill.

We are off to Redesdale on Sunday to sleep out, and fire on Monday. We have been miles today on a drill order and tomorrow I go out again.

The Colonel came to dinner last night and waffled. He is going to try and find out what the policy is for our Regiment. What a hope!

*We are just a lot of forgotten boys off the map. There is one decent pub
down the road and now officers are not supposed to go as it embarrasses
the men.*

Heaps of love to you all,
Your John

Barnes
SW13
29-4-45

My dearest darling,

I expect you are on your way to Redesdale now. I'm sure you
must be finding it bitterly cold, and I do hope you're able to keep
as many clothes on as you can possibly manage; it will be dreadfully
cold if you're sleeping out tonight. I shall be interested to hear what
the policy for the Regiment is, if you ever hear! Personally, I wish
they'd hurry up and demob you. Your family needs your help a great
deal more than the army does!

We are a trifle better here, I think, and Rosemary is beginning to
show faint signs of life at last and doesn't cry quite so much during
the day, but still gets me up two or three times every night. The last
2 or 3 weeks I've been having quite a spot of bother with her about
Jeremy. She seemed to suddenly get very jealous of him: refused to eat
unless I fed her as I do him, and generally behaved like a young baby.
She also snatched all the toys away from him and tormented the poor
little devil by walking round and round the playpen, shaking the
toys at him but keeping them just out of his reach. As soon as I gave
him another so she'd throw away the first and grizzle if she couldn't
have his again. Much patience has been needed when I haven't been
feeling patient at all!

Jeremy simply adores her; lets her do anything to him without
a murmur and obviously thinks she's the cat's whiskers, although I

regret to add that he's a complete 'mummy's boy' and is only really happy when he's got me all to himself, which isn't often! He is the most active child I've ever seen and is never still and never quiet; his vocabulary is coming on, and the rest is 'nonsense'.

I've found an interior decorator. He's apparently an old man, so I don't know how good he would be. Anyway, I shall write to him, and get him to meet me at 'Craiglea' to see what he can do and to give me an estimate.

We all send our heaps of love,
Your Rita

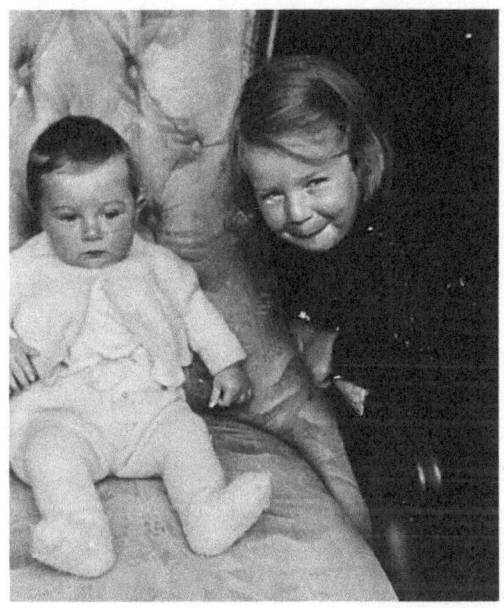

Gosford
1-5-45

My dearest darling,
We got back from Redesdale yesterday after a very cold weekend. Soon after we arrived on the ranges there was a snowstorm which

went on all night and was very thick the next morning. Fortunately I managed to get into a hut at about midnight so was not so bad. It is still very cold up here with snow showers.

The news is really great, and I think the stringing up of Mussolini terrific. I don't think VE Day can be very far distant but what celebrations the army may be allowed, have not yet been announced. The whole day's celebration seems to be completely controlled, according to the news tonight. The best thing they can do is to give us all 72 hours' leave, but we shall see.

Heaps of love to yourself and the two nips,
Your John

Barnes
SW13
5-5-45

My dearest darling,

I wish they <u>would</u> give you 72 hours for VE day, but I don't suppose they will! In any case, I understand that transport will be practically at a standstill. I'd just love to go up to Town and see some of the sights (providing I feel better than at present) – but don't think it's worth risking without a male escort, so shall probably sit tamely at home and listen-in! What an anti-climax! Never mind, let's hope there's a good time coming.

How and when we're ever going to move into 'Craiglea' is completely beyond my line of vision at present! I just don't have a moment, with the two children. I havn't been able to fix anything up with decorators yet. I've been feeling terrible and still am! – am hoping that it's only the M&B's but don't think they should cause the pain that I've had. Sarah has again completely lost her voice, and Mummie is bad today, so we're all in the soup again! The two children are so far the best. Jeremy continues full of beans and Rosemary is continuing to improve gradually. I think it probably has been Whooping Cough, as the hard dry cough is now disappearing at last, tho' she got me up again last night.

Cheeribye for now, darling. We all send heaps of love to you, especially

Your Rita

Gosforth
6-5-45

My dearest darling,

I am afraid you are right about VE Day leave. We are to have two days off duty, but no one is allowed to travel, so I am afraid that is not much good to me. I am longing to see you again, darling, and will try and make a trip after Whitsun.

The war in Europe is really going full throttle and I don't think will last much more than another week. It must be a very thrilling time out there just now.

I quite agree, dear, get the decorations done as soon as the tenants move out. As for demobbing, the whole thing is very uncertain, but it looks as if I shall come out some time during the winter which is not so good. But whenever it is, I am going to take plenty of time off and we are going to have a damned good holiday. Just be thinking about where and what you would like to do.

Heaps of love, my darling,
Your John

Barnes
SW13
7-5-45

My dearest darling,

I'm glad my letter arrived on Saturday; the posts must be speeding up as I have had yours today.

I didn't really expect anything different for your celebrations of VE day.

It won't make the slightest different to me – I can't even have two days off! I'd love to have gone to a party with you – or something like that – but as things are I'm far too tired and dispirited to enjoy myself, so perhaps it's just as well!

I'm quite sure that no-one who hasn't experienced it for a period of time could possibly imagine how tiring two babies are, and how much work they make. Jeremy is not pot-trained at all and is so bouncy that I have to wash out nearly all his clothes nearly every day! Then there's the drying and ironing.

We all send you tons and tons of love darling,

Your Rita.

P.S. The children were delighted with their letters and will 'write' later.

Gosforth
8-5-45

My dearest darling,

The great day has arrived, and I keep thinking of you and hope you are enjoying yourself as much as possible. I tried to phone last evening when we got the great news but, as expected, it was impossible, so I sent a telegram which I hope you have received.

Today has been rather like Christmas Day. We let the chaps have a lie-in this morning until 9:30. Then a short service in the grandstand followed by the best lunch the cooks could provide. The officers and sergeants served them with all the beer they wanted.

A few drinks with the Colonel at Regimental Headquarters, some more with the sergeants in our mess and we eventually got lunch at

14:30. We listened to Churchill and the various recordings on the wireless and I have just had a good bath. We are to go over to the sergeants' mess this evening and after that we hope to get into town. We go back to normal tomorrow, but I expect you have heard that we get 48 hours leave and I am putting in for those days.

I do hope, darling, you are all well. We must start our peacetime life in the best of health.

Heaps and heaps of love to yourself and the children.

I love you very much,

Your John

Barnes

SW13

14-5-45

My dearest darling,

Jeremy's quite a different child now; he seems to have come to life with a vengeance. I'm very proud! I've noticed that it's much harder work carrying him lately(!) so took him in to be weighed on Saturday. A good average gain at his age is 1 lb in a month, but he's put on nearly 3 lbs in five weeks. He looks in the pink and, with the sunshine, his cough has gone, as has Rosemary's. I love having him. I wouldn't part with him for anything. I'm sure you'll be pleased when you see him.

Rosemary still looks pale but mostly sleeps through the nights now. The two are very sweet together and look a dear and charming little couple when we go for walks. Jeremy never looks clean and tidy for more than the first two minutes and when people peer into the pram to see him, they are confronted with his rear part only, waggling about in some violent gymnastic feat, after which he comes up scarlet and puffing and blowing, with everything disarranged.

We took the two VE days off (as far as we could!) and it certainly did us all good. We took Rosemary to church the first morning, but it was the most dull and dismal service I'd ever been to, and the poor little thing was very disappointed. Afterwards, Mummie unearthed a large Union Jack flag and tied it to a long broom handle, which she then triumphantly hung out of the front window.

In the afternoon, I took the children out for a walk to see all the bunting, etc., and in the evening, Mummie and I took a stroll round to see the sights. Well, they were so well worth seeing that I ran home, got Rosemary up and dressed her, and took her, clutching her toy rabbit 'Dear Dear', round with us to the biggest bonfire, where all the children were playing games. The houses were all lit up, with their wirelesses in the open windows, playing the same musical programme, and decorated with flags and fairy lights in V-shapes. It really was pretty, and I thought Rosemary might remember it for always. She was thrilled with the streetlamps, and thought they were stars dropped from the sky. She was an angel and went straight off to sleep again when we returned.

Well, darling, I shall hope to see you soon and do love you an awful lot,

Your own Rita

Gosforth
22-5-45

My dearest darling,

Thank you so much for your letter. I don't know what you have to done to Jeremy, but it sounds as if you have raised a giant, and I shall have to see him before passing an opinion.

I am looking forward to coming home soon for good and being with you and the children for the rest of our lives. That is what we must strive for now. I can hear you saying, "All phoney." We must have a date to aim for to move into 'Craiglea'. I am sure once we're together we

will be able to please ourselves and life will turn much brighter.

News this end is not much. We had a visit today from the General who just peered round. VE night we all got quite pixilated in the mess after having found all the pubs downtown run out of beer.

Heaps of love to yourself, and R and J,
Your John

29-5-45

My dearest darling,

What a grand weekend's leave. Our first together in peacetime. I hope you got back home all right yesterday and found the children OK. I got back in quite good time, but the train was very crowded; people were standing all the way up. I got a tram and arrived in the mess before 11:00 p.m. where there was a great cry of welcome, and of course I had to make up for lost time. They had all been down to the local during the evening and succeeded in driving a tram back, a thing I have always wanted to do.

Anyway, the party warmed up very well and after I had given The Lion and Albert (and a few others you don't know) we let off some Verey lights and thunder flares, eventually succeeding in setting some of the furniture on fire which was duly attended to with promptness and vigour. We broke up at 2:30 this morning and are not feeling too good today.

I forgot to bring a ration card with me so am sending one, as I know even a little helps.

Heaps and heaps of love, my darling, to you and the children,
Your John

Barnes
SW13
30-5-45

My darlingest Mr Snippet,

I'm very glad you had some of the party, which sounds pretty hectic! I expect you'll have quite a few of those coming to you when you're demobbed, under the heading of 'reunions'!!

Yesterday I took both the children to have their hair cut. Jeremy looks very grown up now, and more like his daddy than ever with it all shaped to his head. I took Rosemary to dancing today and stayed in the room to watch. She really is very funny!

Stokes, the painter I've found, is an awful old chatterbox, and says he can't do any decorating in the way of painting, so it looks as if we'll have to busy ourselves with getting 'Craiglea'. ready for us all.

He agrees that all the ceilings ought to be done, and says he thinks the whole house could do with a paint up. I shall have to get a license for it to be done, but he thinks I shall get it all right.

The leaded windows will take about three months to get and put in, and it'll be some weeks before he can even begin the ceilings. So, it looks as if we'll be about ready to move in by September, if we're lucky!

It was simply grand to see you and I missed you dreadfully on Monday night. I must admit I shall be very, <u>very</u> glad when we can live a normal married life. I do find 'nothing and then all' exhausting, as I'm sure you do too! Never mind, not much longer now and then we can settle down to a much more satisfactory and less exhausting life! Oh boy, won't it be grand!?

XXX from R and J, and all my love,

Your Rita

Medals awarded to Captain Edward John Reed

1939-1945 Star
1939-1945 France and Germany Star
1939-1945 War Medal
1939-1945 Defence Medal
Territorial Efficiency Medal
Chevalier de l'Ordre de Léopold II avec palme
Croix de Guerre 1940 avec palme

P/113175

2nd. January,1946.

Sir,

    Now that the time has come for your release from active military duty, I am commanded by the Army Council to express to you their thanks for the valuable services which you have rendered in the service of your country at a time of grave national emergency.

    At the end of the emergency you will relinquish your commission, and at that time a notification will appear in the London Gazette (Supplement), granting you also the honorary rank of Captain. Meanwhile, you have permission to use that rank with effect from the date of your release.

        I am, Sir,

           Your obedient Servant,

Captain E.J.Reed,
  Royal Artillery.

Epilogue

Dear Reader,

I had no idea of the precious and wonderful paper trail that my dear mum had left to me until I began piecing together this unique story. I have felt humbled and honoured by the extraordinary opportunity I have been afforded to tell John and Rita's story and have done so to value and ensure that narratives such as these are not forgotten.

As I read about my grandparent's love, joy, hope, and fear, exhaustion, stoicism and challenges, I experienced a kaleidoscope of emotions. I laughed, cried, and empathised with them both, and recognised that whilst I could try to imagine what they each lived through, to truly understand was an impossibility.

These are the experiences of real people; civilian and military; set amongst world-shaking events. Forging their way through unpredictable times, and at points living with a constant pressure that each tiny everyday decision might have a life-or-death consequence.

Having pieced together John's story I am infinitely proud of the part he played alongside those of his comrades. John always showed humility and immeasurable respect towards all those involved. Whether they were lost or left behind on the sands or in the waves, among the fields and hedgerows, amid villages or towns, or lucky enough to return to their homeland. Now I have a greater understanding of his experiences I hope that bringing this story to life acknowledges the part he and so many others played.

John did not like to share details of his service in the 63rd (Midland)

Medium Regiment RA (TA) with the British Expeditionary Force (B.E.F.). It is only from his letters and my research that I have discovered that as a result of the Germans breaking through the French Lines in May 1940, his corps was forced to fall back, and due to reduced ammunition supplies they were unable to disrupt the German advance into Belgium. It was soon after this that the Belgians surrendered and the B.E.F. was compelled to retreat to Dunkirk. It is said that the Medium Regiments are worthy of recognition for holding the German attack, firing almost continuously until their ammunition supplies were depleted, whilst enabling the B.E.F. to enter the perimeter of Dunkirk, and evacuate.

John entered a second theatre of war during the summer of 1944 when, as part of the 8th AGRA, he landed on Gold beach and served in the North-West Europe campaign and Battle of Normandy, subsequently being injured on his approach to Caen and evacuated.

Years later, when I was with my mother and grandparents in a London-street, a man with a Yorkshire accent approached my grandfather and said: 'Hullo Sir'. It was my grandfather's reaction that was so notable in that he showed such utter delight in introducing his wife, his daughter and with great excitement, me, his young granddaughter. It was only later when talking with my mother that I realised the significance of this and that this man had served in one of John's troops. Perhaps this was a moment in a future that at one time, neither of them would have dreamed to be a possibility.

My grandmother, Rita, never fully recovered from the illnesses she suffered, but she loved life and people, and made the very most of the times when she was well. Reading how she lived through waves of bombings, gas attack threats, the multifaceted complexities of daily life, her constant yearnings to have her young family together and never knowing what tomorrow might bring I have learnt how stoic, brave and determined she was.

It has been wonderful to get to know and understand the people my grandparents were in their younger years before they grew to be the people that I knew and love. I was very close to them both and recognise that many of my personal values and beliefs are moulded by the times I spent with them, including my grandfather's wonderful habit of always having a bottle of champagne chilling in the fridge ready for any type of opportunity to celebrate!

As a family we are the lucky ones and immensely fortunate that when so many families lost those they loved, John made his way back, albeit injured and carrying with him the aggravating and painful effects of the residue shrapnel in his shoulder for his remaining days, but able to live a full life after the war. Both John and Rita never forgot these times and placed their energies into living the fullest of lives with hope and love; always considering how they could make a difference to others be it through a small friendly gesture or by supporting charitable concerns. Perhaps an inspiration to us all today?

With my very best wishes,
Roseanna

John and Rita with Roseanna 1974

Little Troopers

Supporting the Next Generation of Forces Families

Being separated from loved ones for long periods of time is one of the hardest aspects of serving in the military, and children of our Armed Forces personnel can find this separation particularly challenging. This remains just as true today as it was for Rita and John's children during World War II.

Thousands of British Armed Forces personnel are still deployed overseas on military operations each year, and despite advancements in technology, communication with their families back home is still limited, sporadic and often reliant on the written word. The connection between a parent and child often requires nurturing during this time, which is why the charity Little Troopers was established in 2011 by British Army veteran, Louise Fetigan.

Louise's husband also served in the Army, and their daughter struggled to cope with having a parent in the forces, particularly during the Iraq and Afghanistan conflicts. Unsure where to turn for help, Louise set up Little Troopers as a tri-service charity so that all children from Royal Navy, British Army and Royal Air Force families, who have one or both parents serving, have somewhere to turn whenever they need it and wherever they are living in the world.

Growing up with a parent in the forces is a unique way of life. It can bring amazing adventures, memories and friendships, but it can also bring a lot of change and uncertainty. Frequently moving house and school is another aspect of military life that can be challenging for young people, with some children attending up to ten different schools during their childhood.

Through its resources, programmes, events and initiatives, Little Troopers supports thousands of military children each year. Many of the charity's resources can be accessed by families at home, such as the Little Troopers Separation Pack, which supports children while their parents are deployed or away for long periods of time, and the Little Troopers Letters Pack, which aims to ease the anxiety children might feel when they have to move home to a new military posting by encouraging them to stay in-touch with old friends. The charity also has a dedicated Little Troopers at School programme, empowering teachers to support military children in the classroom, and a programme of in-person events called 'All Together'; connecting children through shared experiences. Both at home and in school, Little Troopers is always working hard to ensure military children feel recognised, included and celebrated.

If you would like to support Little Troopers or learn more about the charity's work, please visit www.littletroopers.net.

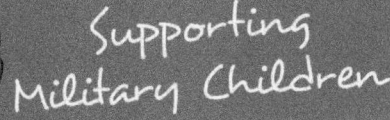

Supporting
Military Children

TEXT LITTLETROOPERS
TO 70085 TO DONATE £5

OR SCAN THIS QR CODE:

Acknowledgements

Having lived through both World Wars, my grandparents John and Rita had adopted a careful approach to the objects and resources they gathered throughout life and would only throw away something if was rendered truly broken or useless. For years, they had joked about what would one day be found in their loft, including the boxes of family papers that had been stored away and left untouched. John and Rita, thank you for being who you were and for your love of keeping hold of things in case one day 'they came in handy' or because 'they are precious'. I think of you both each and every day and so wish I could share this book with you.

When I first started to sort through the letters and diaries, I simply thought of transcribing them to share with family, but it was in conversation over dinner with my lovely friends Tony and Matthew Sim-McMahon that they helped me to start visualising the first beginnings of an idea for this book – their imagination can be infectious. I was further encouraged during a train journey with my wonderful friend Elisabeth O'Hanlon, who couldn't think why it wouldn't work and convinced me it could be something – I love how she always gives me something to think about. Two hours, drinking coffee under canvas in the pouring rain with my fabulous friend Jennifer Davie helped me to map out a plan and believe that, in celebrating John and Rita's story and love for each other, it could be possible to make a difference to others with a charitable connection. I believe that there are times in life when the right people stand beside you at the right time and say the right things to help you to start considering starting something new. Thank you all for your wise counsel and support, without which this book might never have been started.

I then began to share the idea of 'the book' with family and friends, including my dear uncle, Jeremy Reed. Jeremy, thank you for giving me time to talk through my ideas and findings, and for giving kind permissions to include stories about yourself and photographs from your family collection. I dearly hope you enjoy this book. Thank you also to my marvellous friends Tim and Sam Tarrant, who consistently showed support and belief in the value of bringing this story to print; my gorgeous pal Katharine Copsey, whose continuous excitement and interest has been so encouraging, and the fabulous Adam Walker-Cheetham, whose generous support in all things technical has been invaluable. There are so many more names that I would love to include, and it is my hope that you will know who you are.

Finally, and at a full stop, 'the book' was finished, and there it sat quietly, waiting on my desk, for several weeks. For so long it had been just us two, and it felt as though I was holding my breath, in fear of letting it go; frightened that what I could see in the snippets of stories, others might not. Then it was on a chance meeting during a morning walk that my delightful friend Richard Davis (with one eye on what his dog Monty was up to) quietly and reassuringly challenged my hesitation to send it out to publishers. Thank you, Richard (and Monty).

It was the fantastic team at Cranthorpe Millner who noticed and immediately understood this story, and who have since time and time again shown how they are the perfect publisher for this book. A special thank you goes to Victoria Richards, Senior Editor, for her continued support and sensitive approach, which has meant a great deal to me, and to Becca Stevenson, for the brilliant cover which so simply encapsulates the story.

Interviewing Marie Chovil, Lynn Cogan and Cole Maynard

helped me to understand the benefits and challenges of having a parent serving in the British Armed Forces and how this story links to the experiences of military families today. Thank you so much for the time you all so freely gave and your openness. My first meeting with Louise Fetigan, founder of the brilliant Little Troopers charity, confirmed that for some military families many of the book's themes will resonate, and it is my hope that the collaboration will foster a greater awareness of how children of military families may be supported, advocated for and championed today.

None of this would have been possible without my mother Rosemary, christened by her father John as the 'family archivist' and who carefully looked after these letters, diaries and photographs and gave them to me. She had an insatiable appetite for family history and would have been so thrilled to have shared in this discovery. I know she would have truly loved it.

A big thank you to Teddy, my dear four-pawed friend, who has loyally sat at my feet and interrupted my writing days to feel fresh air on my face and walk my thoughts and ideas out.

I have so appreciated the belief and encouragement Olly, Sophie and Togs have shown me whilst compiling and writing this book. I am immensely proud of you all and the lovely people you are, and have been so appreciative of how you have unfailingly listened, encouraged and shown confidence and belief in both this book and me. Your validation and appreciation have been energising, and it is my hope that not only you and other family members, but also future generations, may enjoy this story.

I give my sincerest thanks to Gavin who, whatever idea I come up with, enables me the time and space to fulfil my dreams. You have patiently and unendingly listened to my discoveries, thoughts and plans for the book, and have repeatedly found ways and time to help me research and understand some of the military experiences that John wrote of, whilst simultaneously deciphering some of his terrible handwriting! I so appreciate your support, consideration, constancy and kindness, and love you and the life we share. Thank you for being there in the right place and at the right time in 1990.